MW01322808

End of Arrogance

Africa and the West – Understanding their Differences

Helmut Danner

E.A.E.P

East African
Educational Publishers Ltd.
Nairobi • Kampala • Dar es Salaam • Kigali

Published by
East African Educational Publishers Ltd
Brick Court, Mpaka Road/Woodvale Grove
Westlands, P. O. Box 45314
Nairobi - 00100, KENYA

Email: eaep@eastafricanpublishers.com
Website: www.eastafricanpublishers.com

East African Educational Publishers Ltd
C/O Gustro Ltd
P.O. Box 9997
Kampala, UGANDA

Ujuzi Books Ltd.
P. O. Box 38260
Dar es Salaam, TANZANIA

East African Publishers Rwanda Ltd
No 86 Benjamina Street
Nyarutarama Gacuriro, Gasabo District
P. O. Box 5151
Kigali, RWANDA

© Helmut Danner 2012
First published 2012
Reprinted 2014

All rights reserved
Copyright for the cover image: Bildarchiv preußischer Kulturbesitz (BPK).
Travelling 'colonial style' – in a sedan chair with hammock and sun roof; Togo 1885.
Images of chairs and stools by Helmut Danner

ISBN 978-9966-25-838-0

Printed in India by
Multivista Global Limited

Contents

Preface .... *v*

Greetings .... *vi*

1. Introduction 1

1.1. Non-understanding 1
1.2. The intention of this essay 6

2. History of the relationship between Africa and the West 10

2.1. The unknown history of Africa 12
2.2. The 'discovery' and subjugation of Africa by Europeans 17
2.3. A disturbed relationship 26

3. African social structure 32

3.1. Kenyatta on education and community 33
3.2. Some features of African society 35
3.3. 'Village' and 'City' – tradition and modernity 39
3.4. The 'master-servant society' 46
3.5. 'Kenyan Cowboys' – the need for integration 51

4. Ethics 55

4.1. Social context of ethics 55
4.2. European and African sources of moral rules 57
4.3. Ethics in the encounter of Africa and the West 60
4.4. The 'immoral' side of African politics 65

5. Spirituality 69

5.1 The Western difficulty in understanding African spirituality 69
5.2. More examples 73
5.3. Supra-natural powers 76
5.4. Christianity and Islam in the African context 80

6. Reason and individualism in Europe 85

6.1. Galileo Galilei as an example 86
6.2. The Enlightenment 90

7. Excursion: Understanding and interpretation 101

7.1. Theory of understanding: 'hermeneutics'.. 102
7.2. Understanding the alien, a 'practical hermeneutics' 107
7.3. 'Hermeneutics of development cooperation' 111

8. The encounter of two cultures... 115

8.1. Differences 116
8.2. Enlightenment in Africa 120
8.3. Perceptions 125
8.4. Understanding and learning 126

9. 'Development'.. 130

9.1. What is development for Africa?... 131
9.2. The West as the model?... 136
9.3. Global contexts.. 139
9.4. Democracy and 'pseudo-elders'.. 144

10. End of arrogance... 152

Bibliography 156

Index 164

PREFACE

For the last 25 years, I have been exposed to foreign cultures on the African continent quite unfamiliar to me at the beginning. My job description was to teach the people in Africa how to improve their political structures. With time, I had to step back – sometimes forced by my lack of understanding – to allow those other cultures to speak. Compared to my own German-European background, the differences became obvious to me.

The purpose of this book is to share my experiences and findings, supported by insights of other scholars and practitioners. I see a need in doing this from the observation that the relationship between Africans and Westerners may appear to be burdened by the experience of their common history and by not understanding where the other one is coming from, how he perceives and thinks. Africans can be guided by distrust against Westerners; these patronise Africans in many ways. Both are constrained by that, captives of their own perceptions. The title of this book could be expanded to "End of arrogance and of distrust".

Talking about these issues is an attempt. I cannot maintain that I am right in every respect and detail. The questions concerned are complex and multifaceted. Maybe some may not agree with me at all. But maybe others will recognise some justification in my concern and will pick it up and discuss it thoroughly based on their knowledge. My wish and my intentions are to stimulate a dialogue between Africans and Westerners about their mental and cultural foundations – being aware that understanding is only a first step.

Innumerous encounters have taught me – with colleagues and partners, with friends or sometimes adversaries, in the streets, in meetings or workshops. The learning process was not always easy. But I am grateful to all and regret that I cannot name everybody. In their place, let me mention only these three: Rev. Jephthah Gathaka, partner in civic education, who patiently pointed out what was 'African' in a specific situation; Franz-Joachim Brinck, colleague and friend of many years, who understood much earlier than I did and who tirelessly put thoughts and relevant readings in front of me; and my wife Wambui, who brings me back to the African reality when I act and think 'too German'.

I am also grateful to the Hanns Seidel Foundation, Munich, who supports the print of this edition; I thank Dr Henry Chakava, the Chairman of East African Educational Publishers, for his support of this publication; Jane Mathenge and Benson Shiholo for their professional contribution to its realisation.

Helmut Danner
Nairobi, April 2012

GREETINGS

The Hanns Seidel Foundation is actively represented all over the world in about seventy countries. The daily encounters with very different, often alien, cultures are innumerous – exciting and pleasant and in some cases also frustrating. In spite of good will from all sides, we may fail to understand each other. Or we may even not be aware that we do not understand each other because we are restricted by our own limited worldview.

Dealing with and meeting African partners is no exception in this kind of experience. This is why we welcome the attempt of our former colleague of many years and my immediate successor in Kenya, Helmut Danner, to cast some light into the relationship between Africans and Westerners – how they perceive and think and how different our own perceptions and thinking are. This may help both our African partners and us to have a better mutual understanding of each other. Therefore, we are happy to support the publication of this edition and recommend it to students, scholars, diplomats and the general reader interested in relations between Africa and the West.

Christian Hegemer
Director
Institute for International Co-operation

"The industrial societies of the West who have traditionally understood themselves as teaching and preaching societies have to become learning societies."

(Wolf Lepenies 1995: 6)

CHAPTER ONE

Introduction

1.1. Non-understanding

The crisis of the development cooperation between Africa and the West may serve as an example for a more fundamental question: What is the root of the aid crisis? The crisis as such may be strongly denied by politicians on both sides, by African politicians because they grossly benefit from the inflowing money, and by donors because they have their political interests and a bureaucratic compulsion to keep the development machine moving. The big development institutions and organisations, the 'development industry' in general, may want to close their eyes and ears towards the arguments of practitioners and intellectuals who criticise the development practice. There are many practitioners and theorists who are convinced that the right things are done.

The question is: *Why* is there an aid crisis?
The main criticism and the most general argument against development aid points to the fact that many billions or trillions of dollars could not improve the living conditions of the African population within the last fifty years; to the contrary, their poverty has increased. For, as critics state, aid creates dependence. The bigger the aid, the less the development and vice versa. For, the equation 'more money = more development' is incorrect. Development aid should be drastically reduced if not stopped totally. Through aid, the West dictates what kind of development has to happen. Some, like Dembélé (2010), suspect that there even exists a Western conspiracy against Africa.

There is agreement on one essential reason for the failure of development aid: the *power elites* who are corrupt (not seldom in collusion with Westerners), who enrich themselves, who monopolise the income from national resources, who do not care for their ordinary citizens and, by that, impoverish them. In spite of all criticism, some representatives of the West insist that 'we have to help', considering the poverty and misery in Africa.

Westerners and Africans play the blame game: corruption and selfish leaders against colonialism and neo-liberalism. Much has been said. But what has really changed? There is helplessness and perplexity on the side of the critics, stubbornness and blindness on the side of governments and of development business. There is no need to repeat all details of the criticism of development aid.[1] Rather, we should ask: *why* does it not work? When Moyo (2009) says: *aid* spoils the leaders, makes them corrupt and lazy, and when Ayittey (2006) or Kabou (1991) blame the leaders directly, we should ask: *Why* do corrupt leaders accept to be spoilt by aid? Why are they not taking responsibility for the common good? What is the *underlying* mind-set that makes them behave as they do? A similar question applies to the Westerners: Why are they driven to help, to save, to develop Africa? Above all: Why do they think they have to interfere and are allowed to do that? What is their underlying mind-set?

Many critics from the West ask themselves: *What* do *we* have to change? This shows that they still consider themselves to be the players of the African development.[2] At the same time, they reflect on different *methods* and *techniques* for development cooperation in order to improve it – for example: budget aid

1. Examples: Shleifer (2009); Gerhardt (1988); Kabou (1991); Hancock (1992); Ayittey (1993, 1999, 2006); Shikwati (2006); Moyo (2009); Mbeki (2009); Seitz (2009), Neubert (2009) who is criticising Shikwati; and the discussion forum on the Website: www.bonner-aufruf.eu.

2. Seitz (2009) displays a wide range of arguments why development aid does not work. His main argument is: Africa is governed to become poor because of her leaders. But already in the subtitle of his book he also expresses: 'How Africa can really be helped'. Under the headline: 'What has to be changed' (171–196), Seitz prescribes what *has to* be done. Again, a Westerner takes responsibility for the development of Africa. He knows. It is *his* view under the perspective of the Western context.

or micro-financing, aid through governments or through NGOs. However, it is neither the West who is responsible for Africa's development, nor is it primarily a question of the *methodology* of the aid cooperation. What matters is the *attitude towards* development cooperation and towards Africans in general. The same applies to the African side: Africans have to reflect on *their attitude* towards development cooperation and to the West as well.

The crisis of the development cooperation between Africa and the West may rather have its roots in *attitudes,* in the *perception* of each other, in the *relationship* with each other in general, than in agreements, procedures and money transfers or projects and methodology. This *technical* side may only be the *consequence* and expression of the underlying mutual perception and understanding of each other.

> "Under the perspective of Europe and North America, programmes for development aid are designed and implemented which without further consideration presuppose that Western political, economic, and cultural conditions will be created or can be created all over the whole world. There hardly exists a profound knowledge on the specific conditions of other cultures; it seems, this does not play any important role for those designs." (Kimmerle 2002: 57)

If this is true, then the *approach* to development issues between Africa and the West has to change its scope and attention. The approach must change from *measuring* social and economic data to *understanding* what constitutes those data; then, the scope would shift from those data to the *people* who are the source of them. Both sides – Africa and the West – should be ready for this change of approach and scope if development cooperation is to be of benefit for everyone. Westerners should be willing to understand and to respect Africans; Africans should try to understand the Westerners. Understanding, first and foremost, means to *grasp* what constitutes the other side; secondly, it means to *accept* the other side – without being obliged to assimilate to it; it also means, hopefully, to *respect* the other side.

On this basis, the *roles* in development cooperation and the *concept* of this cooperation would have to be defined anew. Then, as an extreme consequence, the whole development machinery may have to be dismantled; hundreds of thousands of 'aid workers' in ministries, NGOs, World Bank, IMF would have to be sent home. Then the West would have to *listen to* Africans and leave their teaching and preaching attitude behind. Then the present corrupt African leaders would have to refund their loot and be locked up and serious Africans would have to take responsibility for the welfare of their countries. Of course, this is a radical thought and it will not happen. Strong powers on all sides will do everything to maintain the *status quo*.

Directing the focus on the dimension of the underlying mind-sets and world views to understand why development cooperation does not work satisfactorily shall not serve as a mono-causal explanation. It is an attempt to shift the attention to a neglected and basic dimension. This does not mean that there are no other causes of the failure of aid or indeed other explanations.

The slow African development may, at least partly, be the result of *non-understanding,* of a communication that seems to never meet the other side. A well-known joke may illustrate this:

> A Minneapolis couple decided to go to Florida to thaw out during a particularly icy winter. They planned to stay at the same hotel where they spent their honeymoon 20 years earlier. Because of hectic schedules, it was difficult to coordinate their travel schedules. So the husband left Minnesota and flew to Florida on a Thursday, with his wife to be flying down the following day. The husband checked into the hotel. There was a computer in his room, so he decided to send an email to his wife. However, he accidentally left out one letter in her email address, and without realizing his error, sent the email. Meanwhile, somewhere in Houston, a widow had just returned home from her husband's funeral. He was a minister who was called home to glory following a heart attack. The widow decided to check her email expecting messages from relatives and friends. After reading the first message, she screamed and fainted. Her son rushed into the room, found his mother on the floor and saw the computer screen which read:
>
> *'To: My Loving Wife.*
> *Subject: I've Arrived.*
> *Date: October 11, 2010.*
> *I know you're surprised to hear from me. They have computers here now and you are allowed to send emails to your loved ones. I've just arrived and have been checked in. I've seen that everything has been prepared for your arrival tomorrow. Looking forward to seeing you then! Hope your journey is as uneventful as mine was.*
> *P.S. Sure is freaking hot down here!'*

The widow has read the email in her specific context, which is the loss of her husband. Of course, *the change of context changes the meaning of the message.*

Are Africans and Westerners aware that the other side lives in a different mental context, in a different mind-set? Can they 'read' the context of the other side? Are they able to formulate their message in a way that the context of the other side is met? And are they able to decipher a message and an action from the other side, interpreting it in its original context?

When an African has a plate of food in front of him and another one passes by and picks something from his dish, the African will say: 'Please, take more!' A Westerner would grumble: 'Can't you get your own food?!' When somebody hits himself, stumbles or drops something, an African will tell him: 'Sorry!' A Westerner will bark: 'Can't you take better care?!'

A Westerner will arrive at a meeting or at an invitation at the given time. An African will come when it suits his other businesses. For a Westerner coming late expresses impoliteness. Arriving at an African home at the given time may be rather impolite. For the West it is important that something is done *in time*. For Africans it is important that it *happens* at all.

Acholis of Northern Uganda with a traditional orientation are willing to *forgive* the criminals of the Lord's Resistance Army who have robbed, mutilated, and raped their citizens and abducted boys and girls to serve as child soldiers and sex slaves. The Western approach is to *sue* them.

The African older person enjoys respect and privileges, being surrounded by his/her family. The elderly Westerner has just the same recognition like the younger generation – if at all – living in a home for elderly people. Africans support their relatives, within the larger family and beyond. Westerners depend as individuals on their public social system and on insurances. In the West, an event is explained as the effect of a cause. Africans tend to magic, religious, 'irrational' explanations.

There is no encounter with another person without an African asking 'how are you?' Be it a private or a business meeting, at first one would talk about personal and general matters, only then, often at the very end of the meeting, the real issue will be discussed. The guest is offered tea or another drink. One talks in a low voice, touches each other occasionally and laughs a lot. Problems are not addressed clearly and directly, the counterpart is supposed to understand the message. As one does not want to disappoint the other person, one will never say 'No!' or that something is not possible. Obviously, in the African context, the other *person* is more important than the matter; the relationship first and foremost is a *personal* one. Contrary to that, in a meeting, a Westerner will quickly concentrate on the matter of concern, talk in a distant manner, seldom offer a drink, speak bluntly about problems and is not shy to deny what is not possible. The emphasis lies on the function of the meeting; it is a *functional* relationship. No wonder that a Westerner is considered by an African to be cold and rude.

These are only a few observations that give a hint to the very different contexts based on which Africans and Westerners are thinking and acting. Does development cooperation take these differences of world views and conceptions of life in consideration? Or does the West take in consideration only what fits into the Western way of thinking and what can be measured and demonstrated in figures: as facts, data, statistics, percentages, graphics?

1.2. The intention of this essay

What are the deeper reasons of the crisis of development cooperation? As I have said above, there is no need to repeat the arguments of the critics why it does not work and of those who do not see a problem and want to maintain the status quo. I rather wonder whether we are confronted with a development crisis as such. Is it not rather a problem and crisis of the *interaction* between West and Africa in a wider sense? How do Westerners and Africans perceive each other? How do they *encounter* the other side? We may have to look at the *underlying* mind-sets of development cooperation, the underlying world views, in order to be able to understand what is going wrong there. 'Underlying' shall mean that there is something that is real, effective and determining, but usually unnoticed, un-reflected and therefore unconscious – like the rules of a society for 'what is seemly' and what not, the relationship between individual and community, values and norms, religious, non-religious and moral convictions, attitudes and behaviours. Thus, the Oxford Dictionary (2006) describes 'mind-set' as "a set of attitudes or fixed ideas that somebody has and that are often difficult to change" and 'world view' as "a person's way of thinking about and understanding life, which depends on their beliefs and attitudes".

All this is culturally conditioned, expression of a certain culture characterising a society. Individuals adopt those norms, convictions and attitudes through education and socialisation; even if they reflect on them they appear to be self-understood and unchangeable. As every society perceives itself this way, non-understanding and conflicts are the result when cultures meet that are foreign to each other.

"We can't solve problems by using the same kind of thinking we used when we created them." In the spirit of this insight, attributed to Albert Einstein, this essay pleads for a *shift of the approach* in the relationship between Africa and the West. The essay intends to elaborate on *underlying aspects* of African and Western encounter through shifting the focus of the discussion, taking the criticism of the development cooperation as an *occasion* to scrutinise the relationship between Africa and the West as such. Therefore, the essay does *not* contribute to the 'North-South dialogue' in the sense of the report of the Brandt Commission. "North-South – A Programme for Survival"[3]. In a wider context, the essay is asking: What determines and characterises Africa against the West? What distinguishes them? What does that mean for their relationship?

---

3. "The report called for an emergency programme to help the world's poorest countries, especially in water and soil management, health care, solar energy development, mineral and oil exploration, and infrastructure for industry and transport. It also called for an end to mass hunger and malnutrition through increased food aid and food production, helped by agricultural research and land reform. The report proposed diversion of funds and skills from arms production to peaceful needs; a change in the pattern of world trade so that developing countries can have a bigger part in processing, marketing, and distributing their own commodities; an increase in international aid whether funds came from governments, international financial institutions, or private financial bodies; a strengthening of the United Nations system with a high-level advisory body to monitor various organizations and supervise a World Development Fund to spread wealth from the rich to the poor." (Mazrui 1990: 206).

This will also mean confronting truths. They are not meant to disrespect the one or the other side or to hurt – although truths may sometimes be difficult to accept. Above all, I will abstain from advice on what has to be done in a technical sense. The only wish I have is that this essay may contribute to depicting and clarifying from which backgrounds Africans and Westerners are thinking and perceiving. The guiding question shall be: What are their mental foundations? This essay intends to describe and to point at aspects that underlie any encounter between the West and Africa. For, all endeavours in business, development aid, political cooperation or private encounter can only be satisfying if the mental foundation of the counterpart is *understood* and respected, i.e. their culture, beliefs, values and norms, forms of life, social structures, etc. The minimal effort each side should take is to *attempt* to understand the counterpart.

One of the truths, I am afraid we have to face, is that the relationship between Africans and Westerners is *deeply disturbed*. The African/Western relationship is the result of experiences like these ones: the destruction of traditional cultures by the missionaries; the cruelty and brutality of colonisation, such as the inhuman suppression of the Congo by Leopold II of Belgium, the slaughtering of Hereros by the Germans, 'Britain's Gulag' in Kenya; the exploitation of humans and natural resources; the apartheid – not only in South Africa; the Western attitude of setting others right, of advising and preaching (W. Lepenies 1995); in general, the master-servant attitude that Westerners are used to take. The incidents are innumerable. The result and the reality of this historic experience reflect on the mutual perception today. Often, Westerners still have a tendency to look down on Africans and to set them right, sometimes in utter arrogance, sometimes concealed as friendliness, mainly as the perception that Africans are the needy ones. Africans counteract either by being submissive or by rebelling against the West and seeing only mischief and conspiracy in everything the West is doing or saying, and often they perceive Westerners as those who have money and who have to hand-out. I maintain that these attitudes can be found through all social classes in the West and in Africa, and they do not exclude government and development organisations. Whether Africans and Westerners like it or not, they are the captives of their common history.

If this is true, even only a part of it, and if a way out should be found from this captivity, it may be necessary to reflect on a few issues have been neglected in the past, last but not least in the development relationship. The first issue has to consider the *approach* to the other side. On either side, this approach has to be *understanding* instead of measuring quantitative facts or preaching by the West and instead of being guided by deep distrust on the side of Africans. The West should overcome colonial attitudes, and Africa has to leave anti-colonial resentments behind.

Secondly, the West should acknowledge that there is a mostly unknown but impressive African *history*. Both sides should read their *common* history as the story which tells what has gone wrong in the relationship between West and Africa. The third issue concerns basic *differences* between Africa and the West: the different features of societies, values and beliefs, the role of the Enlightenment here and there.

Finally, from there *development* aspects can be reflected anew. These aspects shall be the focus later on.

A few clarifications on some expressions are necessary. On the one hand, it is incorrect to speak of 'Africa' and 'Africans' in general. For, there are hundreds of ethnic groups and languages in Africa; related to these are different cultures. Therefore, a uniform 'Africa' does not exist. On the other hand, it can be justified that we speak of 'one Africa'. Partly, it is the one continent with the pan-African dream of the 'United States of Africa'; it is the negative picture of Africa that is mainly drawn by the West. But primarily, I would like to follow Etounga-Manguelle (2000: 67) who says about Africa:

> "The diversity – the vast number of subcultures – is undeniable. But there is a foundation of shared values, attitudes, and institutions that bind together the nations south of the Sahara, and in many respects those to the North as well."

The "shared values, attitudes, and institutions" form the unity of Africa; the ways how these are realised and lived constitute the many different African cultures.

In a way of comparison, the *distinction from the West* also defines what is 'African'. Returning from Geneva, Muriithi Mutiga notes:

> "It is impossible not to admire the efficiency in delivery of public services [there.] [...] But something which is in great supply in Nairobi is virtually missing: laughter. The spontaneity, the generosity of ordinary people to be found in Africa is the one thing you miss most whenever you have to spend time in a Western city."[4]

Further, in the following I will often use a generalising term for the counterpart of Africa: 'the *West*' and 'the Westerners'. This term shall have a more geographical meaning compared to 'Europe' and the 'Europeans', which form the philosophical core of the Western mind, having influenced and shaped North and South America. Of course we have to be well aware that there are also great differences within Europe and America and between them as well. However, those 'Westerners' represent a certain (European) mind-set, a certain way of thinking, perceiving, behaving and acting, which differs from the African way of thinking, perceiving, behaving and acting. The contrast to 'Africa' allows us to speak of 'Europe', the 'West' or the 'North' in a unifying and summarising way. The comparison with 'Europe' justifies speaking of 'Africa' and of 'Africans' as well. The contrast to the foreign side is unifying and levelling. (Schmidt 2005: 14)

The following reflections and elaborations are guided by three major theses:

- The *relationship* between and the encounter of West and Africa is disturbed due to their common history.
- *Better knowledge* of each other is pertinent to a relationship that is based on mutual respect.
- The approach to reflect on these issues has to be *understanding.*

4. *Daily Nation*, 2 January 2011.

This study is an *essay* – in the double meaning of the word: an *attempt* to approach this obviously difficult relationship of 'developed' nations and African 'developing' countries; and it is an 'essay' in the sense of *style* of writing, supplementing the academic findings by reflecting on experiences in the 'development business' as project manager and representative of a German political foundation for nineteen years, and by referring to the fact that I am not only living in Kenya, but also within the Kenyan society. Some statements may be guided by these circumstances. As far as reference is made to Kenya, this has to be taken as *exemplary* for Africa; however, reference is also made to a variety of African countries and regions. I am aware that what I want to say can only be a *sketch,* hoping to be able to point to a few essential aspects. Others have to be omitted although they are important, too, like cultural differences, African literature, songs, music, dancing, art. Above all, it is neither possible nor am I able to address the huge variety of cultural particularities that characterise Africa. "Cultural analysis is intrinsically incomplete [...] the more deeply it goes the less complete it is." (Geertz 2000: 29)

The biggest challenge for a Westerner is not to be trapped by what Kenyatta[5] (1965: xviii) describes as the "*professional friends of the African* who are prepared to maintain their friendship for eternity as a sacred duty, provided only that the African will continue to play the part of an ignorant savage so that they can monopolise the office of interpreting his mind and speaking for him." Thus, the task will be for a foreigner like me to *listen* and to *learn,* to be open for African arguments and to be corrected, at the same time to observe and to think independently without becoming a "professional friend of the African". In addition, we will not only look into the African underlying world view, but also into the European mind-set. A certain tension and perhaps frictions may be unavoidable. But these are apt to stimulate the discussion, a discussion that fosters better mutual understanding.

5. Jomo Kenyatta is mostly known as Kenya's first president. He is less known as an anthropologist who presented a study on his own Kikuyu tribe "Facing Mount Kenya". By that he delivered a key to the structure of African society and the nature of the African mind.

How can a constructive approach towards Africans develop when Westerners look down on them? Is it astonishing when the attitude of Africans towards Europeans is characterised by bitterness, suspicion, and distrust?

CHAPTER TWO

History of the relationship between Africa and the West

Barack Obama's election as president of the USA has been celebrated as a 'historic event'; historic because he is a black American and Blacks have been considered not to be fit for such a position. The racist opposition against his election radically underlines this opinion. The Kenyan *Saturday Nation* reports on 13 March 2010 the following events and utterances:

> After Obama's Democratic nomination for president on 3 June 2008, on 8 June 2008 six people are arrested with stockpiles of assault rifles and home-made bombs. They intend to shoot black people and predict a civil war should Obama be elected to the White House.

> On 24 August 2008, in Denver, three white supremacists are arrested with high-powered rifles and camouflage clothing. They are talking about assassinating Obama.
> The day after Obama's inauguration, on 21 January 2009, a white man is arrested in Massachusetts, having allegedly killed two black immigrants and injured a third. He says he was "fighting for a dying race".
> "The hatred that's there is very real", says one analyst of right-wing activity. "It's more than a gut-level hatred of having an African-American as president, it's also ideological – these people see black people as sub-human."
> White supremacist forums that provide closed talking shops for members only have been abuzz with anti-Obama rhetoric. In one such talk board, monitored by a watchdog group, a correspondent writes: "I never thought I'd ever see the day when a monkey ran my country and I'm 34. I weep for our children."

African-Americans are depicted here as "sub-human" and as "monkeys". Certainly, that is not the view of the majority of the Americans; otherwise Obama would not have been elected. But there is no denying the fact that this understanding exists, perhaps secretly and more common than the West may admit, and it has existed for centuries. What image of Africans was conveyed to those in the West still in the second half of the twentieth century? In a book like "Tintin in the Congo"[6]; through a song about the "ten little Negroes"; via a cartoon showing a half-naked fat African in front of a big pot boiling a white man in it; through another picture where an elephant is pulling an African by his nose; by the statements that Africans are savages, who have just recently lived on trees? From there it is not far to consider Africans as 'sub-human' and as 'monkeys'. Those Whites who grow up among Blacks as descendants of the colonialists are in general socialised, i.e. programmed, in a way that they perceive Blacks as nothing else than servants, not able to perform in the way Whites do. On the other hand also, Africans should reflect on how they acquired their image of the people from the West, maybe in a similar distorted way.

To understand the relationship between the West and Africa, it may be helpful to look into the history of this relationship, beginning with the history of Africa as such. In our context, we do not have to and we cannot rewrite this history which, by the way, still seems to need a lot of research and a racist-free approach.[7] Here, it can only be a simplified approach. Our question rather is: What does this history *mean* with respect to the relationship between West and Africa? For this, it is necessary that we make ourselves aware of the African and the African-European history.

6. Hergé (1931). In the foreword of the English Casterman edition of 1991 we read: Hergé "depicted his Africans according to the bourgeois, paternalistic stereotypes of the period".

7. Not only is there contradiction in theories, but also in dating.

First of all, the West has to acknowledge that there is an African history *before* the so-called discoveries of Africa. Long before the Portuguese sailed along the African coasts and set foot on the continent, there were African kingdoms, well organised societies, large cities, and trade within and beyond Africa, mining for gold, iron and copper, metal casting and 'art'.

2.1. The unknown history of Africa

Calling Africa's history as 'unknown' refers to the ordinary knowledge about it, even that of educated people. There are, of course, palaeontologists and historians who research on the early up to the recent history of Africa. But who, in general, is aware of African historic facts? Is Africa not considered as the *'dark* continent'? Dark, because in general the Westerners do not know it? But this ignorance shapes their view on Africans.

Among experts, Africa is widely considered to be the *'cradle of mankind'*. Findings in Hadar (Ethiopia), Koobi Fora and Olorgesailie (Kenya), Olduvai (Tanzania) and Swartkrans (South Africa) tell us about ancestors who lived about 2.5 million to 1 million years ago. They are called 'homo habilis', they were tool makers, i.e. they produced and used stone tools. (Oliver 1992: 1–15; Ansprenger 2002: 10)

> "Although other no less valid definitions of man might be proffered, such as upright posture or a cranial capacity of more than one thousand cubic centimetres, the tool-making criterion is certainly a very convenient one. If we accept it, we can say that our genus is of African origin and that it is approximately 2.5 million years old." (Oliver 1992: 3)

Also a much younger hominid, the homo sapiens sapiens, can be identified in the Cape Province of South Africa, "well over 100,000 years ago", which is much earlier than his presence in North Africa and in Europe 35,000 to 40,000 years ago. (Oliver 1992: 27–29). The *Homo sapiens sapiens* is the genus of the modern human. They replaced the Neanderthals in Europe who disappeared some 35,000 years ago. Thus, the roots of the modern human have to be seen in Africa (Connah 2006: 15–16). Another theory assumes a development of the modern human in *different* regions of the world. As Ansprenger (2002: 10) remarks, this may flatter the racist pride of white Europeans, because then they have to recognise in the black Africans only someone like their cousins and not brothers or sisters or even remote parents. However, the genetic research supports the other theory according to which the modern mankind has only *one* origin, namely Africa. And this, of course, is embarrassing for those who look down on Blacks; for, so to speak, genetically we are all Africans. Racism is rather a social fact and less a biological one.[8]

---

8. "Racism, wherever and however it occurs, is a repulsive, endemic and deeply atavistic human characteristic that appears to be present in most of humankind. Whether racism is openly practiced or hidden, it is inexcusable." (Courtenay 2005: 611)

Africans not only gain historic importance because of the Westerners' biological relationship with them. They also very early developed their own and specific civilisations, independently of the West. Pre-historic findings document, for example, that the Khoisan/San created drawings and carvings on rocks in Namibia, Botswana and South Africa 26,000 years ago. Rock and cave paintings which are 8,000 to 5,000 years old give testimony of people who lived in the Sahara. (Connah 2006: 28–41) Although we do not fully understand the meaning of such pictures of animals, of hunting and dancing people, of women harvesting, etc, we have to recognise that the pictures are a human expression of reflection; maybe, certain pictures have a magic meaning. They are a basic way of documenting and recording something and, at least for us, they are a form of information. Do we have the same respect for those African people as we have for those who created the rock paintings of Altamira in Spain or of Lascaux in France, both around 17,000 years ago?

In the West, at school we usually do not learn any African history; the earliest we may hear at school about it is the colonial time. However, there exist astonishing historic findings before the 15th century which are hundreds and thousands of years old. In the following, I will mention a few examples of African kingdoms and cities that date back to the time before the Europeans 'discovered' Africa. Roland Oliver (1992: 90) points out that in the eastern part of Africa, at least during the later Iron Age, there were cities only on the coast of the Indian Ocean. "Only the courts of chiefs and kings attracted quasi-urban concentrations". Otherwise, "homesteads tended to be spread more or less evenly across the countryside, so that even villages were rare". However, in western Africa, "there was an indigenous tradition of *urban settlement*, which went back, in some places at least, to the very beginnings of the Iron Age, and perhaps a little further" which means to about 1500 BC.

One of the important and early kingdoms in West Africa was *Ancient Ghana.* It was situated in the area of the Senegal River and the Upper Niger River, which belongs today to Mali and southern Mauritania. The first kings of Ancient Ghana ruled from about 300 AD. But through territorial expansion it developed into an empire by the eighth century AD. At the height of its power, this empire also included parts of modern Senegal and Guinea. This was at the eleventh century AD. Old Djenné was one of the early cities of this era "that dated back to 250 BC. By 500 AD, it had a population of 20,000 people" – which is astonishing compared to cities in Europe of the same period. "Old Djenné was a centre of long distance trade in which they were the middlemen". Gold was one of Ancient Ghana's trading strength, but they also sold slaves, salt and copper in exchange for textiles, beads and finished goods. However, already "before 250 BC, evidence of a prehistoric Ghanaian culture exists. Large stone masonry villages were excavated [...] West of *Kumbi-Saleh*", the capital of Ancient Ghana from about 300 to 1240 AD. These stone villages "flourished already from around 1100 BC". (Walker 2006: 359–361)

From a historian of the fourteenth century, Ibn Khaldun, we learn about Ancient Ghana and its capital:

> In the 7th century AD "merchants penetrated into the western part of the land of the Blacks and found among them no king more powerful than the king of Ghana. His states extended westwards to the shores of the Atlantic Ocean. Ghana [i.e. Kumbi-Saleh], the capital of this strong, populous nation, was made up of two towns... and formed one of the greatest and best populated cities in the world". (Walker 2006: 363)

Ibn Khaldun refers to Abu Ubaid Al-Bakri who in 1067 AD describes Kumbi-Saleh:

> "The royal town was called Al-Ghaba ..., encircled by a wall, the king had a castle and domed buildings. There was a Royal Court of Justice. Near to the court stood a mosque built for visiting Muslims. Outside Al-Ghaba was a guarded area of cottages and groves where the traditional priests kept their icons. The prisons and royal cemeteries were also there. The second town, originally six miles away from Al-Ghaba, was a Muslim quarter that included twelve mosques... Eventually, the space between the two towns became filled with suburbs creating a large city. Stone houses graced suburbia, standing in gardens. Other buildings were of stone with beams of acacia wood." (Walker 2006: 365)

Two other kingdoms followed Ancient Ghana with even larger areas: Mali and Songhai.

Farther south and several hundred years later flourished another kingdom, the kingdom of Benin, with Benin City as its capital. It was situated in modern Nigeria west of the Niger delta. The speciality of this area was its location within the Nigerian rain forest. The development of iron smelting 2000 years ago in this area of Africa and the use of iron tools facilitated in conquering the rain forest. About 1000 years ago, neighbouring settlements defined their area by digging deep trenches and establishing earth walls. By that, over the centuries a network of earth walls encompassing an area of 6,500 square kilometres with a total length of the walls of about 16,000 kilometres was established. This immense construction has been compared to the Chinese Wall. Finally, more than 500 years ago, Benin City was fortified, again by trenches and earth walls. The height from trench bottom to the top of these walls is supposed to be seventeen metres and the city wall is eleven kilometres long. These are not only impressive physical data, but they also document an elaborate political and administrative system that made these achievements possible.

Benin City with a palace quarter was the residence of the kings of Benin Kingdom. It was supported by highly productive agriculture. Benin City has become famous because of its technically perfect artefacts: brass casts, ivory carvings, wrought iron, ceramics, etc. The beautiful and impressive bronze and brass casts have been produced in the rare and difficult lost-wax process where the intended sculpture is modelled in wax, the wax encased in clay, then the wax melted and drained, and finally the empty space filled in with melted brass or bronze. (Connah 2006: 134–139)

> "Benin's history continued until 1897. In that year the British army invaded and plundered the country, exiling the Oba [king]. The conquerors stole thousands of priceless artefacts that are still held by London institutions and private collections. Following this outrage, they burned the city." (Walker 2006: 341)

We find another example of African urban developments again farther south in *Great Zimbabwe.* Connah (2006: 168) considers it as "one of the most remarkable and certainly best researched archaeological sites of Africa". Great Zimbabwe gave the modern state of Zimbabwe its name, and it is located in the south-east, lying between the Zambezi River in the West, the Limpopo River in the south and between the coastal plain of the Indian Ocean in the east and the Kalahari Desert in the west. Being on a plain at a height of 1,000 metres, it had a moderate climate and no tsetse flies, which allowed keeping cattle and other animals. However, the rainfalls were unreliable, which resulted in adverse natural conditions. The clan elders had to manage this situation, deciding on the proper and timely use of the arable land as well as pastures. This gave them social, religious and political power and, consequently, economic advantage. They were rich with cattle and grain, and they traded goods inland Africa and with the coastal settlements on the Indian Ocean. Under these conditions, Great Zimbabwe developed as the first big town in the southern African hinterland.

Before the time 1700 years ago, the place consisted of a small agricultural settlement. There were many more similar settlements in the area. An important one, Mapungubwe, in the very north of South Africa, preceded the importance of Great Zimbabwe and reached the peak of its development about 800 years ago. However, about 1000 years ago, the first stone walls were constructed which made Great Zimbabwe famous even now. Those walls are built with carefully dressed, brick-shaped stones of granite, put together without any mortar. One of the most impressive enclosing walls is 244 metres long, up to five metres thick and ten metres high. Just below the top of the wall runs a decorative band. A conical tower, nine metres high and five metres thick, stands within this enclosure. These impressive walls and the tower are extraordinary stone constructions representing power and richness of the rulers. About 500 years ago, Great Zimbabwe had about 18,000 inhabitants and dominated the region for about 200 years. Power and richness of Great Zimbabwe were based on its healthy agriculture and on its trade. Within Africa, they bartered goods including iron tools and weapons, copper, salt and gold. The traders at the coast delivered glass pearls, Persian and Chinese ceramics, valuable objects of glass and metal, and they received gold, ivory, copper and slaves. (Connah 2006: 168–173)

At the north-eastern part of the Ethiopian plateau, more than 2000 metres high, there flourished for 500 years a city and kingdom with the name of Aksum. It had developed out of the pre-Aksumite civilisation that flourished 2000 to 3000 years ago. Thus, the beginning of Aksum can be dated to about 2000 years ago. It was a highly developed civilisation with its own script (Ge'ez) and own coins from gold, silver and bronze. The businessmen of Aksum had connections to the inner Africa and to the Mediterranean Sea, trading with ivory, gold, perfumes, hides, salt, copper, iron and slaves, with goods from ceramics and glass, textiles, wine, sugarcane, spices. Obviously, it was a structured, multi-class society, with the king at the top and with craftsmen and experts, workers, farmers and slaves. They had developed manifold sophisticated skills and important technological expertise. An outstanding example is the production of high, narrow stones in a single piece (steles) representing several storeys of windows and a door and used to mark the burial sites of important persons. One of them is still standing; it is 21 metres high, reaching three metres into the ground, showing nine storeys. The tallest of those steles is 33 metres long and weighs about 500 tonnes; however, it has fallen down. These steles are about 1,700 years old. (Connah 2006: 74–82)

The most astonishing civilization on the African continent, of course, is the *Pharaonic* one, dating back at least 5000 years. It is so well known and popular that in our context we do not have to go into details. It is sufficient to remember that Ancient Egypt was *African*. To which extent their population and rulers were Black Africans, historians have to decide. Diop (1974) strongly argues that they were indeed Black.

These very few examples – Ancient Ghana, Kingdom of Benin with Benin City, Great Zimbabwe, Aksum and Ancient Egypt – represent many more indigenous African important civilisations – for instance, Gede[9] at the east African coast or the famous Timbuktu[10] in Mali – that date back hundreds and thousands of years.[11] "Historically, Africa has been a land of movement, migration and, above all, commerce. Far from the image of a continent frozen in time before the colonial period, Africa was always involved in local and long-distance trade" (Chabal 2009: 115). Though there existed early Christian influence – and since the 7th century Islamic influence – those who traded and created the mentioned civilisations were Black Africans. Seen from within and looking at Africa's history, Africa has never been a 'dark continent' and the labels "sub-human" and

9. Moslem historic city at the Kenyan coast south of Malindi; 12th to 17th century; trade with Europe and Asia.

10. City on middle Niger River; founded at the beginning of 12th century; important trade centre; major centre of Islamic learning with famous university and library. See Hunwick (2006: 31–49).

11. The German sculptor Fritz Koenig has collected African objects which date back hundreds and some perhaps thousands of years. As a sculptor, he was interested in them as 'art', i.e. as aesthetic objects with their specific beauty, strength and power. On the one hand, those objects are witnesses of indigenous rich African cultures; on the other hand, in the context of a collector of the West, they are alienated because they have lost their meaning and their purpose. (Eisenhofer 2000: 8, 10) This raises the general question: How can persons from the West adequately encounter not only African objects, but also cultures and the persons who have created them and belong to them? What does 'adequate' mean here?

"monkeys" are ridiculed alone by historic facts. Connah (2006: 188) argues that Africa's past is much too important that not only scientifically educated people should read its historic documentation. It should be appreciated by the whole world, not only by Africans. Unfortunately, in general, the rest of the world is not aware of Africa's rich history.[12]

2.2. The 'discovery' and subjugation of Africa by Europeans

Until the 15th century, Africans traded with other continents and countries. But the trading points were limited to north and north-east Africa and to the coast of the Indian Ocean. These outside relations changed when in the 15th century, on the search for a way to India, the Portuguese started to settle on the western African coast. They set up fortified trading posts, for example, in 1484 one close to the mouth of the Congo River or more than 500 years ago the Fort St. George at Elmina situated in today's Ghana – the Fort São Jorge da Mina. The relationship with Africans was at first friendly, then their contracts were dishonoured and the Portuguese began to dominate. Many more trading posts were erected, however, not only by the Portuguese, but also by the Dutch, English, Danish, Swedish and Germans. (Connah 2006: 181–182) About 400 years ago, the Portuguese erected Fort Jesus at Mombasa in East Africa. Later, the merchants were followed by adventurous explorers and the first missionaries: Mungo Park searched for the course of the Niger River in 1795; Johann Rebmann, a missionary, 'discovered' Mount Kilimanjaro; and David Livingstone, a missionary as well, the Victoria Falls in 1855; in 1862, John Speke found Lake Victoria and considered the river on its West side to be the source of the White Nile; and Henry Stanley searched for and found sick Livingstone close to Lake Tanganyika in 1871.

Ali Mazrui (1969: 661) points out that those explorers can be seen as historical figures *and* as "intellectual symbols". In other words, Mazrui asks for the *meaning* of those 'explorations' and 'discoveries'. Ansprenger (2002: 42) offers an interpretation:

> "It is not so long ago that 'white' Europeans prided themselves to have 'discovered' the 'dark' continent Africa – as if before their arrival no human eye has ever seen the peak of the Kilimanjaro [...] The inner Africa formed a large empty spot only on the maps of the Europeans until far into the 19th century, never in the heads of the Africans".

The 'white spot' on the map and the 'discoveries' are white spots and discoveries only in the *European* perspective. For there existed African people in Africa with their social, economic, technical, political and cultural forms of life. But Europeans

12. See also Rodney (2001: 31–71), chapter two: "How Africa Developed before the Coming of the Europeans – Up to the Fifteenth Century".

perceived Europe and themselves as the centre and the peak of the world. And their 'discoveries' of the African continent were the expression of this Eurocentrism, of a European superiority complex and arrogance – typical for all conquerors all over the world at all times. Other human beings outside Europe did not count, the same as the ancient Greeks called all other peoples 'barbarians'. Seen from a human rights perspective and not from the point of view of conquerors, European merchants and 'explorers' have to be considered as intruders, not appreciating their position as mere guests – as which Africans had treated them at the beginning.

Eurocentrism exclusively characterises European self-confidence, philosophy and science until very recently. Eurocentrism had functioned as a justification for the occupation and 'development' of Africa. The question to Westerners today is to which extent they have overcome their Eurocentric perception of Africa, and the question to Africans is to which extent they are no longer caught in a counter-reaction to this Western Eurocentrism.

***

One of the most sensitive issues about the relationship between Africans and the West is *slavery*, specifically the enslavement of more than eleven million West Africans who were shipped across the Atlantic Ocean to North and South America. Slavery and colonisation play a big role in the African demand for development aid. The argument is that Africa as a whole has suffered a big loss due to the European enslavement of their people; this should be compensated. On the other hand, it appears that slavery is a very *complex* issue that cannot be exhausted by simply pointing at the transatlantic slave trade. Without downplaying the individual human tragedy and the losses and damages to the African people, it is necessary to consider the circumstances and facts of slavery in Africa as a whole. This may contribute to reduce the emotions that accompany the discussion on slavery in the African/Western relationship.

The transatlantic slave trade between the 15th and the 19th century was historically speaking not a unique event. Slavery was known in the orient already 3000 years BC; there were slaves in Israel of the Old Testament; state and society of ancient Greece and Rome were based on slavery, getting slaves from neighbouring countries as captives of wars. Also, Europeans and other peoples became enslaved. (Flaig 2009: 33–79). Concerning later times, Flaig (1995: 979) mentions the Church as "the biggest slave-owner". Obviously, over thousands of years, slavery was considered to be something 'normal'; it was self-understood as part of life and society; there were no moral reservations against it (Eckert 2007: 61).

But also in Africa, slavery had a long tradition even before the 7th and 15th century, i.e. before the Moslems and the Europeans came (Flaig 2009: 107; Marks 2006: 71). Mainly, the captives of warfare – men, women, children – became slaves. They were used for work and they experienced different treatment in different parts of the continent – from being totally deprived of their rights to being freed after some time. There were slaves in Pharaonic Egypt and Nubia. Ramses II is said to have provided the temples with more than 100,000 slaves during his rule. Slave trade was going on among African peoples in Central Sahara as well as in sub-Saharan Africa. In the kingdom of Congo, the slaves may have outnumbered the free in the 16th century. (Oliver 1992: 117)

Before the arrival of Europeans in Africa and up to the early 20th century, the *Arab/Islamic slave trade* played an important role in Africa. This affected mostly the northern half of Africa, but also occurred as the trans-Saharan slave trade and on the east coast of Africa. Slaves were not only captured as a result of wars, but 'holy wars' – jihad – were fought for the purpose of enslaving people, i.e. jihad was practised more to get slaves than to gain converts (Oliver 1992: 85). Egon Flaig (2009: 83) considers the Islamic rule as the largest and most durable system based on slavery in world history. Due to the Arab slave trade, Black Africa became the biggest source of slaves. Those slaves were transported out of Africa:

> "The Muslim era saw a great increase in the trade [of slaves] from North-Eastern Africa into South-Western Asia, and in later medieval times the African entrepots of this trade proliferated southwards down the Indian Ocean coast, while its points of delivery extended eastwards to western India, Bengal and South-East Asia." (Oliver 1992: 123)

According to Flaig (2009: 148–149), in the time between 650 and 1920, at least 17 million Africans became victims of the Islamic slavery – compared to about 11.5 million victims of the transatlantic slave trade between 1450 and 1870.

The *transatlantic slave trade* to South and North America has to be seen from this background. The Portuguese found an existing commercial system of trading in slaves in Africa. In addition, it was not the Europeans who hunted for slaves. This was done by Africans themselves, often making captives in the course of warfare. African traders sold African people enslaved by themselves or by other Africans. African elites – kings and chiefs – dictated the conditions of the slave trade. (Flaig 2009: 170–174) The Portuguese, after 150 years joined by the Dutch, English and French, made use of the offer on the slave markets. At the beginning, i.e. in the 15th century, the numbers of slaves transported, at first, to South America and the West Indies was about 1,000 per year. This number increased to 80,000 per year in the 18th century, which was possible because of increased wars among Africans. The estimate of enslaved Africans who were shipped across the Atlantic is about 11.5 million. All of them came from West Africa, one third of them from Africa south of the Equator, between the Cameroon estuary and the Kunene River. The difference to the slaves who remained in Africa was that in the transatlantic slave trade, two thirds were male because men were demanded as plantation workers while the inner-African slaves consisted mainly of women and children. (Oliver 1992: 123–128)

Africans have to face another fact: *Slavery was not terminated by Africans*. There were, indeed, slave rebellions in South and North America. The most successful one was on Haiti from 1790 to 1794, which resulted in the establishment of an independent state of Blacks in 1804. However, slavery was not fought in Africa, but in European countries and in North America. Rousseau argues in 1762 that human nature as created by God is indispensable and cannot be legitimately suppressed by humans. In 1772, Diderot follows this argument: It is not the slave who has to be considered as an incomplete human being – as Aristotle has maintained – but the slave owner. (Flaig 1995: 982) North American Quakers, the English evangelical movement, Dutch abolitionists were in the forefront of fighting slavery as a sin and crime against Divine Providence. Political steps followed: The Paris National Convent declares the abolition of slavery in 1794; the British Parliament forbids slave trade in English harbours and the import of slaves to British colonies in 1807 and about forty years later the possession of slaves; in 1861, President Abraham Lincoln provokes the American Civil War by announcing the liberation of all slaves; in the 1880s, slavery is no longer allowed in Cuba and Brazil; the Berlin Conference of 1884/5 declares the fight against slavery. (Eckert 2007: 62–65)

But these European efforts to end slavery did not stop it within *Africa*. For example, the Islamic Caliphate of Sokoto – between Northern Nigeria, Northern Cameroon and Lake Chad – was one of the biggest slave owner societies ever. Around 1900, there were 1.5 to 2 million slaves in Sokoto, more than half of the total population. In Zanzibar, slavery was a well-functioning institution in the 19th century. There, the sultans of Oman imported slaves from the East African coast and inland and exported them to Asia or used them on their own plantations. Because of the African resistance to abolition of slavery, the image of Africans changed in Europe from being victims of slavery to being enslaving tyrants. And even in the 21st century, Mauritania and Sudan are considered to practice slavery. In West Africa, parents sell their children to cacao plantations. Many children in Africa are enslaved as soldiers today... (Eckert 2007: 64–68) Only in 2004, slavery was officially abolished in Niger. Even today, there are allegedly still 40,000 slaves in Niger. Sold, lawless, inherited, abused, beaten or raped.[13]

When Africans blame the West for human exploitation through slavery, these facts have to be taken in consideration: Until the 18th century, slavery was usually considered as something 'normal' all over the world; slavery existed in Africa before Europeans came to the continent; the transatlantic slave trade between 15th to 19th centuries found an existing system and market for slave trade in Africa, i.e. Africans were deeply involved in the transatlantic trade of slaves; the abolition of slavery originated in the West, not in Africa where slavery continues in some parts of the continent until today; the Islamic slave trade has played an immense role

13. See also Flaig (2009: 210–214): "Humanitarian colonialism – abolition in Africa". For contemporary reports, see e.g.: *Daily Nation,* 28 October 2008, 10 and 18 November 2010.

on the African continent since the 7th century, being bigger by numbers than the transatlantic slave trade, but it is hardly mentioned by Africans, above all not in the context of claiming development aid.[14]

Taking the modern point of view of human rights – which was not the position of that time of slavery – we have to see the tremendous injustice done to the respective Africans by being enslaved. Their communities suffered a big loss of population. Slave hunting destroyed families and larger social and economic structures. In addition, many were killed in this process, maybe as many as those who were captured as slaves. The transport to and on the ships was cruel. Life as a slave consisted of humiliation and brutality. However, the question of moral blame concerning slavery is related to the change of the image of the human being. When dignity was recognised in every human being, certain violations of this individual dignity were no longer acceptable. This change happened in Europe; dignity and equality of all humans mark ideals of the Enlightenment. Because of the acceptance of these ideals, i.e. because of the change of ethics, the question of guilt concerning slavery arises.

Mentioning this change in (European) ethics and the African involvement in slavery is not meant to deny the Western responsibility for the inhuman treatment of many millions of Africans. But Africans have to take their share of responsibility, too. The moral blame of slavery in Africa has to be shared between and acknowledged by Africans, Moslems and Europeans. Each part has to admit their contribution to the injustice done to those slaves.

In addition, active involvement in slavery is not only a historic question. In the context of today's relationship between Africa and the West, we have to ask whether the *attitude* of the Westerners (and Arabs) towards Africans is still affected by the image: Africans were slaves and, therefore, even today they have to be looked upon and treated as sub-humans. But the same question has to be directed to Africans themselves, particularly to their *'elites'*. Is their self-image still the one of being masters and all others are servants, if not slaves? On a more theoretical level: Did the change of *ethics* happen in Africa – and in Islam – in the same way as it happened in the West? Are the human rights really universal? Are they recognised and even followed in Africa and in the Muslim-Arab world in the same way as in the West? Or as the West pretends to follow them?

***

Missionaries contributed a great deal to forming the relationship between Africa and the West as well as to the gradual change of the African societies. At first, missionaries came to Africa together with the merchants. The first ones were Franciscans who

14. See also Flaig (2009: 215). Hunwick (2006: 75–89), does not give any figures concerning the Arab/Islamic slave trade.

arrived as early as 1420 and 1431 together with the Portuguese.[15] Soon, some African kings converted to Christianity. In 1498, the first Christians are reported in Kenya. But it seems that Africa was not a priority for the various missionary societies of different countries and different denominations during the 16th and 17th century because there was not much missionary activity in Africa compared to later ,and to South and North America and to the East. The interest in Africa increased in the 18th century and continued until the 20th century and up to today. In the 19th century, missionaries also came as 'explorers' such as the Protestant Livingstone and the Anglican Rebmann. About 16,000 missionaries were active in Africa south of the Sahara in 1910.

The missionaries' intentions went beyond the conversion of Africans to Christianity – whichever denomination they were representing. The African heathens should not only be saved from the evil, they were also to receive 'culture' and 'civilisation' and, therefore, they were taught reading and writing. Livingstone's motivation to go to Africa was the "mission enterprise" *and* "the development of commerce, the elevation of the natives, or abolition of the trade in slaves".[16] Introducing (European) education and establishing schools definitely was one of the contributions of the missionary movement. For example, the Benedictines in East Africa not only offered academic schooling but also technical training for craftsmen and farmers. The missionaries produced the first African elites who, on the other hand, did not care for the rural masses. (Meredith 2006: 7)

The colonialists were interested in classifying the peoples of Africa and, by that, created tribes that did not originally exist in the self-perception of Africans; examples are the Abaluyia and the Kalenjin in Kenya. This was supported by missionaries who documented local customs and traditions, spreading the notion of ethnic identity. Missionaries also transcribed languages that were only spoken, reducing Africa's innumerable dialects to fewer written languages. (Meredith 2006: 154–155) One example for documenting a language, namely Kiswahili, is Ludwig Krapf who in the 1840s wrote the first dictionary of this language and translated parts of the Bible to Kiswahili.

Certainly, Europeans are convinced of the important influence that their missionaries had on Africans: giving them the 'proper' religious faith, bringing order into their social structures, elevating their spoken languages to written languages, and, above all, introducing European education. However, what missionaries never talk about and what they do not like to be confronted with is the destruction of African culture that happened by their doings. This is what Jomo Kenyatta (1965: 259–261) thinks about the European influence:

> Missionaries "condemned customs and beliefs which they could not understand [...] the African was regarded as a clean slate on which anything

15. http://en.wikipedia.org/wiki/Timeline_of_Christian_missions <Accessed 15 March 2011>

16. Livingstone (1857: 693), cit. Ansprenger (2002: 85–86).

> could be written. He was supposed to take wholeheartedly all religious dogmas of the white man and keep them sacred and unchallenged, no matter how alien to the African mode of life. The Europeans based their assumption on the conviction that everything that the African did or thought was evil. The missionaries endeavoured to rescue the depraved souls of the Africans from the 'eternal fire'; they set out to uproot the African, body and soul, from his old customs and beliefs, put him in a class by himself, with all his tribal traditions shattered and his institutions trampled upon. The African, after having been detached from his family and tribe, was expected to follow the white man's religion without questioning whether it was suited for his condition of life or not."

The Nigerian Chinua Achebe (1959/1994) describes how "things fall apart" because of the European influence. A similar account is given by Ngũgĩ wa Thiong'o (1975), a Kenyan, in his novel "The River Between". These African voices should be taken seriously when we try to understand the impact of the common history on the relationship between Africa and the West: *Those who are perceived as destroyers cannot expect to be trusted.*

Kenyatta (1965: 260) quotes Daniel Thwaites (1936: 3) to show how little respect the Europeans had for the Africans:

> "It was deemed unnecessary for white men to have any special training before dealing with and being put in charge of natives. It was a common assumption that work on the colonies required men of less education than work at home, so the colonies became a sort of clearing-house for failures and worse. This unfortunately applied equally to the missionary[!] as to other callings, and until recently it was the prevalent opinion that the Gospel could be better preached and interpreted to ignorant and degraded savages by less intellectual and less educated men. Of course, in this case the whole line of reasoning was wrong, for the natives were not as savage and degraded as was supposed".

Again, we have to critically ask where we stand today and which kind of respect Westerners have towards Africans.

***

Colonialism certainly had the strongest impact on Africa and on the relationship between Africa and the West – and it still has if we follow the view that development aid is a continuation of colonialism. The Portuguese established the first colonies in Africa; in 1498, they occupied what is today Mozambique[17]; in 1520, they conquered the sultanates of East Africa; in 1576, Angola became a Portuguese colony. Similar to the missionary activities, there are hardly further colonial

17. For details see the time table in Barth (2007: 124–127).

endeavours in the 17th and 18th centuries. But around 1800, the Cape Region becomes a British Crown Colony, originally occupied by Dutch settlers since 1652. And then, during the 19th century, England and France establish numerous colonies or protectorates in West and North Africa. King Leopold II of Belgium annexes the 'Free State of Congo' as his private colony in 1884. Between 1883 and 1885, the German colonies of "German East Africa" (Tanzania without Zanzibar, Burundi and Rwanda) and "German South-West Africa" (Namibia) as well as Cameroon and Togo as protectorates are established. Germany has to give them up after the First World War and they are distributed between England and France. Kenya becomes the British "East African Protectorate" in 1895.

The 1880s are considered to be the 'Scramble for Africa', culminating in the Berlin Conference of 1884/85.[18] There, thirteen European powers and North America agree on the partition of Africa as colonies and on trading rights. Slave trade is forbidden. Virtually the whole of Africa remains under the colonial rule of Europeans until 1957 when Ghana as the first state gains independence and when afterwards all other countries follow, Namibia being the last one in 1990. Strictly speaking, the really last one is the Black population of South Africa when in 1994 apartheid was abolished.

Ngũgĩ wa Thiong'o (2010: 80) gives an example of how colonialism looked like for the Kikuyu in Kenya:

> "From 1902 onward when Europeans stole our lands they turned many of the original owners into squatters by force, or guile, or both [...] to get money for taxes one had to work for pay, somewhere. Then after the First World War more Africans had their lands taken from them to make way for soldier settlement. Some of them went to the Rift Valley, increasing the squatter population. Then in 1941, even as our men went to fight for them in the big war, European settlers started expelling squatters from their farms, displacement a second time. Ole Ngurueni, near Nakuru, was a resettlement area for some of those who had been displaced. But then, three years after the return of our soldiers from the Second World War, the colonial government decided to expel the residents of Ole Ngurueni, yet again, a third time."

What is the *ideology* behind the European colonialism? What is the ideological *justification* for it? In the Middle Ages, a complicated doctrine of the 'just war' had been developed that was again applied to justify the conquests in South, Middle and North America in the 16th century. In the 1770s, a British member of parliament, Edmund Burke, protested against the despotism of the East India Company in India because Europeans had no right to interfere by force with other civilisations. At the same time, Rousseau idealised the "good wild". On 12 March 1828, Goethe says to Eckermann (1994: 699): "Often one would wish to be born as a so called wild on one of the islands of the Pacific, only to enjoy human existence at least once

18. See Pakenham (2003): The Scramble for Africa.

in a pure form without a bad tinge". On the one hand, one had a justification for conquests and colonisation; on the other hand, an upcoming conscience rejected the brutal treatment of people who were secretly admired.

Between 1770 and 1830, Europe experienced a political, economic, scientific, technical and moral change. The 'West' was at the top of a 'historic progress'. A political revolution happened in France; around 1800, a new type of state emerged, i.e. an interventionist and educationist state. In England, the industrial revolution changed society, economy and technology. At the end of the 18th century, an evangelical revival boosted the missionary movement, followed by the Catholics after 1850. The abolitionists can be taken as an example for a change of ethics: slavery was now considered inhuman. (Osterhammel 2007: 45–49)

Such revolutionary developments in Europe gave Europeans the understanding that they were representing a 'civilised world'; the European culture was perceived as a universal standard. Therefore, the Europeans believed in having to fulfil a *'civilising mission'* by bringing European civilisation to the rest of the world, of course, including Africa. Being the creators and representatives of a technically and morally superior civilisation, the Europeans felt called upon to rule the world. But this was not only an unselfish motivation; it also had a strong economic drive. Natural resources were perceived as not properly exploited by Africans. As Europeans felt to be on top of the 'historic progress', they not only assumed the right but even the duty to use those natural resources. (Osterhammel 2007: 46–50)

Three keywords for the motivation of colonisation are attributed to Livingstone, which he borrows from Thomas Buxton in 1840: *Christianity, Civilisation and Commerce.* The first one, of course, refers to the missionary motive of converting Africans to the Christian belief. 'Civilisation' covers several aspects of activities – the fight against slavery, but also against African customs that were considered 'barbaric', the introduction of technical progress, of health care and hygiene, of education. In education, the different approaches in colonization become obvious: The British offered higher education for administrative staff while the French aimed at the assimilation of a small elitist group, often sending them to France for education. The Belgians fully denied higher education to Africans. Primary education was either offered by missionaries or in state schools like in German colonies.[19] Ngũgĩ wa Thiong'o (2010: 72) describes the role missionary schools played in Kenya:

> They were schools "that were deliberately depriving Africans knowledge, in favour of training them to support the colonial state, which initially limited African education to carpentry, agriculture, and basic literacy only.

19. Ansprenger (2002: 84) questions the role of the colonial schools: "Most of the colonial schools were Christian mission schools, mainly where Islam did not determine the social life. Up to today, Africans like to confront Europeans with a saying [...]: 'When you came to us, you had the Bible and we the land. Soon afterwards, we had the Bible – and you the land.' Which role did the Christian mission really play in Africa's late 19th and early 20th century?"

> Command of English was seen as unnecessary. The white settler community wanted 'skilled' African labour, not learned African minds."

Certainly, 'commerce' was a strong motive for the colonisers. African colonies offered economic opportunities, land for settlers, raw materials, but also prestige in the imperialistic competition. In 1907, the German minister for colonies, Bernhard Dernburg, expressed the commercial benefit from colonies as follows:

> "Colonization means to make use of the soil, its resources, of the flora, the fauna and above all of the humans for the benefit of the economy of the colonizing nation." (cit. Koller 2007: 76)

Here, nothing is left from the philanthropic approach of the 'civilising mission'. It is exploitation at its best.

2.3. A disturbed relationship

This brings us to the question: *What has European colonisation meant to Africans?* Definitely, they were distressed and they resisted. To mention a few examples of African uprisings: the Asante (Ghana) who resisted the British for half a century until 1874; the Zulu of South Africa who defeated 8,000 European soldiers in 1879 or the Shona and Ndebele peoples in Zimbabwe in 1896/97; the leader Samori Toure of 'West African Sudan' fought the French for two decades until 1900 when he was captured; the Battle of Adowa in Ethiopia in 1895 when 4,000 Italian soldiers were killed; there were the Maji-Maji Uprisings in Tanganyika in 1905–1907. Such revolts demonstrate the Africans' rejection of the 'civilising mission' of the Europeans. The Africans experienced it as usurpation. For, this was not only 'benevolent', though guided by a cultural superiority complex, in the sense: we bring you a better civilisation. It was definitely and increasingly malevolent because of a humiliating *racism:* You are subhuman; you are not even educable; therefore, we can do with you what we want, leaving all humanity behind us.

The 'civilising mission' was *alien to the Africans* who were not even asked whether they wanted the European 'blessings'. The European cultures were imposed upon and, by that, the African social and religious customs destroyed as they were declared as 'evil'. The expropriation of land has to be seen on the same level, as land, for instance for the Kenyan Kikuyu, has a spiritual meaning, not only a material one:

> "[...] land tenure [is] the most important factor in the social, political, religious, and economic life of the tribe [...] Communion with the ancestral spirits is perpetuated through contact with the soil in which the ancestors of the tribe lie buried." (Kenyatta 1965: 22)

When you take away someone's land you separate him from his personal past. Have colonialists ever understood and/or respected this? Other African tribes may not have the same attachment to their land. But their social and spiritual roots may have been destroyed by Europeans in a similar way. One example: during a ritual among the

Kamba of Kenya, rain or drought was predicted by a person who had contact with ancestors; villagers say it has been successful, but now it is abandoned because of Christianity.[20] Also here, this is not a question of an 'objective', scientific correctness but of a loss of tradition.

The 'civilising mission' revealed its selfish side when Africans were forced to labour, when they had to pay taxes, e.g. the 'hut tax' in Kenya, when Africans had to serve in European wars without being rewarded, when it came to suppression of rights and humiliation. Apartheid is not a South African invention; there, it was 'only' legally and politically institutionalised and perfected.[21] A story told by Njenga Karume (2009: 82) illustrates how apartheid was practised also in Kenya. Around 1950, as a young man he entered a shop to buy a newspaper. He had not seen the sign 'Europeans only'.

> "A strong hand suddenly gripped my collar and I was dragged out [...] and was warned never to step into the shop again and then shoved with such force that I fell to the ground. That moment opened my eyes to the contempt that the white man held for the African. I could not understand why I had been hurled out [...] I then understood that the African was treated as though he was a dog and I felt bitter about the humiliation and injustice of it all."

Separation in Kenya also meant that there were quarters reserved for the British and quarters for the Black Africans and others for the Indians; separation also meant that only Whites were allowed to grow certain cash crops like tea or coffee.

Contradicting the European 'higher morality' and, above all, the claim for 'Christian ethics' that should be brought to Africa through the 'civilising mission' are the testimonies of the atrocities and brutalities committed by the Whites. As an example: in King Leopold's Congo, workers were killed or mutilated when they did not deliver according to the demand of a supervisor. In Kenya, the Mau Mau uprising was suppressed with utter brutality. Caroline Elkins (2005) calls her report about it "Britain's Gulag:[22] The Brutal End of Empire in Kenya". In her preface, she summarises her findings and judgement:

> "I came to learn that the colonial government had intentionally destroyed many of [the] missing files in massive bonfires on the eve of its 1963 retreat from Kenya." (x) "I've come to believe that during the Mau Mau war British forces wielded their authority with a savagery that betrayed a perverse

20. *The Star*, 1–15 February 2011.

21. "The racism shown by the English-speaking whites in Kenya and the British colonial administration was every bit as bad as it was among the diehard *Boere* in South Africa. Only in this place they were free to put their hate into daily practice, [...] by killing hundreds of black civilians without fear of official prosecution under the dual euphemisms of 'suspected Mau Mau' or 'attempting to escape'. It was open season on the blacks and it brought out the worst instincts in many whites." (Courtenay 2005: 573).

22. 'Gulag' was the Soviet forced labour and concentration camp system. See Aleksandr Solzhenitsyn: The Gulag Archipelago. San Francisco 1973; also: Anderson (2005).

> colonial logic: only by detaining nearly the entire Kikuyu population of 1.5 million people and physically and psychologically atomizing its men, women and children could colonial authority be restored and the civilising mission reinstated." (xiii) "I now believe there was in late colonial Kenya a murderous campaign to eliminate Kikuyu people, a campaign that left tens of thousands, perhaps hundreds of thousands, dead." (xiv)

To illustrate what she is talking about: my Kenyan wife's uncle was *buried alive* by the British – an act of brutal inhumanity. In 2010 and 2011, the British government tried to argue in court that the claims of Mau Mau victims should be taken care of by the *Kenyan* government, as if the Kenyans were committing those atrocities to themselves. This is arrogance and cynicism to the extreme and the opposite of coming to terms with the past.[23]

Colonialism ended at independence for most of the African countries before and after 1960. Many have fought for it like the Kenyans in the Mau Mau revolt. Up to now, the colonial powers are trying to cling on to their influence in the former colonies through contracts, business, military support, organisations such as the Commonwealth, by interfering behind the stage, and last but not least by development aid. Their influence was strongly felt during the Cold War when political power overrode moral considerations, for instance by supporting African despots who diligently learnt from the colonialists how to suppress and exploit their own people.

At the end, was the 'civilising mission' 'successful'? The outcome reveals two sides: The ideology of supremacy and 'civilising' the Africans perverted itself because of the inhuman treatment of the Africans: destruction of African cultures, uprooting people, racism, exploitation of resources, expropriation of land, forced labour, apartheid, brutality and atrocities, etc. On the other hand, the new African states inherited – although not everywhere – an infrastructure of roads, railways, an administrative and health care system, and (European) education with the minimum of reading and writing. However, Aimé Césaire[24] reminds us that such 'progress' was paid with loss, suffering, and blood:

> "I am told about progress, about 'achievements', about healed sicknesses, about a living standard that exceeds the original level by far. But I am talking about societies who were alienated, about trampled cultures, about eroded institutions, about confiscated land, about murdered religions, about destroyed art, about extraordinary *possibilities* which have been suppressed. I am confronted with facts, statistics, figures of kilometers of roads, canals, railways. I am talking about thousands of sacrificed humans for the construction of the railway".

23. Peter Mwaura stresses the need for the British to apologise for their atrocities, in: *Daily Nation*, 16 April 2011.

24. Césaire (1968: 23); cit. Bouchentouf-Siagh (2010: 94).

Equipments and institutions were alien to the Africans, leaving them with the 'hardware' and not with the 'software' to manage those goods. 'Software' means the mental setup that has created them and which makes proper use of them. In addition, not every inheritance was and is a blessing, for instance: the artificial national borders as designed by the foreigners at the Berlin Conference, the political 'democratic' structures or the confusing land distribution. The state borders often divide indigenous peoples all over Africa – for instance the Maasai, the Luo, the Oromo, the Somali in Kenya and neighbouring states. Up to today, politicians and people are struggling to adapt to something like 'democracy', building up a 'democratic' facade to please former colonial powers and donors, also lacking the 'software' for it. In Kenya, the British have thoroughly confused the land ownership. They chased away the Kikuyu from the most fertile land; made shoddy contracts with the Maasai and the Kisii; are still occupying large tracts of agricultural land or sold land which they had acquired through forceful occupation. The land issue was one of the main causes for the clashes in Kenya in January and February 2008.[25]

Once more, was the 'civilising mission' 'successful'? Taking a *pragmatic* perspective – which may not be easily shared by Africans – we have to consider the presence of Europeans in Africa from the arrival of the Portuguese in the 15th century and especially during the intensified colonisation in the 19th and 20th century until the end of colonialism in the 1960s as an *enforced preparation of Africans for the global world* of the 21st century. This global world is strongly shaped by the European 'historic progress' that I have mentioned earlier, namely determined by the changes that came with the scientific, technological, industrial, political and ethical revolutions. Those changes intensified at the end of the 18th and the beginning of the 19th century and gradually dominated the whole world. Whether we like it or not, this globalisation process is driven by the European mental set-up. This does not entitle Europeans to nourish a superiority complex, last but not least, because globalisation has created a *one-sided* way of life suppressing other rich possibilities of life. At the beginning of the 21st century, it seems that the European/American domination could come to an end. The question today is how globalisation will continue and in which way other countries and civilisations will influence it – like the Chinese and the Indian.

---

25. The Kenyan Ministry of Lands presented the "Sessional Paper No. 3 of 2009 on National Land Policy", published in the *Sunday Nation* on 16 May 2010. There, direct reference is made to historical land injustices (No. 178): "Historical land injustices are grievances which stretch back to colonial land administration practices and laws that resulted in mass disinheritance of communities of their land, and which grievances have not been sufficiently resolved to date." Therefore (No. 179): "The government shall (a) Establish mechanisms to resolve historical land claims arising in 1895 or thereafter. The rationale for this decision is that 1895 is the year when Kenya became a protectorate under the British East African Protectorate with the power to enact policies and laws under the Crown. It is these colonial practices and laws which formed the genesis of the mass disinheritance of various Kenyan communities of their land".

As brutal and inhuman this 'civilising mission' may have been for the Africans, it has taken Africa on board of the global development. Africans may answer to this: Left alone, we would have made the necessary development on our own. Then, Africa would have gone which way? It would have been a *different* mental, spiritual, social, economic and political way.

However, this is speculation; history can no longer be undone. Colonisation and globalisation have to be accepted as facts. The pragmatic question rather is: How can Africa cope with globalisation *today* and at the same time maintain her own social, spiritual and ethical identity? How can Africa participate in shaping globalisation? And above all, how can Africa become *independent* as an equal global partner? When we take the use of the mobile phone in Africa as an opinion poll for the acceptance of globalisation, at least on the technical level – over 25 million Kenyans used a mobile phone in June 2011 – then the vote is a clear Yes. But of course, technology is not the whole life.

The other and very important question is: *What did the 'civilising mission' do to the relationship between Africa and the West?* I repeat what Njenga Karume (2009: 82) is saying: "I [...] understood that the African was treated as though he was a dog and I felt bitter" and I quote where Karume (2009: 31) describes the relationship from the African perspective:

> "Europeans had invaded the country, made all the land their own and forced Africans to become servants on what had been their own property. Indeed, Kikuyu traditions revered land as being under the custody of ancestral spirits and for the purpose of economic sustenance. But the Europeans destroyed centuries-old traditions and killed Africans for strange and arbitrary reasons that the African did not even understand. In short, the traditionalists considered European economic and cultural activities evil and therefore a great many parents forbid their children to have association with anything European. European education was seen as a form of indoctrinating African children against their own culture and traditions."

As a critical European, Patrick Chabal (2009: 20) describes the relationship between the West and Africa:

> "Africa is that part of the world where Europeans projected most forcefully and fancifully their own pride and prejudice. This means, among other reasons, that it is in Africa that they revealed most clearly their own vision of mankind, extolled most loudly their own colonial (missionary) project, deployed most skilfully their own justification for enslaving and exploiting 'others', justified most casuistically their own sense of racial superiority and, today, revel in their most self-serving display of guilt and regret."

The purpose of sketching the history of Africa was to create awareness of the current relationship between Africans and Westerners. The widely unknown, but interesting and rich history of Africa before the Europeans arrived in the

15th century should make Westerners rethink their notion of Africa as the 'dark continent' and of Africans as 'savages'. The overall approach to Africa was guided by Eurocentrism, pushing aside the fact that Africa has been populated by human beings who deserved respect as such. This culminated in the transatlantic slave trade, which has to be judged upon within its historic and inner-African context, also keeping in mind the African participation in it; only a change in European ethics ended slavery by and by. Eurocentrism also guided the European 'discovery' of Africa and especially the colonisation period between 1800 and 1960. Eurocentrism had negatively developed to a superiority complex and to racism on the side of the Europeans. Confronted with this attitude of Europeans, Africans experienced expropriation, apartheid, brutality, dehumanisation, and alienation of their own cultures. Even missionary activities and the inheritance at the time of independence, such as infrastructure and education that could be judged as something positive, were alien and destructive in the African context.

Looking at this historic encounter that was mostly painful for Africans – which attitude and feelings towards Europeans can be expected from Africans? Is it astonishing when the relationship between Africans and Europeans is characterised by bitterness, suspicion, and distrust? And when Europeans have always looked down on Africans – how could a healthy and constructive relationship with Africans have developed? I am afraid, this is not a historic observation, but under the surface it is still valid today, at least in many cases.[26] This disturbed and unhealthy relationship can only change when both sides perceive the historic facts as such and decide to leave them behind. It is true that many Africans have developed a healthy self-confidence – Kenyans perhaps more than many others – and that many Europeans have true business and warm personal relationships with Africans where mutual respect dominates. Only this attitude can be the way forward.

26. For example, many writers in the internet forum "The African Executive" express anger and distrust against Whites. Often they may get the facts wrong; but this is not the point; the attacked Whites should rather notice the disturbed relationship that comes afore.

"The African individual can only say: 'I am, because we are; and since we are, therefore I am'."

(Mbiti 1999: 108–109)

CHAPTER THREE

African social structure

My thesis is that Africans and Westerners have to *understand* the other side if their relationship is to be a fruitful one and, based on this, if development cooperation were to be successful. Although this seems to be obvious, *this is not the case* in general. A brief glance at the history of Africa and the common history of Africa and the West gives a hint of what constitutes their relationship today. Now, we should try to see how Africans understand themselves as human beings, what is meaningful for them, and how their social structure is formed.

I intend to pursue this aspect by looking at education in the Kikuyu tradition, which reveals their social structure, by referring to Chabal's findings concerning features of sub-Saharan societies, by discussing 'Village' and 'City', i.e. tradition and modernity, by means of some examples, and, finally, by describing a certain group of Westerners, the 'Kenyan Cowboys'.

3.1. Kenyatta on education and community

To get a preliminary answer to the question about 'the African', we can refer to Kenyatta's description of the Kikuyu "system of education" (1965: 95–124). This may sound strange at first. However, Kenyatta shows clearly that Kikuyu education does *not* mean to teach certain abstract knowledge to a boy or a girl for the purpose of enriching an *individual* through this knowledge. Education here means to introduce boys and girls into the *community* and, by that, to perpetuate and to renew the community through educating the young. The *content* of this education is the social structure itself and what supports and constitutes it. Therefore, following the course of this Kikuyu education will reveal the structure of the Kikuyu community.

In the following, I will summarise Kenyatta's elaboration on the Kikuyu "system of education": Here, education means above all formation of the *character* of individuals, which is formed primarily through relations with other people (117[27]). This happens within the *family* circle and then within the *local* group, and finally within the whole *tribal* organisation. This is not *school* education; it is related to and happens at the *homestead*. The mother and the nurse are the first educators. Very soon, the *history* and *tradition* of the family and the clan are carried on through the medium of lullabies. The child is left free to listen to these songs. But later when the child is able to speak, he or she will be asked questions to test how much he or she has learnt. When it comes to physical education, i.e. sitting and walking properly and how to use one's hands – also related to tribal activities – parents take an almost equal responsibility. Co-education is introduced in the form of children's games. In their games, children will *imitate their elders*. (95–98)

After babyhood, the father takes charge of the boy's education and the mother of the girl's and a part of the boy's education. The father who is a farmer will take the boy to the field for practical training and he will teach him names of animals and plants. In any case, also when the father is a craftsman, he will teach the boy *by examples*. In addition, there is general training. For instance, the boy is taught about family, clan, and tribal lands; their boundaries are carefully pointed out to him. In contrast to European education, strong emphasis is laid on training of *observation* and *memory*. For, counting, especially of animals and people, is a taboo for Kikuyus; it is considered to bring bad luck to the people or animals counted. (This is a highly interesting and consequential aspect. I will refer to it later – 8.1.) The mother introduces her daughter to domestic duties and agricultural works. She teaches "both boy and girl the *laws and customs*, especially those governing the *moral code* and general rules of *etiquette* in the community". (99–100)

Kikuyu education emphasises a particular act of *behaviour* in a concrete

27. Page numbers in this part refer to Kenyatta (1965).

situation. This kind of knowledge is strongly practice oriented. It is taught mainly *by doing,* related to particular occasions and insofar always *within the experience* of the child. Furthermore, this teaching is based on *personal relations.* The core of this education is that the person, i.e. as a child and at the later stages of life, has to learn the manners and behaviours proper to his or her position in the community. The children and everyone else have to *know their place*, giving respect and obedience where it is due. This place is strongly determined by *age,* for the whole Kikuyu society is *graded by age* and the prestige which accompanies a status in age-grouping.

> "It determines the different salutations used, the manners people may adopt in eating certain foods, the different tasks in homestead or garden; it rules habits of dress or demeanour in the community; and it explains the rights of different people in judging cases, in exercising authority in the clan or family, in ceremonial or religious proceedings." (102–103)

As Kenyatta says, one example for paying respect is the way of saluting. Europeans find it strange when an African does not look at them in the eye when he is greeting – but this is meant to be respectful. The Kamba may appear to be rude because they seem to be reluctant to greet – they have to wait to be first greeted by an older and respected person.

Education in the Kikuyu society is not limited to childhood and youth; it is understood as a life-long process. Education accompanies important events in life, e.g. circumcision when a boy or a girl becomes a full member of the community.[28] Another stage of life and learning relates to marriage and becoming a parent. Only when the first child is circumcised and ready for marriage can a man become an elder. Each step in the social ladder is marked by a corresponding standard of manners and behaviour. Sex education is given with a social reference. Thus, boys are taught to look forward to marriage as a duty to themselves, to the clan and the tribe. A girl is also taught grade privileges and knowledge. She is supposed to behave like a "gentlewoman, not to raise her eyes or voice talking to men in public, not to bathe in the open, not to eat in the presence of men other than those of her own age or kinsfolk". (104–108)

The *parents* have to be seen as custodians of tradition representing the public teaching about life and duty. Therefore, they and immediate relatives are the most respected persons. Being cursed by a dying father or mother because of having violated their respect is the most dreadful thing that can befall a son or a daughter. This curse cannot be purified and will be inherited by their children. The father also represents the proper means of communication and fellowship with the *ancestors*. By that, he plays a kind of a religious role and respect to him is even more essential for this reason.

---

28. See Thiong'o (2010: 122–126) about the traditional meaning and ritual of circumcision. This of course does not reflect the Western and modern criticism of circumcision.

Besides the parents and other close relatives, the *age-group* is a dominant factor in the life of an individual. The peer groups represent fellowship and unity, but not only locally; they bind men or women from all parts of the whole tribe; they emphasise the social grades of junior and senior, inferior and superior. These social bonds – family and age-groups – are supported by the principle of *reciprocal obligations*. "House-building, cultivation, harvesting, digging trap-pits, putting up fences around cultivated fields, and building bridges, are usually done by the group" (–113).

This principle of mutual contribution is still true today. The small Kenyan village Nduriri in Kiambu District gives a striking example: Without government support, over the years the villagers have established a primary school, a church, a secondary school and a health dispensary.

> Kenyatta concludes:
> "[...] to the Europeans 'Individuality is the ideal of life', to the Africans the ideal is the right relations with, and behaviour to, other people". There is "no really individual affair, for everything has a moral and social reference." Even "marriage contracts and ceremonies are the affairs of families and not of individuals". "The habit of corporate effort is but the other side of corporate ownership; and corporate responsibility is illustrated in corporate work no less than in corporate sacrifice and prayer." (113–118)

3.2. Some features of African society

This picture of African education and society may be questioned by two comments. First, one can argue this one is limited to the Kikuyu in Kenya. What does it say about African societies in general? Second, "Facing Mount Kenya" by Kenyatta was first published in 1938. What relevance does this description of Kikuyu society (and education) have in a modernised world even if it exemplifies general African features?

At first, I would like to show that the insights we get from the geographically and socially limited findings about the Kikuyu society can be applied to Africans in general. For example, very similar to Kenyatta, Gebrewold-Tochalo (2003: 97–99) says about education of the Kambata, an agricultural society in the southern part of Ethiopia, that the family is the place where the growing children learn to internalise the social virtues and norms. It is an important value for the adults to make the growing children 'adjusted' social members. "The Kambata children are expected to respect not only their closest relatives, but also all relatives and neighbours on whom the member of the society is indispensably dependent." Similar to the Kikuyu education, by practical doing, the young boys are little by little introduced into the roles of the father; and the young girls come to know the duties of women. Gebrewold-Tochalo recognises another important dimension of socialisation in teaching the history of one's own lineage and clan. "The method of teaching is by narrating some stories about the lineage and the clan or through some improvised traditional songs".

Kenyatta's emphasis that he is talking about an 'African' society also gets strong support from Patrick Chabal (2009: 24–84). Mainly in the first three chapters of "Africa. The politics of suffering and smiling", Chabal talks about basic features of sub-Saharan societies. In principle, these are the same as the social structure of the Kikuyu. Discussing the problem of generalisation concerning his own statements, Chabal (2009: 108) remarks: "The general has emerged from the local evidence, brought to light by a large number of scholars (both African and Western) working on entirely different material. That cannot be coincidental." Chabal talks in a more abstract language than Kenyatta, but the parallels are obvious. What are Chabal's findings?

Chabal intends to find out what (a) the *'being'*, i.e. the existence, of the African individual is, (b) his/her *'belonging'* and (c) his/her *'belief'* system. As Chabal is interested in a political theory of Africa, his parallel and consequent question is what being, belonging and believing mean for political action or "agency". (7)[29] In our context, we can limit the interest to the basic facts as presented by Chabal and, by that, acquire a set of terms that help describe some features of African societies.[30] Later, I will mention a few examples that may illustrate what these abstract terms mean in the African reality.

By 'being', Chabal understands the place and role of individuals within the environment in which they are born and live[31]. He elaborates on three dimensions of the 'being': on origin, identity and locality. The *origin* is strongly defined by the places of birth and burial which are closely linked. One has to be buried where he originates from, for birth and burial have religious, cultural and sociological importance. We have earlier seen the connection between land and ancestors. Land, says Chabal, "is not just a physical attribute but is constitutive of what 'being' means – in the sense that it provides the context within which people define

29. Page numbers in this part refer to Chabal (2009).

30. Overview of Chabal's terminology in the first three chapters (24–84):

Being	origin:	land, ancestors, belief
	identity:	ethnicity, religion
	locality:	gender, age, authority
Belonging	kin:	association, obligation
	reciprocity:	(political) exchange, representation, accountability
	stranger:	economic, political, cultural aspect
Believing	morality:	religion, tradition, obligation
	rationality:	gift, witchcraft
	agency:	cycle of life, public virtue, public good

31. It may be a typical Western approach to ask who the *individual* is in the African context.

and organise themselves in socio-political terms" (28). "By far the most significant aspect of origin is the relation between the living and the dead – or the link to the *ancestors.*" At the same time, "ancestors and land are intimately connected in the very real sense that the ancestors inhabit a concrete world", i.e. the place from where the individual originates. "The link to the ancestors, wherever they are buried, is an integral part of the meaning of origin and of the texture of identity". On the other hand, the "relation between land and ancestors, is [...] the very foundation of the *belief system*, or religion" (29).

Concerning the term *'identity',* Chabal (30–35) at first refers to the definition of identity that was used by the colonialists and after independence, namely the tribe or ethnicity. But historically, ethnicity was flexible, fluid and negotiable. Thus, identity is rather determined by 'locality', i.e. the relationship between individual and community, and by 'belonging', which includes kinship and reciprocity. We can certainly add that the individual's origin bears importance for his/her identity as the community is important within which the individual grows up – as described by Kenyatta. As crucial as the reference to history may be, as indispensable it is to see the contemporary reality. Even if ethnicity was flexible and negotiable in former times, as Chabal maintains, we have to acknowledge the existence of tribes and, for instance the tribal tensions between the Kikuyu, Luo and Kalenjin which were the force behind the clashes in Kenya at the beginning of 2008. The Ivory Coast provides another example of tribal identification. Under the headline "Stranger" Chabal (57–63) elaborates on economic, political and cultural aspects of ethnic differences that are an expression of not-belonging. With respect to the religious orientation, Chabal (34) points to the strength of African religions that have easily adapted "the strange dogma and rituals of the foreigners' creeds". In other words, Islam and Christianity do not also provide a strong support for identification.

'Origin' and 'identity' come together in what Chabal calls *'locality'* (35–42). This notion stands for community and more precisely for the *relationship* between individual and community. In this context, we are strongly reminded of Kenyatta's descriptions. One aspect of 'locality' is the *gender* relationship. Women and men belong to certain groupings who are guided by a specific ethos and by specific values. By that, the groups determine the identity of the individual. Those groups are also *age-groups*. They define the social position within the community as well as the social hierarchy, again determining the identity of the individual. From there, the age-group and the individual within it are equipped with *authority.* "Authority implies a position of trust, competence and wisdom that confers upon those who are endowed with it the force of persuasion, rather than coercion." (40) This is genuine authority contrary to politically misused authority.

Individuals are defined by relations, by *belonging-to.* This is clearly evident in *kinship,* which is a form of *association* with specific *obligations*. Kinship is often interpreted by Westerners as something negative because, allegedly, it hinders the personal development. However, in the African context, being 'human' means to be part of a kin network as kinship contributes to a sense of socially meaningful belonging. And "within a network, an obligation defines how individuals relate to each other as human beings". Therefore, obligations are a "means of sustaining one's place in a network of belonging: that most vital attribute of humanity, sociability and, ultimately, being-in-the-world". "To have no obligation is not to belong; it is not to be fully and socially human." Among general obligations which may be found in the whole of Africa that are related to origin, age, gender or beliefs, the most fundamental obligation has to do with burial. (43–49)

Obligations are based on *reciprocity*. The Western argument against demands of relatives towards somebody who has an income based on education or his stay abroad does not take into account that this person's education or travel to a foreign country has been financed by the same relatives. The father has sold land or cows, relatives have donated money, there have been 'harambees'[32] in the village or in a club in town – in order to pay for the school, the university degree or for the overseas ticket. This is not done for the individual person as such but to strengthen the family or the wider community. The beneficiary of the community effort is obliged to support others in return – the younger sibling or another member of the community. This reciprocity is most obviously expressed in gift or giving (72). A family who visits another family will not go empty handed. In the Kikuyu tradition, one will bring something very substantial – bread, flour, cooking fat, etc., but no luxury goods such as flowers or chocolate; this, of course, is very strange for a Westerner. The visiting family will not leave without vegetables, a pot with cooked food, sometimes with a live chicken. This is not done because the other family is starving but because of the "intimate connection between giving, being and belonging" (73).

> "[...] giving is not merely instrumental but also constitutive of the very identity of the individual-within-the-group. The purpose of the gift is not just to act as a social hedge against future fortune; it is also a core component of self-identification and of the assessment of the morality of the 'others'." (73)

Further on, Chabal discusses reciprocity as exchange, representation and accountability in the political context.

Kenyatta's and Chabal's depiction of the African society is confirmed by John Mbiti (1999: 104–105). He, too, stresses that the deep sense of kinship "has been one of the strongest forces in traditional African life".

> "It is kinship which controls social relationships between people in a given community: it governs marital customs and regulations, it determines the behaviour of one individual toward another."

32. *Harambee* means the coming together of relatives, friends, neighbours and other invited guests to collect money for a specific purpose.

> "The kinship system is like a vast network stretching laterally (horizontally) in every direction, to embrace everybody in any given local group. This means that each individual is a brother or sister, father or mother, grandmother or grandfather, or cousin, or brother-in-law, uncle or aunt, or something else, to everybody else. That means that everybody is related to everybody else."

This structure of the community determines who the individual is:

> "In traditional life, the individual does not and cannot exist alone except corporately. He owes his existence to other people, including those of past generations and his contemporaries. He is simply part of the whole."
> "The individual can only say: 'I am, because we are; and since we are, therefore I am'." (Mbiti 1999: 108–109)

3.3. 'Village' and 'City' – tradition and modernity

Whilst Kenyatta describes a specific African society from within, Chabal generalises characteristics of sub-Saharan societies in an abstract way. According to those authors – Kenyatta, Chabal and also Mbiti – what are the main features of African societies?

In the relationship between community and individual, the emphasis strongly lies on the *community;* the community is represented by and is present in the individual; in simple terms, when you understand the community, you have an indication for understanding the individual. This is difficult if not impossible for Westerners to imagine and to grasp; it is alien in the sense of Sundermeier (see 7.2). For the Westerners' emphasis lies on the *individual*; the society is defined from the point of view of individuals – while the African individual is defined through the community. However, 'community' must not be understood as 'collectivism' which muzzles individuals.

> "The community should not be seen as being tyrannical. Individual talents and contributions were held in high esteem and promoted. In fact, the insistence on the importance of the community can only be seen to have been geared towards making the lives of individuals comfortable and safeguarding their freedom." (Makumba 2007: 130)

The *ancestors* are part of the community and they are *present*. Here, Westerners face a similar difficulty in understanding and accepting the presence of an invisible power. This also relates to witchcraft or curse.

Both basic concepts - the community as the core of life and the presence of the ancestors – have consequences for other features of the society:

The importance of the place of birth and burial;

The respect for age and specifically for parents;

The bond of age-groups;
The network of family, clan and age-group;
The related hierarchies and authorities;
The code of behaviour supporting the hierarchy;
The obligations towards the community;
The reciprocity of obligations;
Teaching the history of family, clan and tribe;
The teaching of behaviour and etiquette;
The introduction to stages of life in the community through education and initiation.

These abstract features of African societies indicate a general tendency; they need to be specified according to the peculiar local situation. But still, the second question that we have raised above remains: What relevance do those social features have in a modern Africa?

In the following, I will mention a few examples, on the one hand, to illustrate those general features and, on the other hand, also to show their place in contemporary Africa, concretely in Kenya.

The first examples demonstrate the 'belonging' of the individual, for instance, showing how school children are part of the whole community – not just of the immediate family – and how they are supported. Before the final school exams, parents, relatives and friends will encourage the candidates by sending so-called 'success cards', which are very important for the boy's or the girl's spirit.

A strong gesture of support can be seen when students, parents, relatives, teachers and friends assemble at the school, perhaps on a Sunday morning, to pray, to listen to speeches and, by that, to encourage the candidates.

After the exams, the results are announced in the newspapers, highlighting the best students with stories and pictures. These examples show that school exams are not a private matter; they are a communal, even national event.

Similarly, marriage is not a private matter. According to the contemporary Kikuyu custom, the extended families of the groom and of the bride visit each other before the wedding, for instance to negotiate the dowry. The bride's extended family wants to see where their daughter will be going. These meetings have a ceremonial character and are part of an order, i.e. they have to happen as certain things *have* to be done. The visiting clan will bring food in baskets and the receiving family reciprocate the gifts. Both clans act as groups, perhaps fifty or more persons on each side, not as individuals. This shows, for instance, in the sitting order: The gathering is seated in rows of chairs under a simple tent, open to one side. The individuals of the two clans do not mix as each clan is seated together and besides a brief greeting they do not talk to members of the other clan. In addition, women and men are seated separately (Only when the formal part is over, one is chatting with everybody). A representative of the receiving family says a prayer. Local food cooked by the women is offered, most of the time very generously. It is self-service, but women will serve elders. The men have slaughtered a goat or a sheep in advance. This meat – in small pieces and as ribs – goes round towards the end of the meal. On certain occasions, the guests will receive special parts of the goat to take home.

In negotiation of the dowry at the home of the bride, elders, men, and women will meet inside the house. The fathers and mothers of both the groom and the bride have to be represented by an elder who also represents the clan; the 'main' persons, groom and bride, are not involved. After the dowry is settled and part of it paid by the groom's clan (payment of dowry is a life-long issue), the groom has 'to cut the shoulder' of a goat in front of the elders. One elder may help him to do it in the proper way. 'Cutting the shoulder' seals the marriage in the Kikuyu customary law. After the elders have joined the rest of the members again – also depending on the occasion – one or sometimes several persons will speak and introduce their own clan members to the other group. Often, a woman from the guests will say a prayer to close the meeting.

This cursory description demonstrates how the family, the clan, the community, is in charge and not the individuals. The bride not only becomes the wife of the groom, she will also be an integral part of the groom's family; she *belongs* to it; she has left her original family.

The closeness and the network of family, clan and age-group also show when it comes to the preparation of a wedding, after the marriage has been traditionally agreed upon and sealed. Many weeks before the event, family and clan members and close friends form a committee that will organise the wedding ceremony in detail: venue, invitation cards, overall programme, financing, music, food, master of ceremony, transport, wedding cake, clothing for the bride's and the groom's companions, place of picture and video taking. The bride and groom are definitely not left alone. Preparation of a funeral is done by a similar committee (By the way, it is unheard of that a wedding or a funeral committee has embezzled money).

An example of 'obligation': When a father dies, uncles, aunts and grandparents pay for the education of his children. This can mean many years of support for several children. The costs are shared among the family members as an obligation towards the family. Such a situation can also reveal a misuse of the family support when, for instance, the mother of the children refuses to contribute adequately.

We can see another example of social closeness and related obligation in the case of somebody's serious illness. Not only family members, but also friends, neighbours and colleagues will visit the sick person at home or at the hospital. Hospitals are crowded during visiting hours because there are always several people around the bed of the sick person. These visitors convey the message to the sick: you are not alone, we are with you.

The Kikuyu way of *naming* children demonstrates the close relationships within a family and a clan: The first born boy receives the Christian and the Kikuyu name of his paternal grandfather, the first born girl the name of her paternal grandmother. This boy will later give his name to his future first born grandson, this girl to her first born granddaughter. And so on. The second born will receive the names of the maternal grandparents. In the same way, an uncle will give his names to one of his later born nephews and an aunt to one of her nieces. By that, a close weave of names is established that relates into the past as well as into the future and at the same time into the present time. Kikuyus do not see that as something superficial but understand it in an existential sense, which is the decisive aspect here. They say: I *am* my grandfather; I am represented and *living on* through my grandson. This identification creates a close connection within the clan that appears to be time-less. For, also the ancestors are represented in this weave of names, and the name-bearer and his ancestors will always be present in their successors. Name giving identifies the child with the clan; the name is not identifying the individual but integrates him or her into the clan. In addition, since the missionary time, Kenyans – not only Kikuyus – bear two given names, a Christian name and a tribal name. By both names, one belongs to two worlds, which is not only symbolic but real.

The following examples talk about other tribes, the Luo and the Luhya, and about the issue of *burial*. On 24 February 1999, the Kenyan *East African Standard* reported that Raila Odinga, at that time Member of Parliament, had proposed that the Luo community should bury their dead outside their ancestral homes. The immense sums that were spent for transport and festivities at the burials should be used for fighting poverty. This news initiated a fierce debate in the newspapers for several weeks. Raila was attacked because he had no respect for tradition; he was adulterating Luo culture; he insulted the Luo community; he was not authorised to change Luo customs. Justice Kwach gave a reason for those attacks:

> "Luos are usually buried in their homes so that they can be assured of secure graves and continue their afterlife (because as a tribe we strongly believe in life after death) within easy reach of the immediate family so that they continue to be available for consultation in case of illness and to assist the women in the complex problem of naming children [...] a Luo's funeral is the very last opportunity he has in the world to call all the members of his clan together, and like any host who holds a feast, it is customary to feed them. Being his last feast, he will feel honoured if his guests are properly fed and go away feeling happy. That is the purpose of the practice."[33]

Interestingly, one writer mentioned the "struggle between traditionalists and up-coming generations" and he advised that the elders "should leave cultural adherence and interpretation to individuals"[34] – which, of course, is heresy to traditionalists.

33. *Daily Nation*, 8 March 1999.

34. *Daily Nation*, 9 March 1999.

As a lawyer, the same Justice Kwach had engaged in a vigorous legal tussle that a well-known criminal lawyer, Silvanus M. Otieno, should be buried at the place of his origin in Luo land and not at his farm close to Nairobi despite Otieno's and his wife's explicit will.[35] Even the dead belong to the community.

Also the last example shows the strength of the tribe, specifically in connection with the importance of a burial. When Kenya's Vice President Wamalwa died in 2003, his Bukusu community, a sub-tribe of the Luhya, had a strong influence on the funeral arrangements. Even the state funeral protocol had to respect this. The proper Luhya funeral is a complicated process with many rules and details. To mention only a few: There must be no post-mortem in any case because the "body of a great leader is sacrosanct [...]. It must be buried whole as a sign of respect". The Bukusu clan buries its dead normally in a coffin. Before it is lowered into the grave, all those circumcised in the same age-group as the deceased will have to walk out of the home. For, people "initiated in the same year are regarded as 'identical twins' and if one was to watch the other being lowered into the grave this would result in a heart attack and, by extension, wipe out a whole generation".[36] The head of the dead has to point to a certain direction related to the main gate of the home. The widow is required to leave her matrimonial home for her parents' home to perform some rites. Then she will return back with food and cook it in her house to 'feed' her husband.[37] The third and the fortieth day after the death require a series of rites. At these stages, Wamalwa's widow refused to fully succumb to the tribal tradition as she said "I am a Christian and I don't believe in those things". One rule would have been to succumb to 'inheritance'; for instance, a close relative of the deceased would have to have sexual intercourse with her. As the widow did not follow all rituals after the burial, the elders revoked the traditional marriage with her deceased husband.[38]

All these examples demonstrate two sides of 'tradition': It guides behaviour that is defined by tradition and it provokes debates, refusal and even the 'un-African' argument to let individuals decide. We have to acknowledge that those who behave according to their 'tradition' are not just simple-minded people, but they are educated, successful professionals and business men and women. They are those who have a *'house'* in the city and a *'home'* at the place of their origin. In the city we meet them in their modern, Western appearance, the men in a suit and a tie and the women fashionably dressed and also the 'workers' with jeans and colourful T-shirts. They speak English or French. Then, at the weekend or at least once a year, they go 'home', they drive up-country, to the village or town of their

35. *Daily Nation*, 25 August 2003 – See a detailed report by Harden (1993: 95–129); also Cohen/Odhiambo (1992).

36. *Daily Nation*, 25 August 2003.

37. *East African Standard*, 28 August 2003.

38. *East African Standard*, 21 September 2003.

origin. There, you can discover anyone of them in a traditional ceremony, perhaps even dressed in traditional gear – like Raila Odinga, the second Prime Minister of Kenya, wearing monkey fur, head gear, spear and shield in his hands when he arrived in Kitale to bid Vice President Wamalwa farewell and to bring along sixty bulls for feasting on.[39] There, they speak their tribal language; there, they listen to their fathers and mothers and to other elders or are elders themselves; they attend a traditional wedding or funeral. There, they have their roots, are nourished by their tradition. And at 'home', they have to be buried.

Thus, 'City' *and* 'Village' are *symbols* or codes for the African life *as it is*. Njenga Karume (2009: xxiv) is shown in his book wearing a grey suit, white shirt and red tie and on top of this a monkey fur coat, his head covered by a monkey fur; the union of 'City' and 'Village' could not be demonstrated in a more obvious way. What Westerners do not realise when they see a smartly dressed African in the city is that he or she is the same person who belongs to a 'Village'. Therefore, it may happen that this African does not act and react in a way that his or her Western appearance may suggest. 'Village' must not be taken as derogatory because it stands for what gives *substance* to the African person, i.e. what is *meaningful* to him or her. The 'Village' is also present in the 'City' – one just has to refer to the examples of visiting a sick person or of attending a wedding: this is modern African life. When we take village and city in a more superficial way with regard to technology and civilisation, then, of course, the city is also present in the village through electricity, mobile phone, television, cars, etc. 'Village' and 'City' as symbols refer to the cultural and traditional sphere.

What place within and what relevance does tradition have for modern African life? 'Village' stands for African roots, for tradition, and 'City' stands for Western, globalised, urban modernity. Are tradition and modernity contradictions? Does tradition hinder modernization of Africa? What is *African* modernization? Does it have to follow the Western modernity? Would this be possible at all? Is tradition equal to backwardness? There is no simple and straightforward answer to such questions. On a technical level, modernity and tradition cannot compete with each other because they belong to different spheres; electricity, mobile phones and cars cannot supplant tradition. For, tradition provides the *life and world horizon* within which a person exists. Insofar, modernity can be integrated as long as it does not undermine traditional beliefs. This is shown by the first mentioned examples concerning the 'belonging' and the 'obligation' to a community. In a technical sense, the people who are mentioned there are fully modernised – by education, professional training, global travels, by being equipped with technology. The friction between tradition and modernity arises where the *meaning* of the traditions gets lost, where on the level of meanings modernity takes over or intrudes the traditional meaningful life and world horizon. This could be the reason for the quarrels in the latter stories about burial rules and rites. Here, tradition is questioned and doubted.

39. *East African Standard,* 6 September 2003.

Chabal (2009: 11) recognises the African "ability to adapt to, and to process, modernity for their own purposes and in their own ways". Chabal (2009: 85–86) further argues "that it is possible *both* to make the effort of accounting for traditions *and* to avoid turning them into a causality of backwardness, doom and despair." This requires "an approach to the question by way of culture":

> "[...] an approach to culture based on the interpretation of meanings gives ample leeway for an account of change [...] making explicit the cultural framework within which meaning is imparted is not to [d]eify that framework but to try to account for the way it changes over time [...] such a cultural approach puts a premium on avoiding ossifying dichotomies such as 'tradition' and 'modernity' since it calls for an explanation of change that looks at how specific 'modernities' are rooted in their own 'traditions'."

We can understand 'City' as the way of life where tradition and modernity are *integrated*. However, the encounter of 'modernity' and 'tradition', of 'City' and 'Village', does not always happen smoothly, it can be confrontational. Radical Islamic societies are the best example for this; they want to shield themselves off the Western influence and, therefore, fight it – ironically, by using modern technology for their fight which is another example of how tradition and modernity can fuse.

Another example of conflict between tradition and modernity can be seen in the circumcision of girls – a common tradition in several African societies.[40] Western human rights groups see it as genital mutilation and promote its prohibition. This polarises the African societies in traditionalists who continue circumcision even against laws that exist in the meantime and in those African women who strive for women emancipation. Female circumcision presents a strong example of the conflict between tradition and modernity because of its function to maintain the African community and its values, on the one hand, and because of the Western view that it violates human rights, on the other hand.

African women embrace modernity in other areas of life as a chance for emancipation; this at least is true for the middle and upper class women. Although traditionally having a strong role in the house and on the field and in certain societies also in trading, by tradition women clearly have ranked and still rank under men, the wife under the husband, the sister under the brother. This is changing in the context of the 'City'. In Nairobi, you find quite a few women, increasingly of the younger generation, in leading managerial and professional positions; others run their own successful businesses. The emancipative aspect becomes obvious when those women refuse to marry because they do not expect an equal partnership with an African husband. Some, therefore, marry foreigners.

40. Headline in *Daily Nation*, 7 February 2011: "Parents disown girls for evading, the cut." Despite efforts to stop performing of the rite of passage, female genital mutilation is still considered a crucial part of culture in Mt Elgon.

Others prefer to live a life as a single parent. This is understandable under the perspective of the Western concept of equality between men and women; at the same time, this makes one wonder what this trend means in a broader sense for the future African understanding of marriage, polygamy, parenthood and childhood and, above all, what it means for the relationship of the genders. It clearly questions the traditional family and clan structure.

Certain features of African societies may be difficult or impossible for Westerners to understand and to accept, such as female circumcision, polygamy or witchcraft. These are simply alien. In our context, where we ask for the relationship between the West and Africa, it may be enough to point to the *fact* of the 'Village' and of the 'City' and that 'Village' and 'City' co-exist, often in great harmony. This has to be recognised and accepted as different concepts of life and world – different to Western concepts and where the 'Village' is not necessarily 'backward'.

Masoga (2003: 270–271) gives a wonderful example how 'City' and 'Village' co-exist in African life:

> "... imagine a young well-qualified engineer driving from Sandton (one of the suburbs in Johannesburg, South Africa) with her new BMW 5 Series and a top-of-the-range laptop computer on the seat next to her, to see her grandmother and ask her to bless her new property. She drives to Giyani kaMalamulele (a village in Limpopo Province, Western South Africa), dusty and remote. On her arrival, a diviner-healer of the clan meets her and immediately sprinkles substances on her car. The ngaka (diviner-healer) then gets a goat slaughtered for this special occasion. Vakokwani (grandmothers) of the entire clan sing praises to the young lady. For some, this may be strange. For African people, it is a daily occurrence. It is central to their lives, philosophies and cultures. Modern life does not exclude this particular part of African spirituality. The ancestors are not outdated, nor out of touch with current developments and the challenges and demands of modern living. They are a living part of life – they know about laptops and BMWs."[41]

3.4. The 'master-servant society'

I try to describe a phenomenon that I want to call the 'master-servant society'. On the one hand, it shows us the relationship between a *lower class* and other higher classes. On the other hand, it is the expression of a political relationship between *ruling elites* and ordinary people.

41. About the life between village and city, also see Warah (2011: 97–101): "Divided loyalties: The African identity crisis".

When a foreigner from the West looks at African contemporary societies and lives within them, then he will be confronted with a certain social structure he is not used to: there are *'servants'* and he suddenly becomes an employer of 'servants', a *'master'*. He is supposed to have a house help, a gardener and helpers for all kinds of works. They call him 'sir' while he addresses his employees as 'Grace' and 'Francis' or whichever first name. Not being used to 'servants', at the beginning, the foreigner may do manual work – or even worse, he may invite his 'servants' for lunch – which will appear strange to his employees. By that, these may even be disturbed or look down on the foreigner because 'this is not done'.

Obviously, there is a lower class of 'servants' or 'workers'. The foreigner is not used to it because the Western societies have changed through Enlightenment and movements of emancipation. The 'workers' serve and do *manual work* for the lower-middle, middle and upper classes: for those who are served and who will usually not do manual work. In comparison, a foreigner in the Western context will do works that are self-understood for him: cleaning, painting or repairing his house, making simple furniture, mow the grass, doing household work, etc. Being a 'servant' in this context is not the same as being employed in the African service business, let us say as a waiter, or being a craftsman who does manual work. In that sense, a worker in the West cannot be compared to an African 'worker' who is perceived as a 'servant'. For a worker of the West is an employee with a working contract, protected by laws and a union, with a salary that allows him to live modestly.

The lower social class of Africa can no longer be found among Western societies in the same form, although it is partly re-introduced due to the arrival of East Europeans in the West or by South Americans in the USA. The Western social structure has been changed based on ideas of the Enlightenment. Humans are (to be) seen as equal, with equal rights and with individual dignity. This does not exclude that abuse and exploitation will happen there, too; but this will clearly violate common understanding of laws and social norms.

Also, the African 'servant' may be supported by laws and regulations, for instance, by a minimum wage set by the government. But quite often, servants are misused and abused. They have to work very long hours with extreme low payment and getting no free time, virtually left without powers and rights. However, there are employers who treat their servants in a caring way; Ttey support them when they or their families are sick, help them with school fees for their children, or get them training to open chances for more lucrative employment. Servants, mostly in an urban environment, try to advance themselves socially; they may open a mini-business. They sacrifice greatly to send their children to school so as to provide them with a better chance in life. To climb up the social ladder is possible and it happens.

Certainly, poverty is the main feature of the lower class of 'servants'. The economic side of their lifestyle determines that, for instance, they have to live in a slum or in the country side, dwelling in a one-room tin-hut with no water or toilet. They never have enough food, which often basically consists of maize, flour and beans – or whatever the local food may be. They have close to no health care; get muddy when it rains and can hardly afford any education for their (too many) children. Both, 'servants' and 'masters', live in totally different worlds divided by a huge gap. This shows, for instance, in the value of money. Ten Shillings (or any other currency) has the same survival value for a 'servant' as a thousand for his 'master'. What the 'servant' earns per month caters for the bill of the 'master' after a meal at a restaurant. This comparison of the value of money is not strictly economic or mathematical, but it indicates the economic situation of both parties.

But it would not be fully correct to reduce the master-servant relationship to poverty alone – although the low income of the 'servant' has severe consequences for his lifestyle. This lifestyle is a consequence of the *relationship* to the 'masters', too, and it cannot be defined in economic terms alone. This relationship is based on the *perception* of the other side, i.e. being 'higher' and being 'lower'. Njeri Mbugua (2005: 103–104) satirically describes the view of the 'masters' on the 'servants' in her novel "Joki":

> "[You] should not associate with manual labourers as though you are a common labourer. All subordinate workers should be ignored, unless they are being reprimanded; otherwise, they'll forget their place and assume equality with us. But we are not equals because God has given us the right to rule over them."

Mbugua's description depicts the 'servants' as *essentially* different to the 'masters', separated from them through a barrier. Therefore, the 'master-servant society' is strongly based on *perception* and *attitude* and 'masters' and 'servants' may not be categorised as 'classes' in strict economic terms.[42] The 'masters' even belong to several classes – lower-middle, middle, upper class, etc. 'Masters' and 'servants' are the expression of a relationship; it is the relationship of mutual dependency. For, also the 'masters' need the 'servants', are in a way helpless without them as the 'servants' depend on the 'masters' for earning a living.

This description of the 'master-servant society', pointing to a class structure, does not intend to be more than this: a description; it is not meant as a criticism of the African society. The lower class which serves others has great economic importance as casual workers and helpers in the informal sector, in agriculture, in factories, as

42. According to Chabal (2009: 77–78), class analysis was deficient to explain African societies. "This was not so much because classes had not yet consolidated in Africa but rather that even where they had begun to materialise, Africans continued largely to behave according to 'traditional' social, cultural and economic logics that class analysis supposed were being transcended. [...] my point here is merely to expose the limits of Western political theories as they were applied to Africa. What is true of class analysis is also true of development theory [sic!], dependency theory and democratic theory [sic!]."

house helps, gardeners, etc. The description as 'lower class' or 'servants' gets its distinctions through the comparison with the Western social structure. It seems to be important to have the described difference of the social structures in mind when we want to understand the relationship between Africa and the West.

The 'master-servant society' takes quite a different meaning and dimension when we relate it to the *political sphere*. Then, we notice only one group of 'masters', the political elite, and the rest of the society are forced to take the role of 'servants'. It is the relationship between the ruling elite and their subjects. The contempt of 'servants' as described by Njeri Mbugua reflects in all kinds of actions and attitudes of the ruling elite towards ordinary citizens: Rigged elections disregard the will of the people; corruption and embezzlement of public funds deprive them of what by law belongs to them and of what a healthy state budget needs; emergency laws, suppression of opposition and of free expression of opinion deny political participation; clinging to power and impunity express contempt of the law; establishing torture chambers and torturing political opponents does not leave room for respect of the victims. This list could be continued endlessly. All examples are an expression of utter *contempt of the people*. They are pushed into the role of underdogs, deprived of their dignity. The abuse by the political elite hits the lowest class – the 'servants' – the most. They are misused for elections when they are bribed and even more when especially the poor youth are incited to fight physically against political opponents. They are the ones who pay the price at the end. The general impression given by the 'masters', i.e. by politicians and public administrators, implies that they *do not care* for the citizens and, even worse, they have utter contempt comparable to the contempt that slave masters have for their slaves.

No doubt, there exist programmes for 'poverty eradication', largely financed by foreign donors – often one gets the impression that foreigners are more concerned for the poor than local officials. However and for that reason, 'poverty eradication' can only work if African 'masters', above all the politicians, would change their attitude towards the poor and if they would not perceive them as 'servants'. For, 'poverty eradication' is not only achieved by an economic effort, but it demands a *social* and *ethical* endeavour accepting the stratum of the 'servants' as equal human beings – as Mbugua indirectly claims. When the *social* attitude of the political 'masters' does not change, then the 'servants' will remain poor and, above all, without rights and powers – with and without 'poverty eradication'. Maybe, it is not by accident that some African countries still practice slavery. Slaves are fully dependent 'servants' and treated as sub-human beings.

Why is an African society characterised as 'master-servant society'? What is the cause of it? The 'master-servant society' as a *class* phenomenon may be explained through the way Enlightenment has taken place or has not taken place in Africa.[43]

43. See chapter 3.4.

Concerning the 'master-servant society' as a *political* issue, an answer can only be given as assumptions and more questions. It is an essential feature of this 'master-servant society' to perceive and to treat others as unequal and even as sub-human. *Equality* and equal rights are substantial issues even in African constitutions. But unfortunately, it is not enough to guarantee equality in a written form only. Equality must be *lived*, first and foremost by politicians. When they behave in the sense of 'neopatrimonialism' (Erdmann/Engel 2006), suppress the ordinary citizens and exploit the state economy for their private purposes, then they *do not care* for their people as equal human beings.

Does the political 'master-servant society' have its roots in *colonialism?* The colonialists definitely treated Africans as 'servants' and shipped them away as slaves. And even today, you can notice the 'master' attitude on the side of Westerners, not only of those who are descendants of colonial settlers. But why did *Africans* continue to treat their own people as 'servants', after liberation and independence? Is it an expression of simply copying the colonialists? Has it something to do with a general inborn human attitude to suppress and dominate others? Does it reflect an original pre-colonial social structure? Or a modern distortion of it?

The hierarchical structure of family, clan and tribe with dominating elders does not necessarily point to a master-servant society. Elders were accountable and controlled; that means the subordinates had rights and powers. On the other hand, one can point out that the rights of elders and of subordinates were not the same. An incident told by Njenga Karume (2009: 33–36) may illustrate this: During the colonial days before the Second World War, Karanja wa Maara was a rich man with large herds of livestock and ten wives. He was also generous to the people; he supported and employed them and, thus, he was respected as an elder. As Karanja did not want to drink from the same source of water as the common villagers, he decided to pipe water to his house, using a spring he found inside a farm that was occupied by a colonial settler. This man discovered the water pipe and confronted Karanja: "Who gave you permission to have piped water in your house, you nigger?" Rude words were exchanged, the settler slapped Karanja and Karanja beat up the settler with his stick. The same day, Karanja was arrested and the next day, the District Commissioner sentenced him to two years in jail. The villagers could not believe that a role model of their society, a distinguished person, an elder, could stay in prison. Therefore, they made the proposal to the District Commissioner that one of Karanja's elder sons should take his place to serve the sentence on behalf of his father. The officer declined; the villagers offered two, three and more sons without success. For them, Karanja was beyond reproach because he was a village leader and a respected elder.

Karume tells the story to demonstrate the bad relationship between settlers and Africans and how a white man could insult and beat an African without being charged. Insofar, the story also exemplifies the colonial master-servant relationship. But this event also reveals how an *elder* was perceived by the ordinary people: an elder cannot be imprisoned, above all, not by the colonialists. Is this today the reason – part of the reason – for the *impunity* that we observe all over Africa when it comes to crimes committed by politicians and other mighty persons? Or rather, is the contemporary impunity the misused respect for an elder, or better: the respect and authority an elder claims to have without being a traditional elder? For, the situation of elders changes in the set-up of a modern state where politicians – on different administrative levels – are perceived as elders and they themselves pretend to be elders without representing a community that can be easily and clearly identified. By that, accountability and control are lost; these politicians are no longer elders but *'pseudo-elders'*[44] who care for themselves and not for a distant, abstract community, but still living with the nimbus of elders and enjoying impunity. Could this be a sufficient explanation for the political master-servant society?

How do we have to judge the fact that Africans were keeping and trading *slaves* even long before Europeans intruded on the continent and that they took part in the transatlantic slave trade? Keeping and trading slaves expresses a 'master' attitude and is the sign of a master-servant society. The decisive question is here: has Africa left this master-slave mentality fully behind? Has Africa adapted to the idea and ideal of the Enlightenment and the French Revolution of 1789, namely to human equality? Or does the master-servant relationship ironically have its roots in the changes of the African society caused by the colonial treatment of Africans and its post-colonial aftermath – an irony, because the Europeans pretended to defend human equality and to export European values to Africa?

3.5. 'Kenyan Cowboys' – the need for integration

The colonial time is still present in Africa. For instance, the descendants of white settlers still live there, in Kenya of British origin; they are now part of an African society, though isolated. The fact that Africans and these Whites share the same history distinguishes them from other minorities of foreigners. We have seen that this common history has been and still is painful for the Africans, disturbing the relationship. Not understanding – or perhaps not accepting – the social structure and all consequential behaviours of Africans certainly are a reason for the colonial attitude. The Europeans have measured and often still measure African society and behaviour with European standards. Condescension and arrogance are the result.

The British descendants in Kenya form a 'tribe' on its own as Gitau Warigi[45] characterises them, living their European life separated from black Africans. Among themselves, they make a clear distinction of being English, Scottish or Irish and more or less despise each other though often only jokingly. As the 'real'

44. See below 8.2.

45. Daily Nation, 14 May 2006.

Whites, they have problems to acknowledge another White as a proper human being when he or she is not English, Scottish or Irish and when he or she has been living among them only for a few decades. In Kenya and specifically in the Nairobi district of Karen – named after Karen Blixen – these settler descendants are half-jokingly called 'Kenyan Cowboys'. Sometimes their appearance is a bit exotic, driving an ancient four-wheel drive, wearing shorts and no socks even in winter. The old shopping centre in Karen reminds one of a town in cowboy films. There, they have a preferred supermarket owned by an Indian.

Certainly, 'Kenyan Cowboys' have their equivalent in other African countries – due to colonialism. A serious aspect of their existence in Africa is their land ownership. In the residential area of Karen/Nairobi, a family may possess plots of five or ten acres, and upcountry, mostly in the Rift Valley, they own huge farms growing cereals or keeping cattle. Kenyan governments did not chase them away like Mugabe of Zimbabwe did with the settlers there and, by that, harming the Zimbabwean people tremendously. However, the disturbance of the tribal land ownership in Kenya by the British settlers has a destructive social impact on the country today; it was one of the deeper reasons for the clashes at the beginning of 2008. For, the British settlers dispossessed and displaced Kenyans, by that mixing up tribes, and those who had to settle on the land of another tribe are now chased away again by Africans.

The descendants of those settlers still live in Kenya among Africans. Understandably, there is no great love between them. The Whites have their own social circles, attending 'their' bars and restaurants. It is like a self-imposed apartheid. At social functions, one can observe a clear separation: Whites sit together and Blacks sit together. At a formal meeting it can happen that all attending Whites are seated on the one side of a hall and all Blacks on the other side. This, of course, expresses a mutual aversion; also Africans tend to avoid the Whites; there is mutual suspicion and sometimes, as it appears, mutual racism.

When in 2005 and in 2006 a grandson of the influential British settler Lord Delamere was accused to have killed two Africans, the charges were dropped by the Attorney General in the first case, and he was convicted of man slaughter, altogether serving three years in jail, in the second case. Whatever the legal facts and procedures were, Kenyans observed those court cases with suspicion. Gitau Warigi[46] commented on those killings and reflected on the position of the descendants of the settlers, saying that a majority of them do not consider themselves to be Kenyans.

> "If you chance to eavesdrop on them at their private parties and conversations, you'll realise that at once. Their everyday talk is tiresomely peppered with narcissistic comments. But you will also hear complaints about everything in this country – about its African leadership, about how

46. *Daily Nation*, 14 May 2006.

> things don't work, about the failings of African servants, and so on and so forth. Their idea of paradise is if this country had remained one huge game park [...], Africans playing an unobtrusive background role as waiters, cooks, game trackers and tour drivers who reverentially mutter *bwana* or *memsahib* when a member of the White caste makes an appearance."

These observations and comments on the Whites in Africa and on the British in Kenya in particular would be one-sided if another side would not be acknowledged, too. For, it definitely is true that there are well integrated and well educated British descendants – and other foreigners – who encounter Black Africans with respect and as equals. There are Whites, like Max du Preez, who fight to be recognised as Africans (Behrens 1999) – the question here is: in a European-style or an African Africa? Also, one has to acknowledge that Whites contribute to Kenya's economy, e.g. through agricultural and horticultural production or through tourism business. Minorities with their peculiar life styles and customs exist all over the world – in Kenya, Indians form a minority, living their secluded life. However, the question remains in any case what such observations indicate concerning the *relationship* specifically between the 'Kenyan Cowboys' as descendants of colonialists (and their equivalent in other African countries) and Africans.

Bennet[47] indirectly confirms the isolated existence of the 'Kenyan Cowboys' when he describes them as a rare species with no contact with the local people as human beings except as 'servants'. They live in their own world far above all others. This becomes obvious when Bennet says about the settlers and their descendants:

> "What they all had in common was self-confidence – not just among the local population, but everywhere! Most were from the high-performance echelons of a nation that ran half the world. The fact that in Kenya they were a tiny minority but totally dominant administratively conferred a sense of privilege and elitism which only reinforced that perception. Their descendants were born into that pattern and [...] knew no other; you begin to see where the Kenyan Cowboys might be coming from, and why their self-assumed status [...] was and is resented in some quarters."

Their self-confidence did not make it necessary for them to get seriously in touch with the local people and to understand them – who were just 'niggers' to them. Indeed, they came from a nation that was a world power during the colonial times. But they did not "run half the world" like benevolent managers. They suppressed "half the world" at a bitter price. The Mau Mau and other uprisings did not arise just for fun; their reason was the expulsion from their land by the British. Therefore, it sounds cynical when Bennet depicts the settlers as "totally dominant administratively" – he forgets to mention the expropriation of the indigenous Kenyans, the system of apartheid they practised, and the brutality of their 'administration'. The 'Kenyan Cowboys' apparently also fade out this part

47. *Daily Nation*, 9 August 2010.

of the not so glorious history of their forefathers but bask in their "privilege and elitism". It is indeed a "self-assumed status", which makes them an exotic and doubtful pseudo-elite.

To avoid a misunderstanding, it would also be wrong to expect 'Kenyan Cowboys' and Whites in Africa in general to walk around with a consciousness of guilt. The younger generation of today have not committed the colonial atrocities and, therefore, cannot be blamed at all. Feelings of guilt hinder a normal relationship to Africans like a superiority complex does. But it seems necessary that 'Kenyan Cowboys' and others *admit* that those atrocities have been committed by their fathers and grandfathers and *accept* that grave injustice has been done to Africans. This admittance and acceptance could be the first step to overcome the superiority complex they still suffer from, a step towards a normalisation of their relationship with Africans. Are they willing to break up their self-imposed cocoon, to *integrate* into the African society, to identify with *African* Africa, leaving their condescension towards 'those niggers' behind because they are on an equal human level? Integration does not mean to give up one's own identity and cultural origin. An Irish will and shall remain an Irish, a German can never deny his German descent as it is impossible to escape one's cultural background. But cultural self-confidence and identity do not justify superiority.[48]

48. A small, but economically important minority in Kenya and other African countries are the Indians, in general called 'Asians'. Under the headline "Hurdles to meaningful integration of Asians in Kenya", Warah (2011: 107) notes about "the 70,000 or so Asians in Kenya": "...Asians will have to try harder to show that their love and loyalty is to this country and its people, and not merely to the fruits of the land. If they integrate politically and economically, they may be forgiven their social insularity."

"Your brother is your brother even if he stinks."
(Makumba 2007: 155)

CHAPTER FOUR

Ethics

Trying to understand the relationship between Africa and the West, we have also to ask by which values and norms they are guided. In other words: What is the ethics of Africa and what is the ethics of the West? On which principles are they based? We will see that these principles have to be related to their social contexts. In addition, they are derived from specific norm orientations in Africa and the West. Which role do moral norms play in the encounter of and in the cooperation between Africa and the West? Finally, we will have a brief look into the actual moral behaviour in Africa's politics.

4.1. Social context of ethics

Western ethics is based on and starts with the individual; the *individual* reaches out to others and forms partnerships, families, groups and political entities.[49] Values and norms are derived from this constellation and guide the individual. The Golden Rule exemplifies this ethic approach: Treat others as *you* would like to be treated. Here, the individual is the measure and the starting point. The individual is representing *all* humans. Ethical norms are valid for the whole of mankind. They are abstract insofar as they are not related to a concrete social unity. They claim to be universal.

For the African social order, the *community* is the core of life and of ethics. Accordingly, to support the kinship, the peer group, the network and the tribe is the base of moral behaviour. We have seen in Kenyatta's description of the traditional Kikuyu education how the social order determines the behaviour of the member of the community. The norms of the behaviour are rooted in the community, not in the individual. The social order demands acknowledgement of the existing hierarchies, i.e. basically to respect the older person. This also relates to the tribal beliefs; for instance, ancestors and the behaviour towards them have to be taken into account. Hierarchies and living with the ancestors impose certain norms.

According to Chabal (2009: 79), the idea that the living and the dead inhabit the same world:

> "stresses an ethics, which puts a premium on the upholding of a certain number of foundational principles having to do with respect for age, the elders and, more generally, matters of long tradition. [...] there is certainly evidence that it does impinge on local frameworks of action, for instance through such phenomena as the belief in the power of spirits, the deference afforded elder statesmen, the continued significance of 'traditional' status or rank, the need to favour place of origin, the reluctance to accept strangers as genuine political representatives, the adaption of universal religions to local precepts, the requirement for politicians to submit to local rituals and accept local spiritual authority, as well as the ubiquitous resort by national leaders to 'advisers' who are supposed to placate the forces of the occult."

Makumba (2007: 155–156) illustrates the powerful moral guidance by the community and the ethical foundation in the community. He draws the attention to the concept of "Shienyu ni Shienyu", which is a Luhya proverb and literally means in English "Yours is Yours" or *"Your Own is Your Own"*. The full meaning only becomes clear when the second part of the proverb is added, although rarely expressed: "Shienyu ni Shienyu khali shihunyi bukundu". Not the literal translation, but the interpretation of this means in English: "Your brother/sister is your brother/sister even if he/she stinks."

> "It does not matter how smelly *one of your own* is, you have an obligation to lend them a hand, almost by oath and under pain of being ostracised. Or to be more precise you have an obligation to 'protect' them – in good

49. There are different approaches in European philosophy, too, e.g. by Ludwig Binswanger (1962), Martin Buber (1962) or Emmanuel Lévinas (1983), emphasizing the 'We' or the 'Other'.

> and in evil! But even then the protection of brother/sister is not limited to the immediate family circle, which is rather obvious, but extends to the members of the clan and of the tribe, sometimes even of the nation."

This concept of "your own is your own" explains many cases of African behaviour where Western understanding fails: A businessman employs relatives and tribesmen although they are not qualified for the job – but they need a job, therefore, he has to employ them. It is not the quality of the work that has priority but the *relationship* to a kinsman does. We see the same in public administration and politics – Westerners call it 'nepotism'. In politics, as Chabal (2009: 50–54) shows, this also depends on reciprocity, i.e. politicians want to secure support by finding someone a job in government or in business. Another political consequence of "Shienyu ni Shienyu" can be seen in the fact that voting happens as a block, i.e. based on a community relationship, not according to a programme or to capability.

Even if "our own stinks", we have to protect him. Of course, his stink does not have to be taken literally. It means he may be an evil person, a criminal even. Whatever a community member does, he/she is protected by the family, the clan, the tribe – or because he/she is Black. The news is full of big scandals. But as soon as somebody, often a politician, is publicly accused, his tribesmen will not condemn the committed crime as such but will maintain that the accusation is directed against 'us', against the tribe. The criminal act is less important than the affiliation to their community, which represents the higher value. The closer the relationship, the higher the priority somebody will get; first comes the family, then the clan, then the tribe. Africans will also protect their 'own' against attacks and accusations from Whites, for instance, when foreigners blame Africans for rigged elections or blatant corruption. A good example for this is Mugabe, who is widely protected by Africans as accusations against his alleged crimes stem from the former colonial power. By the way, the opposite scenario happens, too: Whites will protect their not so moral members against accusations by Africans.

4.2. European and African sources of moral rules

My assumption is that African ethics is primarily and essentially rooted in the community. Values and norms assure the physical, economic, moral and religious *existence* of the community. The physical existence, for instance, is guaranteed by protecting the community land, the economic existence through mutual help. Respecting the different hierarchies supports the moral existence. Keeping a proper relationship with the ancestors strengthens the religious existence of the community.

This orientation towards the community will become more obvious when we compare it with the European sources of moral rules ('Normorientierung', i.e. norm orientation). According to Oelmüller (1980: 27–84), three systems of sources of moral rules can be discerned: (a) nature or *natural law*, (b) the *Christian* God of creation and redemption, and (c) the *human rights*. These systems of norm orientation have evolved in the course of the European history of mind and are still relevant, although the third system, the human rights, dominates today. Here, it is neither possible nor necessary to go into details about what is meant by the three moral norm systems. Only one example for each shall give a hint to their meaning.

Those who condemn homosexuality say that it is against nature; meaning, what is good and right and how we should behave, is determined by what is 'natural'. Charity is a strong value and moral norm that stems from Christianity; although originally it may have been related to the members of the church, charity has become a universal demand, i.e. in the Western context. Finally, human rights are a result of modern times, of Enlightenment; their basic values are the dignity of each human being and, consequently, equality among all humans. The value of 'dignity' demonstrates very clearly that the emphasis lies on the individual; every individual human being has to be respected. Equality also relates to the individual: each individual has equal rights.

When we confront these European systems of moral norm orientation – nature, Christianity, human rights – with the African system of moral norm orientation – community – it becomes obvious that the moral direction through the community is *concrete* because what is at stake is the physical, economic, moral and religious *existence* of a certain community. The moral norms that are demanded by the community secure its existence. By following the moral norms and rules, set by the community, the individual fosters the community and, by that, defines his/her morality. The community is the purpose and the value of the individual's morality.

The moral direction or guidance through nature, Christianity, and human rights relates to a reality beyond the concrete community, it is more general and *abstract,* and it provides moral norms and values *per se.* Also here, following (social) norms benefits the society. But in this case, the norms do not stem from a relatively small group; they have a tendency to be universal *principles* referring to *mankind.* Fulfilling them has an end in itself. Western values such as punctuality, diligence, accuracy, honesty, charity, justice, etc. are considered to be realised as a value in itself; by that, defining the morality of the individual.[50]

In a simplified way we can summarise: The *relationship to,* the affiliation with, a *concrete* community, is the foundation of the African ethical system. This is contrary to *abstract values and norms* that are embedded in the individual as a moral person and which is the Western concept of ethics. The traditional African norm orientation focuses on the community, the European orientation on value and

50. Here, values and moral behaviour tend to have their end in themselves; they are in danger to lose contact to reality. 'Gesinnungsethik' (ethics of convictions) may be the result, contradicting responsibility that takes the real situation into consideration. See Danner (2010: 44–45).

norm systems – nature, Christianity, and human rights. The latter are thought to be *'universal'* as they are supposed to be valid for 'humanity' in general (However, this understanding of 'humanity' had and still has *Europe* in mind, and is, therefore, Eurocentric and indeed not universal).

In reality, African and European norm orientation is *more complex* than depicted here.[51] But at least the tendency of both systems of moral norm orientation may have become obvious. 'Village' and 'City' definitely play a role in the African context; the European norm orientation has strongly influenced the African way of life. In addition, there is an aspect that has always puzzled me: What is the real position of the *individual* within an African community? How strongly does he/she feel and act as a *member* of the community *or* as an *independent* person – not only because of the influence of the 'City', but also because of egoistic, psychological reasons? We have to assume that the nature of all humans is similar to the way Shylock expresses it in the "Merchant of Venice"[52]. In case an African person should feel and think independently of the community, he/she would follow a different norm orientation.

These considerations may appear to be rather abstract. However, they reflect reality on the practical level. The African who has the best interest of his community in mind will not understand a Westerner who insists on an abstract moral principle – and vice versa. An African employee may disappear from work for a day or a week. In his understanding, he has a valid reason – because there is a problem to be solved in his family; but his Western employer will insist on the work contract and on the employee's reliability. A European expects a qualified African counterpart in business, but a position may be occupied by an inexperienced family member of the company owner. An African chief executive officer may be offended because a European has not contacted him – as the boss – but an employee although the employee is the more competent person in a specific matter. Other and quite different examples of frictions between African and European ethics are polygamy and female circumcision. Both have a solid position and justification in the concept of an African community. In the traditional set-up, an African marriage is an institution of the community, and polygamy is acceptable. In the Western understanding, marriage is a partnership between two individuals, a personal relationship that demands sexual faithfulness and exclusiveness. While female circumcision violates the protection from injury from a Western point of view, in the African understanding it is an important step of introducing a member into the community.

---

51. Christine Gichure's "Basic Concepts in Ethics" (1997) elaborates on European ethics from Plato to Leo Strauss without mentioning African writers and concepts of ethics – although she is Kenyan. Interestingly, her starting point of ethics is "human beings' quest for happiness", i.e. the individual is at the centre here. In this context, we would have to regard the orientation for values, taboos and sanctions that were inherent in African traditional religions.

52. "Hath not a Jew eyes? Hath not a Jew hands, organs, dimensions, senses, affections, passions? [...] If you prick us, do we not bleed? If you tickle us, do we not laugh? If you poison us, do we not die? And if you wrong us, shall we not revenge?" (Shakespeare [without year] 235).

Two prominent examples for moral decisions happened around the same time in 2010, which may demonstrate the contradicting African and Western positions: The Kenyan government invited the Sudanese president, Omar al Bashir, for the ceremonial signing of the new constitution. Al Bashir is accused of genocide, violation of human rights and war crimes; the International Criminal Court (ICC) had issued an arrest warrant against him. The Western world, including the American president, protested against al Bashir's invitation; Kenya should have arrested him, last but not least because Kenya is a signatory to the Rome Statute supporting the ICC. What the West considered being a severe violation of international law, Kenya with the support of the African Union (AU) explained as a necessity to have good relations with a *neighbour*. Very clearly, the African ethics contradicts the Western ethical approach – the orientation in the (Eastern African) *community* stands against ethical *principles*. That does not mean that the African approach is unethical; it is guided by a different orientation, namely by the relationship within a certain community and not by abstract principles.

The other example happened in Germany. A board member of the Federal Bank, Thilo Sarrazin, made derogatory and insulting remarks against Muslims, Jews, and Africans. Because of that, the Federal Bank decided to expel Sarrazin from their institution. Sarrazin's ostracism was based on the violation of human rights *principles*. He was not protected because he was one of 'their own'. In an African context, being member of a certain community may have overridden moral principles.

These examples show overt conflicts between African and European ethics. As such, they can serve as hints to more subtle differences that are not obvious in the same way. The obvious should again bring awareness of the permanent need of *understanding* the other side.

4.3. Ethics in the encounter of Africa and the West

Different behaviours with underlying specific norms and values affect the relationship between Africa and the West, including business and development cooperation. To achieve a common understanding on how things shall be done together also needs an understanding about the norms and values that shall guide common activities. Although it will not be possible to *share* all norms and values, there should at least be an attempt to *understand* the morality and ethics of the partner.

With self-confidence, representatives of the West – especially development partners and foreign governments – pretend to possess universal values and norms that have to be followed by everyone. Those 'universal' values and norms are labelled 'human rights'. I fully support the idea of a unifying global ethics. No doubt, it is *desirable;* it would solve many problems on the globe if the whole mankind would acknowledge it and *follow* it. But with good reasons, it can be doubted whether a 'global ethos', one unifying ethics, will ever become a reality.[53] Facts argue against it.

One may argue in favour of universal values and norms because in all cultures there are *common moral norms,* e.g. hospitality. A stranger has to be sheltered and fed, though for a limited time. In general, the *Golden Rule* could provide a common moral ground: Treat the other person in the same way you would want to be treated. Küng (1998: 140) quotes a long list of forms of the Golden Rule in different societies and based on different religions. The weakness of this argument lies in the *realisation* of the Golden Rule; in addition, this ethical principle may apply only to the respective society. This becomes clear in the Islamic formulation: "None of you is a believer as long as he does not wish for his brother what he wishes for himself"[54]. Here, the Golden Rule applies to the 'brother', another Muslim – what about a 'non-believer'?

Development cooperation and any other encounter with different cultures have to face the *gaps* that exist among major civilisations, and gaps in terms of ethics. How can we pretend that we do not experience a fierce *controversy with Islam* all over the world? The wars against Al Qaeda in Iraq and Afghanistan, the fights in Somalia, Muslim suicide bombers in many countries, the destructions of 11th September 2001 in America, etc., are examples for a strong Islamic rejection of the Western way of life *and* of Western values and ethics. Suicide bombers and their ideologists are terrorists who may be convinced that "killing American unbelievers is an honour".[55] But where are the moderate Muslims to correct abstruse religious beliefs and to fight them? Also, moderate Muslims, for instance the majority of the Turkish community in Germany to an extent reject the Western values, insist on their own and may commit 'honour killings'. Whatever the details and the motives may be, there is a large Muslim community in the world that lives on the foundation of their own ethics, often contradicting 'human rights', specifically when they adhere to the Sharia law.

Another huge civilisation that cannot be neglected is the *Chinese*[56] and the Asian in general; there are permanent demands of the West that the Chinese have to respect the 'human rights'. But are these compatible with Chinese ethics? Already, at the "Second World Conference for Human Rights" in Vienna in June 1993, it became obvious that the claim for human rights had diminished since their

53. Küng (1998) considers a "Weltethos" – 'world ethos – to be necessary and a "minimal consensus" to be possible (p. 133). Lütterfelds/Mohrs (1997) present a "controversial debate" in "Eine Welt – Eine Moral?" – "one world – one ethics?" See also Bielefeldt (1997), Berg-Schlosser (1997).

54. 40 Hadithe by an-Nawawi 13, cit. Küng (1998: 140).

55. Moh. Makkawi Ibr. Moh., Khartoum, quoted in *Daily Nation*, 22 January 2009.

56. On China, see the publications by François Jullien.

declaration in 1948. European and North American countries were confronted by a block of fifty countries with Latin American, Buddhist, Confucian and Muslim background, countries without a Jewish-Christian tradition and a tradition of natural law. (Huntington 1997: 312–315) Then, opening the first "International Conference on Human Rights" in Peking in October 1998, the Chinese Deputy Prime Minister, Qian Qichen, underlined the different social systems and the different emphasis on human rights in Asia and Europe. While European countries favour individual rights, Asian countries prefer *rights of the community* and the responsibility for family and society.[57]

Finally, as we have seen, *African* customs may very well contradict the principles of Western human rights. The inclusion of a "bill of rights" in an African constitution does not guarantee that those rights will be respected because traditional customs may still prevail in daily life. Maybe modern African constitutions – as the Kenyan one adopted at the referendum on 4 August 2010 – are paving the way to an approximation to Western ethics?

All kinds of ethics are closely related to certain *societies* and their religious and/or philosophical foundations. Therefore, an ethics cannot claim to be 'absolute' although it is an *'objective'* measure for and within its *specific* society. Even the 'dignity' of the individual – as the cornerstone of the human rights – is a secular form of the Christian interpretation of the human being, i.e. to be a creation of God and God's image (Weiß 1997). Thus, human dignity and *human rights* in general originate from the *Western* hemisphere. When all forms of ethics relate to a certain society – large or small – then a global ethics could only be based on a global society, a 'global family'. Globalisation brings societies closer together in certain aspects of life – economy, technology, politics, but it will *not* (easily) eliminate unique cultures, religious beliefs or other convictions. A 'global family' seems to be a mirage.

If a universal ethics were possible, at least theoretically, it should not only be valid for all societies, it should also have validity for *all times*. This has so far not been true, and it is not plausible to believe this for the future. Forms of ethics are *historical*; they change and develop over times. Historic experiences of extreme injustices – e.g. the European denominational wars, the absolutist state, economic crises – made it impossible to return to former traditional forms of ethics or traditional customary law (Bielefeldt 1997: 259–260). We can add that the process of Enlightenment as a whole, the transatlantic slave trade and slavery in general, the human catastrophe of the Holocaust or, in recent years, the understanding of the ecological crisis,[58] provoked a *rethinking* and a *reformulation of values and norms*. Last but not least, the Universal Declaration of Human Rights,

57. Reported by *Deutsche Welle News* on 20 October 1998. The discussion with China about human rights rather concerns a specific aspect of them: they also mean the rights of the individual towards the state power; human rights are supposed to protect the individual against the state power.

58. Hans Jonas (1979: 36) formulates a new ethical imperative as a response to the ecological destruction: "Act in a way that the effects of your actions are agreeable to the continuation of genuine human life on earth."

adopted by the United Nations in 1948, was a *response* to the atrocities of the Second World War.

One consequence of this insight – forms of ethics are historical – is that it becomes difficult to maintain a universal ethics. Another consequence is that 'guilt' appears more prominently in the light of the ethical reflection on committed injustices than at the time of committing them. This must not be understood as an excuse; it rather points to the consciousness of justice and injustice of those who have committed atrocities. It also raises the question whether relevant moral norms have existed.

What does all this mean for the encounter of Africa and the West, for example, for the development cooperation? Certainly, those who are involved in it in practice do not have to decide the complicated, controversial ethical discussion. But at least, they should be aware of it. That should include the understanding that the Western moral measure of the human rights is not as absolute and universal and desirable as it may appear for the West. The former President of Germany, Horst Köhler (2005), engaged in a positive relationship with Africa and for a more than materialistic development of Africa, is a strong proponent of a universal ethics:

> "I am concerned about humaneness in this one world, about the consciousness that we are depending on each other. Well, I am also concerned about morality and one world ethos. We have to discuss issues of social justice increasingly on a global, not only on a national scale."

Also on the level of 'world ethos' and human rights, mutual understanding and *dialogue* are a necessity. Otherwise, the strong belief in and the conviction of the human rights are in danger of ending up as ethics of conviction ('Gesinnungsethik'), which as such can take rather cruel, inhuman forms. Advocating for human rights, therefore, has to happen with *responsibility,* acknowledging *reality*. This has to include the differences of moral norms. Cautiously, the West can try to convince other societies who follow a different norm orientation that the human rights are a valid platform for human relationships. But, advocating for human rights can only be convincing when this is accompanied by respective moral *action*. Talking human rights and violating them at the same time is not convincing.

This brings us back to an ethical principle and *ideal* that should guide our encounter with different cultures: the Golden Rule – Treat your partner in the way that you expect him to treat you. This sounds simple, but it is difficult in practice – as all of us carry the load of our, sometimes negative, prejudices with us that include our moral norms. Both the principle of the Golden Rule as well as being aware of our 'prejudices' should apply to the West and to Africa. Concerning the relationship between Africa and the West, often it would be helpful if Western diplomats as well as development partners would remember the Golden Rule. Often, they talk to and treat African partners in a way that they would never accept themselves. Sometimes Western diplomats and development partners excel in presumption, haughtiness, and arrogance, exceeding the usual teaching and preaching attitude. And this is definitely not helpful for a healthy relationship with Africans.

One of the Western moral norms definitely is *charity*, the conviction that those who are in need should be helped. For instance, Germans contribute huge amounts of private money to assist in cases of natural and human catastrophes all over the world. There are also many private initiatives of 'development projects' in Africa. This is an expression of good will, sometimes misused by Africans, sometimes rejected as an undue interference. There is a saying in German: Meaning well is the opposite of 'good'. There is some truth in that and, therefore, charity should be handled with responsibility, too. A good deal of Western development aid is motivated by charity; it is not always and not only imperialism, selfish interest and post-colonial interference. Rather, it is motivated by the deeply rooted conviction that one should assist those in need. "There is [...] a moral obligation to take care above all of those who are worse off. This is a moral imperative that goes beyond what is termed enlightened self-interest." (Köhler 2004) More precisely, being "worse off" means to suffer, to suffer physically and non-physically. According to this understanding, development policy must have the aim to diminish human suffering. As human beings we are able to 'co-suffer', i.e. compassion becomes the ethical motive for development cooperation. (Müller/Wallacher 2001: 22–23)[59]

Africans should try to understand and accept the West's ethical approach. On the other hand, the West should welcome Africa's efforts to contemplate on African Renaissance, 'Africaness' or 'négritude' or any other expression for African originality.[60] Ghana, for example, makes an effort to integrate African traditional values in modern development. The New Partnership for Africa's Development (NEPAD) was and is a trial of a new beginning, specifically emphasising African responsibility. These are African endeavours to reformulate culture – including African ethics – in a changed, post-colonial world. This African contemplation should be given room in development cooperation.[61]

59. See also Kesselring's (2003), 'Ethics of development politics'.

60. "Négritude is the whole complex of civilised values – cultural, economic, social and political – which characterize the black peoples or, more precisely, the Negro-African world. All these values are essentially informed by intuitive reason [...]. The sense of communion, the gift of myth-making, the gift of rhythm, such are the essential elements of négritude, which you will find indelibly stamped on all the works and activities of the black man." (Senghor, Léopold: Négritude and African Socialism. In: St. Anthony's Papers on African Affairs, No. 2, p. 11; cit. Mazrui (1990: 134–135). See also Mbiti (1999: 262–277), "The search for new values, identity and security"; Bidima (1995).

61. This is not the case in a type of approach, for instance represented by the Bertelsmann Transformation Index, where political and economic indicators are clearly Western orientated. What is genuinely African has been omitted. (Bertelsmann Stiftung 2009).

4.4. The 'immoral' side of African politics

The Kriegler Commission investigated the electoral process of Kenya in 2007.[62] Their analysis of the causes of the clashes that followed included the Kenyans' embracing of unethical behaviour and action that corrode the institutions, morals and integrity. The Kriegler Report blames the Kenyan society for having "long condoned, if not connived at perversion of the electoral process". Tom Mshindi[63] who refers to this report continues: "Kenyans, and particularly the schooled and exposed lot, have over time exuberantly embraced the perversion of justice and equity."

Misuse of government funds and grand scale corruption lead the list of criminal behaviour in Kenya. Bribes to politicians and kickbacks to public officials are known everywhere in Africa. Also the 'quiet corruption' which does not cause headlines in the news burdens the daily life of Africans.[64] Public servants will often render services only when they receive bribes or they may not be found at their working place at all. "Your file cannot be found" simply means: pay!

These are well known facts of African reality. What ethics – or better what failure of ethics – is behind it? As it seems, the social system of communities guides the moral behaviour of their members; it is "traditional reciprocity" or "reciprocal obligation" (Chabal 2009: 69, 71). Is it possible for the community-related ethics and norms to change *beyond* the borders of the community? That there is no or a weaker moral obligation or loyalty towards those who are not members of the same community? Stealing within and from the community certainly is considered to be a moral offence. However, for instance, the traditional and still on-going cattle rustling points to a moral attitude that does not respect the possession of another tribe; it appears to be a 'way of life' without moral implications. Other moral norms, which are 'ours', seem not to apply to 'others'. Tribal clashes do not abstain from violence and brutality, from looting, mutilating, raping, killing and arson. Also, private business suffers from fraud, cheating and stealing either within companies or it affects their customers. The biggest headache for business people is to chase after outstanding payments because their customers run away from settling their bills. Corruption is systemic in public administration.

What does this behaviour mean? Can it be related to situations where the community-based ethics – "reciprocal obligation" – does not apply? Has it something to do with the 'City' and the abstract society of a nation because anonymity prevails there? I have mentioned earlier that wedding and burial

---

62. *Report of the Independent Review Commission on the General Elections held in Kenya on 27 December 2007.*

63. *Daily Nation*, 19 September 2008.

64. *World Bank News Release,* 15 March 2010.

committees do not embezzle their funds – is it because they are strongly related to their community? What I would like to understand is this well-known immoral and even criminal behaviour: Big scandals may be criticised and discussed in public, 'commissions of investigations' may be set up, but at the end nobody will be legally punished. *Impunity* prevails and indirectly sanctions what is morally wrong. Impunity appears to be the biggest moral deficiency on top of all immoral and criminal acts; impunity expresses a non-existing morality on the side of judiciary and politics. Keguro Macharia[65] writes under the headline "Everyday Kenyan life is built on impunity":

> "Impunity is a Kenyan problem that is not restricted to the political class. [It] is a historically-developed form of social negotiation that structures everyday Kenyan life. [...] impunity is so deeply embedded in our national psyche, and is so supported by the national ethic that urges us to forgive and forget, that we find it impossible to punish anyone. [...] we have a culture where no one is ever responsible for anything, where not only is there no accountability, but it is impossible for there to be accountability."

It would be very wrong to maintain that moral consciousness does not ordinarily exist among Kenyans or Africans in general or it is only tuned to community affairs. Otherwise there would be no public outcry about immoral wrong doings like impunity. Also, I cannot see the only answer in the conflict between "reciprocal obligation" and liberal democracy on the level of politics, between 'tradition' and 'modernity', that Chabal (2009: 67–71) is discussing. Thus, what makes African societies more 'immoral' than others? We find an indicator for this provocative statement in statistics on worldwide corruption where many African countries are at the top. That question certainly has many answers, simple ones like poverty, or more complex ones like the encounter of African and Western values.

However, as we try to understand African moral behaviour, at the same time we have to consider the corresponding *Western moral behaviour*. For instance, this strongly applies to cases of corruption when Western companies heftily bribe African politicians in order to get business from their governments. Then, immorality is found on both sides in the same way and we can ask who does the first step. Another example of questionable moral behaviour of the West is the tolerance of and the cooperation with dictatorial regimes like in North Africa; it needed their citizens to stand up against the dictators; the democracy-preaching Westerners had no problem with them *before* the actual revolutions.

Christine Gichure (2000) sees a solution for the African fight against fraud in the hope for an African Renaissance. To demonstrate the extent of fraud in Africa, she refers to a study by Deloitte and Touché on 17 countries. Only one, Botswana, showed an improvement in the fight against fraud. The main reason given was "a strong economy and a good example set by leadership" (Gichure 2000: 240).

65. *The East African*, 19 January 2009.

Gichure names *greed* as a reason for fraud and draws an analogy to hunger. Instead of sharing with others when there is finally food after a period of hunger, usually people grab as much of it as they can "unconcerned for what others may suffer":

"Applying the example of hunger to Africa's situation one can understand why there is a growing tendency in Africa today to take as much as possible by whatever means when an opportunity for gaining money presents itself. The question as to the justice and morality of the action does not take precedence. What matters are oneself and one's immediate family, and then the clan and the village." (Gichure 2000: 242)

I would agree that greed may be the driving force behind fraud. But large scale fraud is usually committed by the rich, by those who are not 'hungry'.

Gichure (2000: 243) gives another reason for fraud, or perhaps better: a justification for it. She refers to the *gallant* in traditional Africa who with valour and prowess obtained "what would lead to greater fame in the eyes of the public, even if force was required to do so". He became a rich and powerful hero admired by the people. Although times and values have changed "the gallant of days gone by is still admired". But "the quest for warrior values translated to the modern economic setting in business and professional life produces not heroes but crooks that are far different from the gallants of old". It is remarkable that Gichure refers to an African tradition to (partly) explain a contemporary occurrence. I would rather agree with Gichure that fraud is nothing else than the expression of greed as a human feature, independent of time and place.

In any case, the question remains: Where is the ethical framework to reign in an all too human motive? On the one hand, Gichure gives an answer to this by proposing a *partnership* of politics, private sector, media, academia as well as religious leaders. On the other hand, she refers to an *African Renaissance* which

> "should be a renewal and a reform in artistic and intellectual activity, a re-discovery and a reclaiming of any African values that may have been lost or spurned through the domination of alien cultures, and it should also be a movement towards the economic growth of the whole continent" (Gichure 2000: 237).

To stand up against fraud would need "values rooted in our cultures". Obviously, Gichure notices a contemporary *vacuum of values*. Therefore, she says Africans "need to believe in a cause and [...] to face the challenges that the ideal of an African Renaissance requires". This necessitates a change "of the social order, where we need to widen the horizons from the smaller clan to the wider clan, which is the nation, rather than the tribe or race". And there "are the challenges of competition in an urbanising world" (Gichure 2000: 247). In expressions that I have used earlier: The 'Village' has to take on the dimension of the nation – but can the obligations and reciprocity of the 'Village' be transferred to the anonymity of a nation? Does the 'City' not only provide new economic and technical opportunities but also new values and norms to realise them in a human, i.e. morally valuable, way? Referring to an ideal that exists as an idea and as a *hope*, namely to an African Renaissance, as Gichure does, makes us wonder whether there is an *actual* African ethics that can be referred to in a case like fraud.

"The physical and spiritual are but two dimensions of one and the same universe. African peoples 'see' that invisible universe when they look at, hear or feel the visible and tangible world."

(Mbiti 1999: 57)

CHAPTER FIVE

Spirituality

5.1 The Western difficulty in understanding African spirituality

The belief in a reality, in a power that is not visible, seems to be characteristic of Africa. Therefore, it is necessary to talk about it if we want to understand Africans. At the same time, by that, we enter an area that is difficult if not totally impossible to comprehend – at least for non-Africans. It may already be wrong to call that reality 'not visible' as it *is* reality for an African, visible for him or her not in a physical, but in a spiritual sense. Therefore, for a foreigner like me, it is hardly possible to talk adequately about this reality. Also, there are *many forms* through which that reality is manifested: witchcraft, sorcery, magic, healing, voodoo, devil worship, mixtures with Christianity and Islam, etc. Strictly speaking, it needed a careful description of them and distinction between them – by kind and by geographical practice.

Another fact makes it difficult to talk about this African spiritual reality. Although African religious beliefs and practices show "probably more similarities than differences" (Mbiti 1999: 103), they have different importance for different African peoples; they either believe strongly or less strongly in these forms of spirituality. This applies to the whole continent. West Africa seems to be more indulged in sorcery than East Africa as a whole, although it can be found there, too, mainly in certain tribes. For instance, the (modern) Kikuyu in Kenya give the impression to be quite 'sober' in this respect; witchcraft hardly plays a role in their lives; it is the relation to the ancestors, the curse of an elder and – still – the oath taking where the 'invisible reality' becomes important for them. However, the Kamba, neighbours of the Kikuyu, are strong believers in sorcery. A Kamba friend wanted to sell his car; for many months he did not find a buyer; this *convinced* him that somebody must have bewitched him. This friend is not a simple, uneducated person; in his profession he deals with huge sums of money. Among other Kenyan peoples who are involved in witchcraft are those of the coast, e.g. the Mijikenda and the Swahili. When Kenya suffered from the bloody clashes at the beginning of 2008, the rioters at the coast were told that they would be bewitched if they continued – they reduced rioting and returned the loot.

Finally, sorcery and all other forms happen in *secrecy*. Their activities are hidden and secluded, often performed during the night. A sorcerer or a healer does not talk about his doings. When Bitala (2002) as a journalist wanted to interview a Tanzanian witchdoctor, he simply experienced refusal. Signer (2004: 19) reports that he had to get practically involved himself in order to learn and understand about sorcery in West Africa. The only time when I came across some witchcraft myself was in Egypt when I discovered a charm – sort of a small scroll of paper and a tiny stick bound together – among the clothes of somebody else; this charm probably was either meant to do harm or to protect against evil witchcraft.

Here, it is neither necessary nor possible to elaborate on all kinds of magic and witchcraft. Above all, it is not possible to go into a description and explanation of their practices. However, their *effects* and *results* pop up here and there; for instance when a whole boarding school has to be closed because the students are haunted by spirits, when a dozen of villagers are killed under the suspicion to be witches, or when babies are raped as a remedy against AIDS. Certainly, there are cases – like the latter one – which can be denounced as 'superstition' and as 'backwardness'. But many other reported examples point to something that Western logic and understanding cannot easily push aside; full incomprehension has to be admitted. This may be illustrated by an example that we find in Mbiti (1999: 195). The event happened in Ghana at around 1960 at the construction site for a new harbour near Accra. The construction work took place under European supervisors. Neal, who tells the story and who was an Investigations Officer there, was told by a supervisor "that one tree was giving them a headache."

"Neal went over to see the tree which he found standing alone in a large compound where all the other trees and shrubs had been cleared. It was a small tree. The supervisor told Neal that all the mechanical equipment had failed to uproot that tree. The African foreman insisted that it was a 'magic' tree, which could be removed only if and when the spirit living in it agreed to forsake it and go to another tree. A traditional 'priest' [...] was summoned, who asked for a sacrifice of three sheep and an offering of three bottles of gin to be given to the "spirit" and for some money "as his payment". When the sheep had been killed and their blood poured at the foot of the tree, and the gin poured as libation at the base, the diviner became a medium and conversed with the spirit, persuading it to leave that tree and go to another and even better tree. When the rite was over, the European supervisor ordered tractors and bulldozers to uproot the tree, but the diviner stopped him telling him that a few African labourers could pull out the tree. This they did with the greatest of ease – to the amazement of European spectators and satisfaction of African onlookers."[66]

Western mind immediately asks for an explanation, wants to know cause and effect according to natural science. But according to the African view of the world, the Westerners are missing out on something – the reality of spirits, of spiritual power. This power is not fiction as Europeans would like to interpret it; whatever it is, it is a reality for Africans; it is part of their world. Here, Western understanding hits a wall; it is confronted with something totally alien. But instead of denouncing this non-understandable as nonsense, superstition, hoax or deception, Westerners should accept it as *real*, as it exists for those who believe in it and practice it.

'Good magic' as well as 'evil magic' are part of African life – with all the variations of tribal, geographical and certainly educational differences. Definitely, the difference between 'Village' and 'City' plays a role here although also in this context the 'City' has its roots in the 'Village' – we remember the story of the educated and rich young lady who drives her BMW to her village to receive traditional blessings there.

In general, formal *blessings* and *curses* are considered to be powerful and important. Therefore, an African will behave in a way that will avoid a formal curse. Spiritual power is used in a positive and a negative way as 'good magic' and as 'evil magic'. The medicine-man provides 'good magic' for *protection* in forms of charms, amulets, powder, rags, feathers, figures, special incantations or cuttings on the body. 'Evil magic' – or 'witchcraft' in a popular understanding – "involves the belief in and practice of tapping and using this power *to do harm* to human beings or their property. It is here that we find sorcery at work [...]. We

66 . J.H. Neal (1966): Ju-Ju in My Life. London, pp. 19–24, cit. Mbiti (1999: 195).

must point out, however, that a great deal of belief here is based on, or derives from, fear, suspicion, jealousies, ignorance or false accusations which go on in African villages." In fact, we can observe in daily life that for Africans "nothing harmful happens 'by chance'; everything is 'caused' by someone directly or through the use of mystical power". (Mbiti 1999: 197–202) This is especially true for the death of a prominent person. He or she is not supposed to have died a 'natural death'; some evil power has to be assumed as its cause. Western education or even medical training cannot hinder somebody to perceive and to think in this way.

David Signer (2004) got intensely involved in studying 'sorcery' in West Africa. Like Mbiti, he identifies *envy* as the thriving force behind witchcraft. When somebody possesses more than the others, he will be harmed by witchcraft. As a counter-action, he has to find protection from a witchdoctor. Certain rites and sacrifices have to be performed. Signer concludes that envy and related witchcraft form a system that impoverishes African societies and, therefore, talks of the "economy of witchcraft", which does not allow African economy to prosper. A report by Michael Bitala (2002) confirms Signer's findings and assumptions in Tanzania. Sixty one per cent of Tanzanians not only believe in witchcraft but have at least once sought the help of alleged witches and witchdoctors. Jealousy and mischief form the basis for the widespread belief in witchcraft. Nobody is supposed to possess more than what is adequate to his social standing. When he/she exceeds this, he/she will be controlled by the use of witchcraft.

Bierschenk (2005) does not deny that Africans believe in the existence of invisible, super-sensible powers that influence events in the sensually recognizable world. But he objects Signer's idea of a 'system' of witchcraft that allegedly hinders economic accumulation and individualism. The existence of modern African capitals with high-risers and beautiful villas proves that there is accumulated wealth that has not been hindered by witchcraft. Indeed, one could point to the impressive skyline of Nairobi or to big business enterprises belonging to Africans. Among them is the earlier mentioned Njenga Karume (2009). In other words, the phenomenon of spiritual powers in the African context has to be approached in a more subtle way, appreciating the various differences: sorcery, magic and oracles, esoteric, spiritism and shamanism, natural medicine and religious spiritualism of Christian and Islamic origin (Bierschenk 2005). The subtitle "Why there are no skyscrapers in Africa" of Signer's (2004) "Economy of Witchcraft" is a simplification and, therefore, misleading. But this does not answer the question what mischief and the related witchcraft mean for the development of those African societies, who are intensively practising it, and: what does it mean for the whole of African development?

5.2. More examples

The following additional *examples* illustrate what was mentioned before in a more abstract way and demonstrate – though not systematically and comprehensively and without comment – how 'spiritual power' is present in African daily life. Most of these examples stem from Kenya, but represent many other African countries. Many more and detailed examples can be found specifically for West Africa in Signer (2004) or K. Palmer (2010).

Earlier, we learnt the importance of the ancestors. They are not gone; the *spirit of the dead* is present. The "living and the dead inhabit the same world, [...] the dead continue to play an active part in the affairs of the community" (Chabal 2009, 79). This was quite vividly expressed in the statement of Justice Kwach: A Luo's funeral – reckon: he is dead! – "is the very last opportunity he has in the world to call all the members of his clan together [...] Being his last feast, he will feel honoured if his guests are properly fed and go away feeling happy."[67]

How witchcraft can affect and *change a person* for lifetime is narrated by Signer (2002):

> A man from Burkina Faso "had been trained and examined as a pilot. After two weeks he was supposed to start his work. He took this time to visit his village. There he became crazy. He spread the papers and maps on a table in front of him and shouted:
> 'Pull up stairs, fasten seat belts, prepare for departure, full power ahead!'
> Failing to appear for his work at the airport after two weeks, his boss was told that he had become crazy. The boss did not believe it and visited the pilot in his village. He confronted him:
> 'Why did you not come to work?' The man answered: 'No problem, boss. We start with the work immediately. Please, fasten your seat belt, we will start after a few minutes. Please, stop smoking and put your seat in an upright position...'
> His boss returned to Ouagadougou, the man has been staying in the village until today where he is collecting his food from the garbage. One would not believe that he really was a pilot. But here, what grows too fast is beheaded."

Sacred trees show a positive, constructive side of the belief in spiritual powers. For example, the Kikuyu have the Mugumo as a sacred tree, the Maasai the Oseki or the Embu the Mururi. Under these trees they not only gather, but the sacred trees also have the power to give *peace*. Reconciliation of past events – like cruelties during the Mau Mau uprising – or of contemporary fights is negotiated under these trees. This goes together with the 'healing of the earth'. After the loss of human life due

67. *Daily Nation*, 9 March 1999.

to diseases, natural disasters and conflicts, the land has to be cleansed. 'Healing of the earth' "is both a memorial service as well as a ritual to acknowledge the earth [...] often referred to as the Mother who has been hurt and angered".[68]

Also, a *medicine man* who practices the religion of his ancestors and draws his power from ancestral spirits has constructive, positive intentions as he offers traditional herbal services for healing and fortune-telling. With his face painted white, murmuring in a strange language he uses paraphernalia like antelope horns, water buck horns, impala jaws, eland hair, pieces of reptile skins. He is confronted with suspicions from church members who consider him to be a sorcerer performing witchcraft.[69]

The existence of medicine men and herbalists coincides with the clients who seek help from them and who believe in their power. Demand and supply stem from the same spirit. No wonder that questionable help is offered like one-time medical cure or solutions to social issues like failed marriages, rivalry, jealousy and joblessness. Clients have suffered from taking 'medicines'. Although healers in Kenya have earlier received licences from the Ministry of Culture, the Ministry of Public Health and Sanitation ensures protection from unqualified doctors and traditional healers who fail to adhere to safety standards.[70]

The Kamba in Kenya practice a deadly oath or curse to address theft, fraud or murder that police and a court cannot resolve. It is called *kithitu*. Because of its dangerous consequences, the 'kithitu' requires an official permit. An official, like a Chief or a District Officer, has to be present when it is performed. This happens in public, often in the presence of a big crowd; all who participate have to be warned of the effects. The executor of the ritual has to be naked. Depending on the issue, different rites have to be observed.

In one case, two cows were stolen. The farmer obtained the permit for a 'kithitu'. But before it was administered, the grandfather of the suspected thief intervened and pledged to replace the cows and to pay for the expenses incurred in search of the offender. By that, he avoided deadly harm to his family. In another case, a boy was killed. After the 'kithitu', several members of the suspected killer's family started dying, one after the other. "Only those who went to the boy's father [...] to plead for forgiveness were spared". In 1983, 'kithitu' was also applied to free voters from an oath that they had performed in 1963 and by that they had bound their votes to Ngei – a politician. After the cleansing from the oath they could vote for another politician.[71]

---

68. *The People*, 1 November 2002.

69. *East African Standard,* 11 January 1999.

70. *Daily Nation,* 17 August 2010.

71. *Daily Nation,* 12 November 2003.

Now and then, stories are reported in Kenya about *schools* that have been closed because of 'jinns' or 'demons' attacking students. At a secondary school close to Machakos, male students reported that they were strangled during the night and that they felt terribly tired in the morning. Girls said they were sexually assaulted during the night, they heard screams, and the beds were shaking.[72] At a primary school in Nairobi, a teacher who was a member of an evangelic church prayed in the class in the morning. During his prayer, seven girls collapsed, yelled, rolled on the floor and later claimed that they had been possessed by 'spirits'. This caused a big turmoil by parents.[73] Under a big headline – "Satan threat to Kenya schools" – a newspaper reported about the infiltration of *devil worship* in schools and colleges. The manifestations of this were writings, symbols, signs and numbers, paraphernalia, code names and slang, and pornographic literature.[74]

However, devil worship obviously was not limited to schools. In 1995, a government commission consisting of clerics had investigated and prepared a report. It related devil worshippers to usually wealthy and prominent people who drive expensive cars. "It said rituals common with the cult included human sacrifice, drinking and eating human blood and flesh, Black Mass, cannibalism, incantations in unintelligible languages, sexual abuse and rape (especially of minors and children), black magic, nudity of participants in rituals, use of narcotic drugs, snakes, signs and paraphernalia". The newspapers also published descriptions of some cases. However, the public discussion did not concentrate on the *content* and the allegations of the report, but rather criticised it as such, and the commission. Some claimed that devil worship was not forbidden.[75]

Herbalists that heal by means of natural medicines have to be distinguished from witchdoctors. These are considered to be able to *fight evil witchcraft*. There was a self-confessed healer in Kiisi with a big crowd of followers who hunted witches, going into their houses, accusing them of being witches and taking away their paraphernalia. He involved administrators in order to avoid mob justice of the public against the alleged witches.[76] At the Kenyan coast, a famous witchdoctor, Akiba Bakari, was called by villagers to conduct exorcism by which he chased away all witches. A female witchdoctor in Nairobi claims she can undo the spell from people who have been bewitched. After that she protects them from witchcraft.[77]

In many other cases, alleged witches are simply *killed* by the people. Here is one story:

> "The verdict was swift and the sentence brutal. The [villagers] decided that the elderly woman was guilty of bewitching her neighbours. She was to die! In a split second, they stripped her naked and forced her to walk down

72. *East African Standard,* 7 June 1998.

73. *Daily Nation*, 16 July 2002.

74. *Daily Nation*, 6 August 1999.

75. *Daily Nation*, 5, 6 August 1999; *Sunday Nation* 8, 15, 29 August 1999; *East African Standard,* 5, 11 August 1999; *People*, 6 August 1999.

76. *The People*, 10 November 1999.

77. *Daily Nation*, 27 February 2004.

> the streets of the dusty Migwani estate near Machakos Town. In the process they humiliated her, beat her up and when they were tired, poured paraffin on the defenceless woman and set her ablaze."[78]

In Western Kenya, villagers raided homes of suspected witches. A seventy year old man was stabbed and burnt. Ten houses were set ablaze.[79] At the Kenyan coast, villagers said they were tired of what they termed demonic spells and unexplained misfortunes. They have taken it upon themselves to deal with the perpetrators of the alleged evil and put eleven 'witches' on a death list. In the same area, five suspects had been killed the year before.[80] Witch hunting and killing does not happen in Kenya only. Her neighbour, Tanzania, seems to be sadly leading in this respect. Tanzania's Ministry of Home Affairs claimed that 5,000 victims of witch lynching were murdered between 1994 and 1998. Petraitis (2003) calculated "that between 1991 and 2001, a total of 22,000 to 23,000 Africans were lynched to death by fearful neighbours, as witches" – the majority from Tanzania and most of them elderly women.[81] Tanzania also is on record that there are people who use body parts for their magic cults; innocent people are killed for this purpose; absurdly and shockingly, body parts of albinos are considered to be especially powerful.[82]

5.3. Supra-natural powers

The recounting of witchcraft-related examples could go on and on. But these few cases reported by the media clearly demonstrate the existence of the belief in witchcraft of all kinds. This belief is an African reality, a reality that can end in impoverishment and death. The tragic side of the *fight* against witchcraft is that the fight itself counts on witchcraft, the use of magic, the belief in supra-natural powers – whatever we want to call it. It is a vicious circle. Believing that somebody is a witch is a belief in witchcraft. This kind of belief can be found all over Africa; it is not restricted to sub-Saharan Africa. The North Africans have their jinns, the evil eye and charms. Also, this belief is not restricted to simple villagers or to uneducated people in general. "The real tragedy is that members of parliament and other leaders who should enlighten and guide rural peasants out of ignorance are actually the perpetrators of the archaic and evil beliefs". "More than 60 per cent of Kenyan members of parliament are involved in witchcraft; some carry charms and amulets to

78. *Daily Nation*, 31 July 2006.

79. *Daily Nation*, 27 September 2002.

80. *The East African Standard*, 28 January 2005.

81. Richard Petraitis (2003): The Witch Killers of Africa. www.infidels.org/library/modern/richard_petraitis/witch_killers.shtml, 5 December 2010.

82. *Daily Nation*, 18–20 August 2010. *The East African Standard*, 4 May 2002, reports about Swaziland: "Human body parts are used in a potion that users believe will strengthen them against misfortune, and make them powerful against their enemies."

help them sort out personal problems". Two Kenyan medicine men "confirmed that cabinet ministers and members of parliament in government and opposition frequent their homes [...] their diaries are actually full with politicians' appointments".[83]

The belief in witchcraft – or better: in the spirit world – in various forms is a fact. This does not mean that we can explain in scientific terms how witchcraft works. But there are its undeniable effects – more negative effects than positive ones; people may be healed or reconciled and they can be harmed or killed by it. The effects point to a force which cannot simply be explained by means of natural sciences or psychology, although this sometimes seems to be possible.

Which place does witchcraft occupy within the world that we experience? European philosophy and the subsequent ordinary belief assumed – and still assume – a reality *beyond* the physical world that we experience; since Plato, two worlds are distinguished: the natural world and a metaphysical reality. The Greek 'meta ta physika' can be interpreted as 'beyond the nature'. From this point of view, we may be tempted to call the African spirituality 'metaphysical'. However, the place of the power of witchcraft *cannot* be positioned in the same way. The power of the spirit world is of *this* world, *within* this world and *not beyond*, although it cannot be explained by natural laws. This is the position of the *belief* in witchcraft. Taking the position of natural science, the power of witchcraft, of spirits or God in general could be called 'supra-natural'. This power does not fit into 'nature' as science defines it. Science understands nature as matter that is organised and ordered by (natural) laws. The 'supra' of the 'supra-natural power' must not be understood as the 'beyond' of the 'meta-physical world view'.

To avoid a misunderstanding: The term 'supra-natural power' is not limited to and not identical with witchcraft. Witchcraft is *one* form of the belief in a supra-natural power. This also includes spirits, ancestors, and the permanent presence of God and His actions, even in the meaning of Christianity or Islam.

Supra-natural powers and the belief in them determine the whole life of an African. That does not necessarily mean witchcraft in a more narrow sense. Supra-natural powers are taken as a general fact and they are ubiquitous. "The physical and spiritual are but two dimensions of one and the same universe." "African peoples 'see' that invisible universe when they look at, hear or feel the visible and tangible world". (Mbiti 1999: 57) The African perception expects *'more'* than the factual and visible. As counting on supra-natural powers is ubiquitous, it is also present in the 'City', i.e. in modern life, as partly shown by the above examples.

83. *East African Standard,* 25 September 2006. Examples of African 'leaders' and their relationship with the spiritual world: In his novel, "the nights of the big hunter" (original title: "En attendant le vote des bêtes sauvages"), Ahmadou Kourouma (1999) portrays a West African, though fictive, president whose life is intertwined with magic; Ngugi wa Thiong'o (2007): "The Wizard of the Crow"; Naipul (2010: 3–60) describes the closeness of the Kabaka, the Ugandan king of the Baganda, to spirituality and witchcraft: "The Kabaka is linked to the spirit world; the mediums are linked to the ancestors. This is where the cosmogony touches earth and the Baganda." (35)

To a certain extent, dealing with supra-natural powers is related to the *social structure* of the community, being based on it and at the same time strengthening it. The access to supra-natural powers follows the hierarchy within the community; old people are closer to them than the young; the 'living-dead', the ancestors, represent the strongest supra-natural power. Blessings and curses with their strong effects support and enforce the order of the community and they are uttered by older people. And insofar as envy plays a role in witchcraft, it makes sure that an inferior person – the younger brother, the nephew – does not possess more and does not become more powerful than the older brother or the uncle.

At this point, it seems necessary to mention a certain view on African religiosity: *animism*. In 1866 and 1871, E. B. Tylor[84] described the "belief in Spiritual Beings" as a primitive form of religion. According to this, animals and plants as well as stones, rivers and lakes, mountains, stars and even objects like jewellery are considered to possess "object souls". From this belief, religions developed via the belief in many gods – polytheism – contrary to the belief in one god – monotheism. However, hundred years later, Mbiti (1969: 1999) rejects such a view on African religiosity with strong words: Those earlier descriptions are "inadequate, derogatory and prejudicial" (7). "The theory of religious evolution [...] does not satisfactorily explain or interpret African religions. Animism is not an adequate description of these religions and it is better for that term to be abandoned once and for all." (8) And again fifty years after Mbiti, Heinz Kimmerle[85] insists that the belief in spirits is widely spread in sub-Sahara Africa and that African people are deeply convinced of the reality of spirits. Kimmerle considers the belief that spirits in principle are living in all natural objects – trees, rocks, rivers – as an expression of the respect for nature; this has gained importance for the ecological thinking and action in modern days; therefore, animism should be recognised as a world religion.

It is not the place to debate this controversy about the importance and position of animism. Based on my own experience, I cannot see that Kimmerle can be supported, although it is true that there are sacred trees, as mentioned earlier, or we can remember the story of the tree in Accra that could not be removed without convincing its spirit to leave it. Also, there are known sacred places in Western Kenya, for instance caves, or the Mijikenda Kaya Forests at the coast. The latter have also gained significance for environmental conservation and in 2008 were declared a World Heritage.[86] In our context, again it is important to be aware of

84 . K. Müller (1971: 316); see also Mbiti (1999: 7).

85 . Kimmerle (2006): *Die Welt der Geister und die Achtung vor der Natur,* in: www.philosophie.uni-koeln.de/kongress2/html/Abstracts060706.rtf.

86 . See http://whc.unesco.org/en/list/1231 and the informative article by A. N. Githitho: "The Sacred Mijikenda Kaya Forests of Coastal Kenya and Biodiversity Conservation", which also gives an insight to the spiritual aspect, in: http://www.sacredland.org/PDFs/Mijikenda_Kaya.pdf.

an African world view, different to a Western approach, in this case, to nature. Etounga-Manguelle (2000: 67) quotes the late president of the Ivory Coast, Felix Houphouët-Boigny: "From African archbishops to the most insignificant Catholic, from the great witchdoctor to the most insignificant Muslim, from the pastor to the most insignificant Protestant, we have all had an animist past."

As events are interpreted in the light of a supra-natural power, they are not seen in a cause-effect relationship in the sense of a *natural* cause – although this also follows its own logic (Paul 2008). An accident or becoming rich do not have a scientifically explainable, natural cause – for instance, careless driving or working hard. But it is some power beyond my influence which has caused the accident or my wealth and on which I am depending. I am *not accountable*. The dependency on a supra-natural power relieves me from my responsibility. But also such events which are not within my power undergo a totally different interpretation when they are 'caused' by a supra-natural power rather than by a natural cause. A death caused by kidney failure is something totally different from a death that is 'caused' by witchcraft. Knowing that the kidneys have failed lets us rest; seeing witchcraft in a death forces us to search for the witch and to counter-act.

After these rather 'Western' reflections on supra-natural powers, I want to quote the answer from a South African diviner-healer who was asked by an African researcher: "What do you think about the subject of beliefs, and their social implications for medicinal plants?"

> "There is a problem with the use of the concept: medicinal plants as well as 'belief systems' behind medicinal plants. The idea of medicinal intervention [...] should rather be used instead of medicinal plants conceptualisation. This is because there are a wide variety of plants that could be used for specific interventions. The intervention is important, not the plant. Similarly the term 'belief system' should be replaced by the term 'social reality' [...]. You young researchers suffer from the Western way of looking at things. You come to us with words and expect us to give you the African equations of them. That is simply wrong!! You have got to change the manner in which you conduct your research. African belief systems must have a *holistic approach*. Plants cannot be viewed in isolation from the spirit world. They are also connected with the animal world – both domestic and wild. All are part of an environment that is composed of the forces of air, water, fire and earth! Healing in such a world is always physical, psychological, spiritual and social!" (Masoga 2003: 273)

5.4. Christianity and Islam in the African context

Of course, it would be wrong to limit African religiosity to the belief in supra-natural powers in the sense of indigenous, traditional religiosity. The dominant, first-glance appearances of African religions indeed are Christianity or Islam – depending on their geographical representation. Christianity was established early in North Africa, Egypt, Ethiopia and parts of Sudan. This African Christianity contributed considerably to the formation of Christianity as a whole, for instance through theologians such as Augustine (354–430). In the 7th century, Islam ousted Christianity from North Africa, spread to the south-west, and to the east coast in the 9th and 11th century. (Hunwick 2006: 14–29) Ethiopia and Egypt were the main African Christian countries until the Portuguese brought Christianity to the west coast in the 15th century. The major Christianising began through the missionaries in the 19th century. This was also the time when Islam advanced into the interior of the continent – e.g. to Uganda, Malawi, Congo. Beside the historic expansion, the interesting and important question is how Christianity and Islam interrelate with indigenous African spirituality.

In contrast to contemporary Europeans, Africans in general are very religious. As a rule, they are 'believers'; you will hardly find an 'unbeliever', at least nobody would admit to be an atheist. Sunday masses are full. Churches entertain discussion groups for Bible interpretation that are diligently attended. On the road side, you find preachers with a Bible in one hand and a microphone in the other, a crowd listening to them. References to God and to the Bible are made in normal conversation or in public speeches. Many Africans are able to quote from the Bible by heart. Frequently, all kind of meetings are opened and closed with a prayer. You may observe a receptionist or any other person reading the Bible during his or her spare time. 'God bless you' is often said as a form of thanks. Any kind of wishes will be accompanied by a reference to God's blessings. Similar religious following and behaviour may be observed in Muslim communities.

In a society like Kenya, one will find all bigger Christian denominations represented – Catholics, Anglicans, Protestants, Methodists, Seventh Adventists, etc. But more astonishing are the numerous small churches and sects. Their road signs point to simple tiny tin shacks. On Sunday mornings you can see a group of a dozen people on the road side or standing on a river bank, often dressed in fancy long clothes, one outstanding – their 'bishop'. They drum, sing and dance. Or there are others, the rich ones, occupying a huge compound and putting up a series of large white tents. All over Africa there are innumerous different churches; alone in the area and surroundings of Nairobi you might count hundreds of them. These churches and sects provide a service that is obviously demanded by the population. And it seems that running a church can be good business.

Especially, Pentecostal churches, largely sponsored and influenced by Americans, have a large and increasing following. It appears to be the fastest growing denomination on the continent and it promotes a change of the traditional community-related self-perception of its followers, addressing their sense of identity and their behaviour. On the one hand, Pentecostalism strongly rejects 'traditional' beliefs; on the other hand, it "also advocates a decidedly 'modern' and individualist notion of (economic and political) agency". The conflict with traditional ethics, that is community centred, occurs as personal self-improvement and internationalism are encouraged. (Chabal 2009: 102)

Mbiti (1999: 15, 229–241) draws the following picture of *Christianity in Africa*: In principle, it has to be noted that for Africans, religion determines the whole life, or, the other way round, "the whole of existence is a religious phenomenon, man is a deeply religious being living in a religious universe". This is valid in general, not only for any form of Christianity (or Islam), but basically for being African, i.e. also for traditional religions. But missionaries of the nineteenth century did not understand this, which resulted in a very superficial type of Christianity in Africa. Mbiti blames the "mission Christianity" – as he calls it – for being too closely related to colonialism. Many different churches and sects from Europe and America came over the years to preach Christianity to Africans. They introduced their particular denominational and sectarian interpretation of Christianity in addition to their specific cultural background.[87] Both shaped the kind of Christianity they represented. Thus, Africans experienced a variety of Christian interpretations. Finally, the missionaries in Africa were not well educated; above all, they were no theologians. Therefore, the "mission Christianity" was presented without theology.

As a whole, Africans were confronted with a superficial Christianity that was rather meaningless for them.

> "Mission Christianity has come to mean for many Africans simply a set of rules to be observed, promises to be expected in the next world, rhythmless hymns to be sung, rituals to be followed and a few other outward things. It is a Christianity which is locked up six days a week, meeting only for two hours on Sundays and perhaps once during the week. It is a Christianity which is active in a church building. The rest of the week is empty. Africans, who traditionally do not know religious vacuum, feel that they don't get enough religion from this type of Christianity, since it does not fill up their whole life and their understanding of the universe. Furthermore, African Christians often feel complete foreigners in mission churches." (Mbiti 1999: 233–234)

87. We can add that over the centuries, Christianity had developed away from its Jewish-Biblical origin, having absorbed a good deal of Greek philosophy. Therefore, the Christianity Africans were taught was a Europeanised one.

Chabal (2009: 34) judges the conversion of Africans to Christianity quite pragmatically: they converted out of convenience or interest, rarely out of conviction. At the same time, they did not abandon their own beliefs. "African religions have always been highly adaptable and did not find it difficult to accommodate the strange dogma and rituals of the foreigners' creeds."

A reaction to an empty religious experience has to be seen in the establishment of the *independent churches* and of sects and in the attraction of the Pentecostal churches. Independent churches want to 'indigenise' Christianity; they want Africans to feel 'at home' and to get rid of the missionary and colonial control.

> "Revelation and healing play important roles in the independent Churches. Some of them forbid their followers to use European medicines, teaching their members to depend entirely on God's power through prayer and healing services. Revelation comes through dreams and visions, and through meditation when leaders withdraw to solitary places for varying lengths of time. Emphasis is also laid on the place and work of the Holy Spirit, and during worship services people seek to be possessed by Him. When they become so possessed, they speak in other tongues." (Mbiti 1999: 235)

This appears to be close to African spiritualism, God's power understood as supra-natural power.

Protestants and *Catholics* are blamed for separating Africans from their society. They "made no positive attempt to incorporate ancestors and witches, song and dance, into the Christian scheme". (Mbiti 1999: 237) In *South Africa,* the Church has totally failed and betrayed Africans by justifying racism and apartheid through a twisted theology. The *Ethiopian* Church, though having problems to modernise, is considered by Mbiti (1999: 230) as "truly African". For it has kept African elements such as the belief in "a whole host of evil spirits", the protection against these and other spirits. Everybody carries amulets with inscriptions of magical prayers. The priests conduct exorcism. As a whole, Mbiti also acknowledges positive contributions by the "mission Christianity", namely its cultural inputs like the introduction of formal education and of Christian ethics and morality, by promoting medical care, etc. But also in this respect, one has to ask which traditions and traditional values have been *destroyed* by the missionary churches.

We can assume that today, "mission Christianity" does not exist in the same way as Mbiti has experienced and described it before 1969. One important step has to be seen in the translation of the Bible into various local languages. This has allowed Africans to come closer to its meaning than through foreign languages and foreign mediation. Even the big churches have opened up to African culture and spirituality. Christianity and African spirituality seem to overlap when it comes, for example, to blessing of fishing boats for a safe journey and a rich harvest or to using peace trees to reconcile adversaries[88] and similar practices. Under this perspective, one has to question: Is there a difference between traditional beliefs and Christian belief? Or have the traditional gods, spirits and ghosts just been exchanged for the Christian God, Jesus and Holy Spirit? Both – tradition and Christianity – are expected to do magic?[89] Kä Mana (2005: 62–63) critically asks whether and in which way Christian belief is possible and meaningful if it is lived in Africa, which is far from the intellectual mediation through the official churches who are directly related to the Western world. Was Christianity through the missionary theology and the African theologies not able to encounter Africa in her deep and immanent world view because this encounter was only superficial?

Islam knows less factions and sects than Christianity. Its appearance may be less confusing for Africans than the many Christian denominations and sects. As a whole, there is a mingling of Islamic ideas with those of traditional religions. For instance, the traditional cult of the departed has been embedded within Islamic thought. The living-dead are addressed through offerings and sacrifices in order to appease them; they reveal themselves to their human relatives in dreams. Sacrifices and alms shall help obtain success or ward off evil. Amulets are worn that may contain Koranic verses. "Magic, sorcery and witchcraft have their hold upon the people and, in addition to treating human complaints, the medicine-men perform exorcisms, sometimes using Koranic quotations as magical formulae." The Koran itself mentions many spiritual beings, including angels, jinns and devils. Divination and magic are other areas where Islam and traditional religions converge. Islam as a religion "has done little to add to or alter radically African religiosity except in the (in any case external) ritual side". (Mbiti 1999: 248–253)[90]

***

The above cannot be more than an outline of African spirituality. It proves to be a complex matter, mainly if one tries to understand it from the European perspective. The *belief* in supra-natural powers, of which witchcraft is only one

88. *The People*, 1 November 2002.

89. However, Old and New Testament understand belief in a way that is opposing the belief in magic cults – one example is Moses' rejection of the Golden Calf. Does Christianity not necessarily have to be alien to a culture that is based on the belief in spirits, ghosts, magic, etc? The message of the Old and New Testament talks of monotheism, of the one God who is bound to and revealed by the history of the people of Israel. This is continued in the Christian community, the Church. Therefore, the dimension of *history* and the realisation of the belief in the *community* constitute Jewishness and Christianity. In addition, Christianity preaches the command of *charity*, which radically revolutionizes the social structure because of acknowledging *equality* (within the community of the believers). Can these constitutive moments of Christianity – monotheism, historicalness, community-related belief, charity, and equality – be harmonised with the indigenous African belief(s)?

90. See also Chabal (2009: 35): "African Muslims have long practised a form of Islam that accommodates local religious beliefs and makes space for socio-cultural practices that are nowadays frowned upon."

area, has to be accepted as a reality which produces its more often destructive and even deadly results than positive ones.

Some examples have demonstrated how these effects come to the light in different ways, and that the belief in supra-natural powers is more widespread than a foreigner commonly may assume.

A general feature of the belief in supra-natural powers is to permanently expect more than the appearances show. As the actions of a person are not considered to be the *cause* of certain events, but as these are referred to a power beyond the person, one has to ask whether he or she is considered to be accountable and responsible.

According to Mbiti, "Mission Christianity" was not able to satisfy African religiosity. In a similar way, Kä Mana doubts whether missionary theology and African independent theology were profound enough to meet African existential needs.

Islam seems to be more open for African spirituality and better prepared for it. 'Enlightened' Westerners might be tempted to look down on African spirituality and witchcraft as primitive and backward. They should be reminded of the strongly existing, but hardly talked about *superstition in the West*. It starts with the fear of the number '13' and, even worse, of Friday, the 13th; some have problems to see a black cat crossing the street in front of them. Newspapers and magazines regularly offer horoscopes because they tell the future to those who believe in 'the stars'. A factory owner may hire an important employee based on which month he was born. Esoteric is booming. Not only in Africa, soccer players need spiritual support,[91] also Western players may make the sign of the cross on themselves before the game. A German newspaper reported about the "suggestive power of surgery": some patients become healthy just by being cut open and stitched again.[92] The strong effect of placebos is another example for the supra-natural beliefs of Westerners. Is it heretical to ask: how do we have to understand the Christian belief in literal resurrection, virgin birth or physical ascension of Jesus and Mary?

Obviously, the African belief in supra-natural powers does not stand alone, and Westerners should not look at African beliefs as totally alien. And African beliefs are no reason for Westerners to feel superior to Africans.

91. *Daily Nation*, 20 September 2003.

92. *Süddeutsche Zeitung*, 29 September 2005.

Main features of the European mind: emphasising reason, i.e. critical, independent thinking, and individuality, i.e. the strengthening of the individual in religious, political, economic and social affairs.

CHAPTER SIX

Reason and individualism in Europe

This essay attempts to understand the undercurrent aspects of African/Western relationships. So far, we have seen: The common history of Africa and the West resulted in a disturbed relationship, and the African history before the arrival of the Europeans is richer than commonly known. Quite contrary to the European image of the individual, the African person receives his/her determination and definition from his/her community. From there, we have to understand African ethics where the personal relationship has priority over abstract moral norms. Another determining feature of African life is the belief in a ubiquitous supra-natural power.

By dwelling on those issues, the African society has been depicted – though only roughly – more than the European side. We turn now to the European undercurrent world view and, by that, the African picture may even become more distinct.

As the Westerners should understand their African counterparts, also the Africans should try to grasp from where the Westerners are coming with respect to their world view and concept of life. For, a particular underlying mind-set relates to both, Africans and Westerners.

6.1. Galileo Galilei as an example

What distinguishes the Western world view from the African world view, the Western way of perceiving and thinking from the Western way? To get an answer to this question, we may have a look at Galileo Galilei's work and life. Why him? He is not the only important person during and even before his time who fostered natural sciences through discoveries and publications. Nicolaus Copernicus (1473–1543), Tycho Brahe (1546–1601) or Johannes Kepler (1571–1630) could be other examples, specifically as astronomers. However, Galilei's confrontation with the Church, in particular with the Inquisition, due to his scientific stance clearly demonstrates the central role and importance that individual reasoning plays in the history of the European mind.

Galileo Galilei was born in 1564 in Pisa, Italy[93]. His father, belonging to a patrician family, was a musician; in 1572, he moved with his family to Florence. Galileo returned to Pisa in 1581 to enrol at the university there, starting his studies to become a priest, but which he gave up to study medicine. From there he moved to the study of mathematics – without achieving any degree. In spite of this – which would be a handicap today – Galilei got the chair of mathematics in Pisa in 1589 and then in Padua in 1592. Galilei improved on a telescope that a Dutch, Hans Lippershey, had invented. This telescope helped Galilei discover the moons of Jupiter, the mountains of the Moon, the movements of Venus and of Mars and other appearances in the sky. In 1610, Galilei became the mathematician *and* philosopher to the court of the Medici in Florence.

Publishing his observations of the sunspots, Galilei expressed his position in favour of Copernicus for the first time. Copernicus' thesis maintained the movement of the earth around the sun, which was contradictory to the then predominant view that the earth was the centre of the universe and the sun was moving around the earth. The latter is known as the Ptolemaic geocentric world view. The Copernican heliocentric system also contradicted the teachings of the Church that not only related to Ptolemaeus and Aristotle but also to the Bible, according to which the sun is rotating around the earth. Therefore, in 1616, the Sacred Congregation of the Index banned Copernicus' book "On the Revolution of the Heavenly Orbs". And Galilei was instructed to neither teach nor defend Copernicus' theory. However,

93. Data concerning Galilei's biography and scientific achievements refer mainly to Machamer (2009) and to the time table in Sobel (2000: 387–393).

Galilei tried to prove its correctness by means of observations and mathematical calculations. Consequently, in 1632, he published the "Dialogues Concerning the Two Great World Systems" where he showed the weaknesses of the Ptolemaic system and the strong arguments in favour of the Copernican system. Galilei's book was put on the Index and he had to appear in front of the Holy Office of the Inquisition in Rome. In 1633, he was accused of heresy and forced to recant and sign a formal abjuration which had been formulated by the Holy Office:

> "I have been judged vehemently suspect of heresy, that is, of having held and believed that the sun [is] in the centre of the universe and immoveable, and that the earth is not at the centre of the same, and that it does move. Wishing however, to remove from the minds of your Eminences and all faithful Christians this vehement suspicion reasonably conceived against me, I abjure with a sincere heart and unfeigned faith, I curse and detest the said errors and heresies, and generally all and every error, heresy, and sect contrary to the Holy Catholic Church." (cit. Machamer 2010: 11)

Galilei escaped torture and jail and was put under house arrest which he could finally spend at his own house on the outskirts of Florence. Only in 1835 were Copernicus and Galilei taken off the Index, and finally in 2000 (!), Pope John Paul II issued a formal apology for all the mistakes committed by the Catholic Church, including the trial of Galilei.

Although being under house arrest, being sick and finally becoming blind, Galilei worked on another book: "Discourses and Mathematical Demonstrations Concerning Two New Sciences". This was smuggled out of Florence and published in Holland. The two new sciences concerned corporeal matter and natural motion. Against the Aristotelian teaching, Galilei stated that there was only one element, the corporeal matter, and not five elements: fire, air, water and earth plus ether as the celestial element. Also, there was only one kind of motion on the earth and in the universe. The Aristotelian distinction between terrestrial and celestial spheres was rejected by that. In addition, Galilei demonstrated the *mathematical* nature of matter and of motion. Almost 78 years old, he died at the beginning of 1642.

Here, it is not the place to go into more details of Galilei's work and achievements. In our context where we try to see the differences between African and European thinking and world view, a few essential features of the latter can already be deducted: Galilei used his *senses*, his *reasoning*, his *logical thinking*, to discover and to prove astronomic and other physical facts. By that, he opposed traditional teaching and, in particular, the Church authority. He as an *individual* used *his* reason and challenged the authority of a community, the Church. Although he did not win in this confrontation during his life-time, at the end, an *individual's reason* proved to be the reliable source for the truth against the teaching of the authorities.

These are essential European characteristics: reason and individualism. They belong closely together; we are talking about a person who is using his/her senses and his/her capacity to think, to reflect, to use logic, referring to reality – independently of and even in contradiction to existing opinions and teachings. On the one hand, this sounds fully self-understood – today, as we have become used to this understanding of reason in the European context. On the other hand, we have to notice the shift of authority: from an institutional authority (here the Church and the Inquisition), from a doctrine, in a certain sense from a belief, to the reasoning of an individual. At the same time, it is the authority of reason as such.

Something is true, not because an authority is teaching it but because it is based on facts, reason, and on logic. The individual insight bears authority – not in an absolute sense like a philosophical or theological doctrine – but still as long as it is based on reason and on (disputable) facts. The individual reasoning is more vulnerable than the institutionally supported doctrine; Karl Popper later talks of the principle of falsification. Galilei was not right in everything that he scientifically maintained. For instance, the tides were no real proof for the rotation of the earth as he had thought. Therefore, the individual reasoning depends on the exchange of arguments with other individuals. Important works by Galilei are written in the form of dialogue.

One aspect of Galilei's outstanding importance is shown in his confrontation with the Church authority, in the confrontation of individual reasoning with an institutionalised doctrine. Galilei had the audacity to use his senses, e.g. by means of a telescope, to trust his own observations and to speak out against a teaching that had been proven wrong. Reason gives authority to an individual. Individualism is based on this. Others before and after Galilei had the same audacity to use their senses and their individual thinking – Copernicus, Brahe and Kepler who considerably contributed to astronomy; Martin Luther (1483–1546) who protested against an erroneous interpretation of Christian belief; or before them Christopher Columbus (1451–1506) who reckoned that he could go to India by sailing to the west. These scientists, discoverers and reformers of that time represent a development that has shaped the mind of Europe.

However, this development had started much earlier. The German philosopher Karl Jaspers (1949: 19–22) refers to a change of mind. He notes that during the period of 800 to 200 B.C. – i.e. around 500 B.C. – a change of human mind occurred as the deepest hiatus in history. Jaspers calls this period "Achsenzeit" – *'axial period'* or 'axial age'. For the first time, there were philosophers in China, India and Greece and prophets in Palestine. They became conscious of the Being as a whole, of themselves as thinking human beings, i.e. of consciousness as such, and of human limitations. Convictions, morality and human conditions were questioned and dissolved. Questioning became dominant over inherited answers. The fight against the myth began based on rationality and real experience, the fight for the transcendence of the one God against the demons. Logos stood against mythos – rationality against myth. Philosophers and prophets dared to rely on themselves as individuals. Jaspers considers the axial age as the appearance of reason and personality, i.e. individuality. This change that happened at the same time and independently in China, India, Persia, Palestine and Greece is still the valid foundation to date for thinking and the perception of world.

Two aspects are to be emphasised in our context. The one is the shift or even the qualitative leap from a mythological world view to a rational interpretation of the world – from 'mythos to logos' – as well as the rise of individuality.[94] The era of myths is left behind and there is a new self-consciousness of the human being. It is a *revolution in thinking*. As we have seen in the example of Galilei, 'reason' and 'individualism' will later characterise the European mind. The other aspect we have to note is the *geographical* areas where these developments have happened: in China, India and the Occident. *Africa* is neither mentioned by Jaspers nor by those who are discussing the concept of the 'axial age' after him.[95] Jaspers (1949: 48) classifies 'negroes' as 'primitive races' ("Naturvölker"). What does this mean? Do we have to assume that Africa as a whole, on her own merit, did not achieve the leap from 'myth' to 'logos'? Does Africa have personalities such as Socrates (ca. 469–399 BC), a Greek example of the 'axial age', who stood up as an individual against the community, the 'polis'? Socrates listened to *his* 'daimonion', i.e. *his* conscience. Following his own insight, he preferred to be executed by poison rather than to give in to the teachings of the elders. Does Africa follow the maxim of Horace (65–8 BC), the Roman poet: 'sapere aude!' which can be interpreted as 'dare to discern', 'have the courage to think'? 'Sapere aude' later became a key word of the Enlightenment in Europe.

Galilei stands in this tradition that has started in the axial period. He is a representative for relying on reason as well as for having – or claiming – authority as an individual. As such, he is demanding the freedom of thought and speech. To reason also means to make a difference between appearances and reality (Assmann 1995: 26), between opinions and knowledge, in Galilei's case to make a difference between the teachings of the Church and his own observations.

Therefore, the other outstanding importance of Galilei has to be recognised in his development and practice of *principles of natural science* (Meier-Oeser 2004): His various discoveries are based on observation by using his own senses; extending the capacity of his senses with instruments such as a telescope or a microscope; formulating his experiences as hypotheses; examining those hypotheses through experiments; finally, formulating natural laws in a mathematical language. These scientific procedures in combination with mathematics determined the future

94. Assmann (1995: 26) summarises the aspects of the axial period as: reflexivity, difference, 'communication', individuality, and history.

95 . See Dittmer (1999) for the discussion of Jaspers' concept of the 'axial age'; also Assmann (1995: 24–28, 40–51, 276–277). Obviously, Jaspers has to be corrected in details, but he has recognised something essential in a philosophical sense.

development of natural sciences. They were in clear contradiction to the traditional dogmatic knowledge and teaching which was deductive, i.e. specific statements were logically deduced from a general insight, doctrine or assumption. This had been Aristotle's approach, which was adopted by the Church. Therefore, the inductive approach of science, starting with facts discovered by observation and experiment, brought Galilei in conflict with the Church. It was a conflict between individual authority, based on reason and inductive methodology, and an institutional authority, based on power and doctrines. Definitely, no supra-natural powers play a role in the scientific explanation of nature.

6.2. The Enlightenment

Galilei only represents an example for a development of mind in Europe that has been slowed down in the Middle Ages and that was revived about the 15th century. He exemplifies the use of reason and, based on it, the authority of the individual. Both have shaped thinking, religion, art, society, politics, science, and finally technology in Europe and later in other parts of the world of European influence. This development had a peak in what is known as *'the Enlightenment'*. It means a certain period within this European history of mind, roughly in the 18th century, on the one hand; and it claims the realisation of those concepts – individualism and reason – in a concentrated and consequential way that has been unknown up to then, on the other hand. The driving power behind it was the *consciousness* of the individual reason and subsequently the freedom and authority of the individual. This was documented in publications by intellectuals who increasingly *contradicted* the social and political *reality* in the 17th century. This contradiction demanded a solution. Enlightenment is a step towards this solution.

The Enlightenment was mainly nurtured in England, France, Germany, and in the Netherlands. As different aspects were emphasised in these countries, the beginning and the end of this period varies. But in general, one can date the beginning at the last two or three decades of the 17th century and its end at 1789, the year of the French Revolution. Also, the term as such is ambiguous; partly, 'enlightenment' had the same meaning as civilisation and education. And therefore, there were not only controversies among the representatives of the Enlightenment, but also the historic research on this period is controversial. (Borgstedt 2004; Hinske 1981) In our context, we can neglect the details and emphasise the common ground of the diverse intellectual contributions and discussions of that time:

1. The appeal to think independently, 'think for yourself' ('Selbstdenken');
2. The question: what determines the human being?
3. The criticism and change of the existing societies and political systems;
4. Different forms of rejecting religious institutions or religion in general.

'Think for yourself!' – to think independently – became a classical formula of the Enlightenment. For instance, it meant to avoid the un-reflected adaptation of pre-given teachings, opinions, and prejudices. Also, the religious consciousness should not be fixed by 'systems' and by 'symbolic books'. Rational thinking should not be biased; otherwise something irrational would interfere with reason. The concept of Enlightenment presupposes the idea of a 'general human reason', which is distributed among different individuals. Each human participates in this common, general human reason. But at first, it is limited by various prejudices and interests in *each* individual. Therefore, it is necessary to recognise the contribution to the truth by each position. This needs frank and unbiased discussion. By that, the generality of reason will be achieved step-by-step. The process of Enlightenment is the process of liberating reason by finally unifying singular truths to become the one, undivided truth. (Hinske 1981, XVII–XIX; Hinske 1980: 35–45)

In 1783, answering the question "What is Enlightenment?", Immanuel Kant (1966a: 53) emphasises the use of reason:

> "*Enlightenment is the departure of the human being from one's self-inflicted immaturity. Immaturity* is the inability to make use of one's reason without another's guidance. This *immaturity is self-inflicted* when its cause is not the lack of reason but lack of decision and courage to make use of it without another's guidance. *Sapere aude!* Have courage to make use of your *own* reason! is the motto of Enlightenment."

In simple words: When you always follow the opinions and teachings of others and you do not use your own reason, you are dependent and you are immature. One has to 'depart' from this situation. In this context, immaturity is not a biological fact – you are responsible for your immaturity. As far as an individual and a society strive to be mature, they are on the way to be enlightened. Consequently, when you think independently – what you should do – then you have to be *critical*. 'Criticism' became one of the key words of Enlightenment (Schalk 1971: 622).

The question about the determination of the *human being* is answered in this view: The use of reason is put at one's discretion; you are not only able to use your reason, you are also free to do it and, therefore, you are responsible for your individual enlightenment. Kant does not talk of 'responsibility'; this is a modern interpretation, mainly when responsibility is not understood as 'accountability' or 'duty' but as a personal decision and engagement.[96] Responsibility and individual *freedom* become an important feature of the image of the human being. But this has been and still is not only a philosophical statement and claim. Freedom has to become *real* – as freedom of thought, as freedom of speech, of religious belief, as political freedom, etc.

96. See the distinction between 'juridical' and 'existential' responsibility in Danner (2010: 57–93).

Another aspect of the image of the human being is morality. In the context of Enlightenment, it is individuality and reason that determine European *ethics*. According to Kant (1966b), all *moral terms* have their place and their origin in *reason*.[97] Therefore, a moral law, a moral imperative, is a principle of reason. As an agent of reason, the human being exists as an *end* in him/herself. As such he/she is not to be a means for an end or for the use by another human being. Related to this, Kant (2008: 29) formulates a practical imperative: "Act in such a way as to treat humanity, whether in your own person or in that of anyone else, always as an end and never merely as a means". An additional 'categorical' imperative states that one is only to act in a way that one's maxim of action can *become a universal law* of nature. The human being as a rational being is giving (moral) laws. Moral action based on reason is setting a generally valid law; although it is the action of an individual, it is not arbitrary and unfounded. For

> "Reason [...] checks out every maxim of your will, in its role as giver of laws, to see how it relates to everyone else's will and also to every action towards yourself. It does not do this from any external practical motive or future advantage, but rather from the idea of *dignity* of a rational being who obeys no law except one that he himself gives while obeying it". (Kant 2008: 33)

Dignity represents an *intrinsic value*, it has no price, and it cannot be replaced by anything else.[98]

In a popularised and general form, Kant's categorical imperative can be expressed through the 'Golden Rule': Treat the other human in a manner in which you wish to be treated yourself.[99] In this point, the West has betrayed the Enlightenment. For, who lives accordingly? In general, we can maintain that the Golden Rule is not applied in the encounter with Africa.

Human rights are built upon the moral understanding of the human being where dignity is at the core of them. Accordingly, reason and dignity distinguish the human being and that means *every* individual. Based on this, the individual has rights and enjoys equality. But it was only in 1948 that the General Assembly of the United Nations adopted and proclaimed the Universal Declaration of Human Rights. Its acceptance and realisation are still an unfinished process. For, a culture and a society have problems to accept the human rights as formulated by the West when they do not share the same presumptions – individuality, reason and the related human dignity as intrinsic value – and when for them human dignity is an *extrinsic* value determined by the traditional community.[100]

---

97. I refer only to "Groundwork for the Metaphysics of Morals" (Kant 2008), German: "Grundlegung zur Metaphysik der Sitten", (Kant 1966b), although Kant develops his ethics also in later works.

98. The history of accountability in modern times can be taken as an example for the emphasis on *reason* with respect to the individual. See Danner (2010: 41–44).

99. See different formulations of the Categorical Imperative in Kant (2008: 24–29).

100. Bielefeldt (1997: 259–261) argues that human rights cannot be claimed by or based on the European Enlightenment alone.

Based on these principles – use of one's reason, being an end in oneself, dignity – also a *society* as a whole is changing or better: has to change. When the authority lies in the individual because he or she has reason – and dignity – then all individuals are *equal*. Because of that, estates, classes and villeinage have to be abolished. All members of the society have *equal rights*. A society of (principally) equal citizens can no longer be ruled by an absolute monarchy. His powers and his legitimacy cannot be derived from God or from his office as such. Also, his protective role as a patriarch and the demanded obedience to him have been criticised. *Politics* has to *include the people* and the monarch has to be subjected to the rule of law; he does not stand above the law. Abraham Lincoln, the American president, formulated in 1863: Democracy is the government of the people, by the people, for the people.

Historically, England can point to the oldest development in this respect, i.e. to the development of democracy. Already in 1215, the 'Magna Carta' guaranteed rights for the nobles and the king had to follow the constitutional law. King Edward I instituted a parliament consisting of aristocrats, clergy and other representatives; this happened in 1295. After King Charles I had provoked a fight between parliamentarians and royalists, he was beheaded in 1649, something unheard of before this time. The Bill of Rights of 1689 gave English citizens civil and political rights within a constitutional monarchy; one aspect of it was free expression. The American constitution of 1788 is another milestone in the development of democratic governance; e.g. it separates the powers of the president, congress and judiciary. Shortly afterwards, in 1789, the French Revolution intends to replace the absolute monarchy by a republic and to install the rights of the people. In the 17th and 18th century, these historic events have been inspired by theorists such as Hobbes, Locke and Rousseau, who developed different ideas about a *'social contract'* which is to be a contract between the people and their government to give powers to the government while at the same time controlling the same government.

At the same time, over the centuries, *Christianity* has been liberated from the strict authority of the (Catholic) Church. The individual believer refers to his or her personal conviction, also using reasoning instead of simply relying on the teachings of the Church, e.g. by interpreting the Bible independently. The outstanding personality in the religious controversy is *Martin Luther*. In 1517, with his famous theses, he tries to correct the path of the Church, reminding it of the meaning of the Bible. Luther's protest still happens *within* the Church, although the 'protestants' finally walk away from the Catholic Church resulting in the Thirty Years War (1618–1648).

Movements within the Church, mainly as orders, have been known long before Luther. However, what is new in the context of the Enlightenment is the objection to the *authority* of the institution of the church (es) and finally of the *institution* as such. For instance, a self-declared enemy of the Church was Voltaire (1694–

1778). The image of God changes from the God of revelation in the Bible to a rationally perceived God who is the creator of the universe but no longer interferes with His creation. This is the concept of the 'free thinkers' or of *deism* of the 17th and 18th century. An example is Leibniz' (1646–1716) understanding of God as a clockmaker. A step further than claiming a God by rational means is the total denial of God, i.e. *atheism.* It has been declared at first in the 17th century, though secretly. In 1882, Nietzsche (1966: 127) will say: "God is dead!", which may have become the most well-known expression of atheism.[101]

The appeal to rely on one's own thinking, to be aware of one's dignity, equality and freedom, not only changed the social structures, the political systems and the attitude towards religion, but also resulted in *practical* changes of daily life, caused by *technological* developments. We remember in which way Galilei had influenced and determined modern *science:* through observation by using one's own senses and instruments, examination of hypotheses through experiments, formulation of (natural) laws in a mathematical language, independence of the teachings of an authority, etc. This approach to science became the model for science in general and for the development of many specialised new sciences that we know today. Scientific discoveries and applied sciences fostered the development of *technology*. A criterion of science and technology is *precision*.

Sciences and technology in combination with a new science, namely economics,[102] were the driving power for the *industrial revolution* of the 18th and 19th century. Inventions such as steam power, electricity and combustion engines allowed machine-based manufacturing and industrial production in general; new means of transport such as railways and powered ships contributed to this development; canals were built and roads improved. Sciences, technology and industrialisation changed the European and American societies and economies profoundly, resulting in an unprecedented growth of populations and wealth.

A very significant characteristic of the period of Enlightenment is the *effort to foster* its ideas and practical effects. One, of course, is the *publications* of intellectuals. Just to name a few: In England, these were Thomas Hobbes' "Leviathan" (1651) among many others of his writings and "Two Treatises of Government" (1689) by John Locke.

> "Much of Locke's work is characterised by opposition to authoritarianism. This opposition is both on the level of the individual person and on the level of institutions such as government and church. For the individual,

101. For the criticism and changes in Protestantism, Catholicism and Judaism during Enlightenment see Borgstedt (2004: 34–53).

102. "An Inquiry into the Nature and Causes of the Wealth of Nations" by Adam Smith (1723–1790), first published in 1776, gave a decisive impetus to the science of economics. Also, the understanding of Protestants and the Calvinists that one is free to make money supported economic development. Calvin wrote, "it is even a great blasphemy against God to disapprove of riches [...] For where do riches come from, if not from God?" (cit. Scharf 2008: 6).

> Locke wants each of us to use reason to search after truth rather than simply accept the opinion of authorities or be subject to superstition. He wants us to proportion assent to propositions to the evidence for them. On the level of institutions it becomes important to distinguish the legitimate from the illegitimate functions of institutions and to make the corresponding distinction for the uses of force by these institutions." (Uzgalis 2007: 1)

As we can easily recognise, alone this short description of Locke's political writings refers to important elements of the Enlightenment.[103] France was represented by Voltaire's critical writings against the political regime and religion, and by Jean-Jacques Rousseau's "Discourse on the origin and the foundations of inequality among the human beings" (1755) and "Social contract" (1762). The 'Encyclopédie' published in France between 1750 and 1780 by Diderot and d'Alembert deserves special mentioning due to its strong influence at that time.[104] Immanuel Kant was an important thinker in Germany – I have quoted above from his "Groundwork for the metaphysics of morals" and "What is Enlightenment?"[105]

The above mentioned need of discussion in order to elaborate on common reason and 'the' truth was realised by *enlightenment societies*. (Borgstedt 2004: 62–70) One example is the "Berlinische Monatsschrift" – the 'Berlin Monthly' (Hinske 1981). It provided the platform for publications of a group of politicians, jurists, theologians, philosophers, educators, medical doctors, who in 1783 founded a "society of friends for the enlightenment" and who regularly met to exchange their thoughts (Hinske 1981: XXIV–XXV). The motives of the "Berlinische Monatsschrift" were described by its editors as such: *Publicity* as its main interest; open-mindedness as its permanent character; expansion of freedom of thought, recommendation of purified and clarified terms, fight against dark and emotional philosophy as its purpose; liberation from all ties of irrationality, saving the right of individual investigation and individual thinking as its issues. (Hinske 1981: LXIV) This alone describes almost the whole programme of Enlightenment in general. What is missing here, the aversion against religion, was practised in the Monthly's criticism of Catholicism.

The case of Enlightenment was practically carried forward by some *rulers* who – at least partly – identified with its ideals. One example is Frederick the Great

103. On John Locke see also online:
http://plato.stanford.edu/archives/sum2010/entries/locke/. First published Sun Sep 2, 2001; substantive revision Sat 5 May 2007.

104. Blom (2010) stresses the importance of Diderot, Holbach, Helvétius and others for what he calls the "radical enlightenment" as opposed to the "moderate enlightenment", represented by Voltaire, Rousseau, and Kant.

105. Other representatives of the German Enlightenment are Christian Wolff (1679–1754), Gotthold E. Lessing (1729–1781), Moses Mendelsohn (1729–1786). Besides Kant's importance for the German Enlightenment, his racist prejudices towards Africans have to be mentioned; usually they are not noted like Hegel's racism; see Kimmerle (2002: 57–62).

from Prussia (1712–1786), who participated in the discussion about enlightenment, even invited Voltaire to his residence, and who called himself "First Servant of the State" (Scharf 2008). Frederick also showed religious tolerance; he softened censorship and introduced compulsory school attendance; he abolished capital punishment. These were demands of theorists of the Enlightenment. Recent research on Enlightenment doubts whether the progressive attitude of 'enlightened despots' has been genuine or whether it has also to be interpreted as opportunistic (Borgstedt 2004: 24–30). But in any case, Enlightenment in Germany was closer to the state system than it was, for instance, in France; civil servants got the order for reforms from the top.

For the critics of absolute monarchism, it was clear that a king could no longer derive his legitimacy from God's will. When and where monarchs did not respect the rights of the people, *revolutions* tried to enforce them. This happened in America between 1775 and 1783 with success where the colonies revolted against the British Crown, resulting in the Declaration of Independence (1776), the American constitution (1788) and the American Bill of Rights (1791); this was attempted in the French Revolution in 1789 carried by high ideals – 'liberté, égalité, fraternité' – and with horrifying results: the invention and excessive use of the guillotine, Robespierre's murderous rule, a new Empire under Napoleon and wars in Europe.

Education was the peaceful way for the protagonists of Enlightenment to make their ideas known, not just as an ideological way of teaching, but because education as such enlightens and liberates. Enlightenment, education and emancipation belong together; they further the progress of the society individually, collectively and as humanity. Enlightenment and education can almost be used as synonyms: education through enlightenment, enlightenment through education, but also enlightenment as education. The educators of the Enlightenment fought the thoughtless learning by heart and repetition; they demanded visualisation and learning to think instead of learning thoughts. (Borgstedt 2004: 53–55) The most famous work on education was Rousseau's "Émile or on education", published in 1762. It was distributed all over Europe. An anecdote maintains that Kant, known for his punctual life-style, forgot to take up his regular walk when he was enthralled by reading the "Émile".[106]

The representatives of the Enlightenment not only intended to address children through education, but also the 'simple people' including farmers. For this, *'popular enlightenment'* tried to teach the ideas of Enlightenment to the 'common man' and to encourage him to think for himself. This movement began about 1770 and lasted until

106. Other publications on education of this period: François Fénelon: "Traité de l'éducation des filles" (1687); John Locke: "Some thoughts concerning education" (1693); Heinrich Pestalozzi: "Lienhardt und Gertrud" (1781). The Swiss educator Pestalozzi is understood to be *the* representative of education of the Enlightenment.

about 1848, also facing the problem that the addressed 'simple people' did not always understand or even were not willing to understand. (Borgstedt 2004: 58–62)

Although the ideas and ideals of the Enlightenment may not have been adopted immediately and by everyone, they still contributed to several *emancipation movements* that started in the 18th, 19th and even 20th century. They are an on-going process that has to be initiated and fought for again and again. That is true for Enlightenment as a whole. There is no enlightened final state. Thus, emancipation means the liberation of suppressed, disadvantaged groups that will develop anew. They may be suffering under mental, legal, social and political tutelage and injustice. By that, their human dignity is violated and they are denied equal rights or rights in general. 'Emancipation' can imply that certain rights are *granted* by an authority; for instance, in Roman times a slave may have been liberated by his owner. However, the emancipation movements that followed the Enlightenment have normally been fought for by the concerned social groups as class conflicts – by the citizens, by farmers in villeinage, by the proletariat.

The abolition of *slavery*, beginning in the 18th century, rather was an emancipation that was initiated by concerned Europeans and Americans, although there have also been slave revolutions – as we have seen above in the context of the African history. The *Jewish* emancipation intended to liberate the Jews from the 'ghetto', and this not only in a physical sense, but also spiritually and mentally. Moses Mendelsohn (1729–1786) was one of the first intellectual fighters for the Jewish emancipation, which later in the 19th and 20th century found an expression in the Zionist movement. While the Jews suffered suppression because of belonging to a specific people[107] and to a certain religious belief, the industrial revolution of the 18th and 19th century created another underprivileged group – the (industrial) *workers*. Their labour, their living and legal situation demanded emancipation towards humanly acceptable conditions. Workers unions were founded, enforcing changes by strikes, but also by legal improvements. Socialism and Marxism have their roots in the workers' conditions of the 19th century.

Another group which experienced inequality due to different reasons were *women*. Not only were they affected when they belonged to the working class, but also by simply being the female gender. Their role has been – and often still is – restricted to household and motherhood, being denied higher education, voting, and ownership of property or executive jobs. Thus, the women's emancipation movement began to fight for women's rights all over Europe in the 19th century. More recent struggles for equal rights are concerned about other groups, e.g. children, Blacks, homosexuals, or the disabled.

Those various emancipation movements intended to improve the living conditions of groups *within* the European and American societies. Insofar, Enlightenment had a positive effect on the development of those societies (though,

107 Sand (2011) argues that taking the Jews as a 'people', i.e. an ethnicity, is an invention.

at first, Enlightenment may have been the cause of inequalities as, for instance, for the workers). But Enlightenment can also be seen as having a negative effect on the relationship to societies and cultures that were not European or American. For the enlightened peoples perceived themselves as superior to and dominant above other cultural systems (Borgstedt 2004: 99). Insofar, the ideals of Enlightenment, expressed in égalité and fraternité, perverted to the opposite, namely to suppression and dehumanisation.

> "Africa is that part of the world where Europeans projected most forcefully and fancifully their own pride and prejudice. This means, among other reasons, that it is in Africa that they revealed most clearly their own vision of mankind, extolled most loudly their own colonial (missionary) project, deployed most skilfully their own justification for enslaving and exploiting 'others', justified most casuistically their own sense of racial superiority and, today, revel in their most self-serving display of guilt and regret." (Chabal 2009: 20)

Taking this negative effect of Enlightenment in consideration, one has to be skeptical about the 'progress' that it has brought to the West and to the rest of the world. Obviously, this 'progress' was not purely positive. This is not only a matter for retrospection. Also during the actual discussions about goals, contents, and ways of Enlightenment there were differing views arguing with each other. But in addition, the overall intention of Enlightenment – think independently, be critical – was contradicted. This is not astonishing as certain power positions were in danger – in the Church and in governments. Therefore, churches and religious thinkers argued against the proclamation of autonomy of reason and methods of natural sciences. At the beginning, *Anti-Enlightenment* or Counter-Enlightenment was a matter of religion and theology, strongly supported by Jesuits who objected to church reforms. Around 1780, political opposition also joined the rejection of enlightened ideas. (Borgstedt 2004: 90–98)

As we have seen, Frederick the Great, King of Prussia, was one of the monarchs who were open-minded towards the ideas of the Enlightenment. When he died in 1786, his successor, Frederick William II, replaced the incumbent and likewise open-minded minister of culture by an enemy of the Enlightenment. The new minister immediately gave orders that the 'errors of naturalists and deists' must not be spread among the people in the name of enlightenment. No clergy, preacher or teacher of Protestant religion is allowed to teach those errors otherwise he will be severely punished. In addition, strict regulations and an authority for censorship are introduced. This directly affects the earlier mentioned Berlinische Monatsschrift (Berlin Monthly). The free and unhindered discussion of German Enlightenment is terminated. (Hinske 1981: XXXII–XXXVI)

However, there also exist other motives to oppose Enlightenment, other than power interests. The stress on *reason* and rationality has to be seen as *one-sided*;

it reduces the world view and consequently the human being to rationality. That is clearly the case in the concept of science in Descartes and in Spinoza: Only what can be expressed in the way of mathematics – 'more geometrico' – can be accepted as 'science'. According to this concept, for instance, ethics or philosophical anthropology has to be considered as 'un-scientific'. (Danner 2010: 22–23) But it was felt that the reduction of reality and of the human being to rationality was an impoverishment. Mainly in German literature at the period of Enlightenment, another emphasis was laid on *emotions*. Decisions are made not only based on reason, but also by the 'heart'. For instance, Heinrich Pestalozzi, the Swiss educator, demanded a holistic education by nurturing 'head, heart, and hand'. Wolfgang von Goethe published a novel in 1774, which was enthusiastically received all over Europe: "The Sorrows of Young Werther". The unexpected success of this novel can probably be explained by the fact that it talks of dimensions of the human being that are otherwise neglected by stressing on rationality: of love and passion, of romantic life in the countryside, of sentiments and emotions.

***

The purpose of this outline of the Enlightenment and of the previous period was to create awareness on the *undercurrent* disposition of the Western mind in distinction from Africa. The Enlightenment was a period of contractions and of rich contributions in different countries under various perspectives; last but not least it was attacked by opponents. Each area would deserve a thorough elaboration; some are not mentioned here at all, for instance art. However, the main features of the Enlightenment and consequently of the European mind should have become obvious: emphasizing *reason*, i.e. critical, independent thinking, and *individuality*, i.e. the strengthening of the individual in religious, political, economic and social affairs. The Enlightenment has shaped Europe and the countries of its influence, above all America, with tremendous progress and dubious effects.

However, although individualism and reason have to be seen as important factors of the developments that Enlightenment has initiated, it will be too narrow to consider individualism and reason as the single cause of these developments. For, each area has its own dynamics. For example, in politics this is power, in science it is the quest for knowledge, in religion spirituality, etc. However, the European development of mind and its historic consequences cannot be understood without reason and individualism.

The enlightened developments in religion, society, politics, ethics, arts, literature, science and technology are *parallel* processes that are interdependent. Above all, they have been on-going over many centuries; their roots can be traced to the ancient Greek and Roman times; they were revived in the $14^{th}/15^{th}$ centuries and emphasised through the Enlightenment. They are not completed by today, to the contrary, they are experiencing regression and they have to be revised. Movements such as the workers' or the women's emancipations are permanently opposed by interests of greed and power of other groups – by employers or by men. While in Wyoming women got the right to vote already in 1869, in Switzerland they had to wait until 1971 for the federal level, and the last Swiss canton needed a court decision against the men to introduce the voting right for women in 1990. We notice regression in the suppression of scientific insights by authorities up to date; a historic example for this is Darwin's theory of evolution that is fought up today mainly by religious people. Revision of the whole idea of the Enlightenment appears to be necessary in the face of today's ecological problems – the rational approach to and use of nature has reached an absolute limit. And it seems to be obvious that we have to revise our biased rational and individualistic approach to other cultures.

Enlightenment must not be misunderstood as a programme or an action plan that once had been designed and that had more or less perfectly been fulfilled. It had tremendous effects on society, politics, religious belief and on science and technology. Rather than being a programme, Enlightenment follows *ideals* – rationality and individuality, dignity and equality; Kant's description of Enlightenment as the departure of the human being from one's self-inflicted immaturity is a *continuous challenge* to the individual and to the whole society, hardly fulfilled, more often betrayed. This also applies to the ethical challenge of the Golden Rule. The consequences of the Enlightenment as well as the encounter with other cultures posit another challenge, namely to rethink the basics of Enlightenment.

One way of approaching reality is to collect facts, to measure, to structure data. Another way is to describe reality. Facts and descriptions need to be understood and interpreted in their sense. Sense cannot be measured.

CHAPTER SEVEN

Excursion: Understanding and interpretation

The relationship between Africa and the West is determined by factors that we have described up to now: by their history, by the African social structure, ethics and spirituality as well as by the emphasis of the West on reason and individuality. It is an essential insight and claim of this study that a change of attitudes is necessary – on the side of the West and of Africa. A change of attitudes requires knowledge and above all understanding, i.e. the understanding of the mentioned factors.

This chapter as a *theoretical* foundation intends to elaborate on the process of understanding: What happens, what do we have to consider, when we understand? Secondly, in the line of a 'practical hermeneutics', insights into understanding as an act of recognition shall clarify what occurs and what is necessary when two very different cultures encounter. Thirdly, we will outline a few features of a 'hermeneutics of development cooperation'.

Readers who are less interested in this theoretical part may skip it and go directly to the next chapter, "The encounter of two cultures", and they can later return to it.

One main reason for unsuccessful development cooperation and development politics – using this as an example of relationships – is the lack of awareness of and sensitivity for the cultural and mental environment of the developing country – when for instance goals and strategies are imposed by the donor countries. At the same time, this also applies to their African counterparts who may not be aware of the cultural and mental background of the West – when, for instance, conditions are followed to please the donor without realising the spirit of the conditions. The best example for this is 'democracy', which in many African countries may exist as a facade behind which traditional forms of ruling are applied. In other words: The lack of mutual *understanding* may be one of the essential reasons for an unsatisfying development cooperation and a dragging development. Development efforts can only be successful when the partners are ready to *understand* the world view of the other side, both the 'donor' and the 'receiving' side. Both sides should understand each other, i.e. the culture, the 'mentality', language, social structures, values, norms, beliefs, etc. Accordingly, understanding as a form of cognition should be elucidated in order to take in consideration a decisive component of human life. As a theoretical background of this essay, it seems to be helpful to have a brief look into the 'theory of understanding' – without going into theoretical depths and into too many details here.[108]

7.1. Theory of understanding: 'hermeneutics'

For example, politics of development and development cooperation on a large scale – e.g. through IMF or World Bank – have a strong tendency to see development in the context of measurable facts, of numbers, statistics, GDP, percentages of growth, etc. Also Dambisa Moyo's "Dead Aid" (2009) is an example for an empirical, quantitative, positivistic approach. It is blind towards the inadequate approach of donor institutions to aid because Moyo herself is caught in the same kind of approach. Moyo's criticism of aid, therefore, is the victim of a vicious circle. (Danner 2011a) To avoid a misunderstanding: Quantitative data, measuring, etc., are necessary. But the important question is: What do those figures *mean,* what *sense* do they make? And do they represent the *whole reality?*

There are several ways of approaching reality. One is to collect facts, to measure, to structure that data. Another way is to *describe* reality either in the form of art or in a strict methodological process like in phenomenology. But facts

108. See in general: R. Palmer (1969), Gadamer (1975), Birus (1982), Danner (1995; 2006).

and descriptions need to be understood and interpreted in their sense.[109] For this reason, it seems to be necessary to get acquainted with the basics of the 'theory of understanding'.

This essay is guided by the conviction that the human reality, i.e. everything that is related to humans, has to be perceived under the perspective of *sense.* Language, tools, gestures, social structures, contracts, texts, buildings, structures of settlements, economic and legal order, are something *meaningful* to the related people; they are representing something which has to be *understood.* This – what has to be understood – we call 'meaning' or 'sense'. That does not necessarily relate to a 'deeper' sense or a metaphysical or religious meaning or 'sense of life'. That may be the case; but this is not the meaning of sense we are talking about here. In any case, one thing should be clear: Meaning or sense cannot be measured; it has to be understood.

Understanding has been systematised, analysed and elaborated on in a philosophical and scientific way under the name of *'hermeneutics',* which is considered as the theory or the 'art of understanding and interpretation'. The historic roots of hermeneutics can be found in theology as the interpretation of the Bible, in jurisprudence as the interpretation of legal texts, and in the study of literature as the understanding of (classical) texts. In each case, a specific form of 'hermeneutics' had been developed, but it always was a form of interpretation of *texts*. In the nineteenth and twentieth century, hermeneutics has been reflected on a *general* philosophical level, which goes beyond the pure interpretation of texts, for human reality in general has to be understood and interpreted.[110]

We are familiar with the core term of the theory of understanding in a way that usually we do not notice it; we constantly deal with it, namely with *sense*. Because sense is so commonplace, it is difficult to understand what it means. In our familiar surroundings, we understand spontaneously: what somebody says to us, what we read, a traffic situation, the structure of a building. But suddenly we may 'stumble' over a situation where the fluent understanding is interrupted. The reader of this text, for example, may doubt whether he/she can grasp what the writer is talking about. Suddenly, the question of the sense of this text arises; interpretation is needed.

As the English language uses 'meaning' in a double sense or twofold, it is good to be aware of it and make a clear distinction: The reader may easily understand the meaning *of* this text, but these reflections do not have a meaning *for* him/her. The 'meaning of' is the *sense* of the text; the 'meaning for' the reader is the *importance*

109. Chabal and Daloz (1999) and specifically Chabal (2009) are an exception: They (1999: xv–xxi) refer to aspects of the "irrational" and of culture; in a wider sense, their approach can be called an 'applied phenomenology' and it has features of hermeneutics. (See Danner 2000: 1–2) Specifically Chabal (2009: x) refers to the "key areas of human existence" and asks for the meaning the observed facts. Geertz (2000: 5) says, culture is a web of meanings.

110. For different hermeneutic positions and their historic development, see Birus (1982). More recent developments, for example, reflect on hermeneutics of music, history of art, pedagogic, etc.

of the text for him or her. What we are talking about here is the *sense*. To avoid misunderstandings and to be clear, we will use 'sense' as the term of our interest.

Another occurrence of sense may happen in the context of nature and in contrast to it. Imagine you are walking in a remote area; you are surrounded by pure nature: stones, grass, bushes. But all of a sudden you notice a small pile of stones. It strikes you that this pile cannot be natural. It is obviously man-made. You immediately ask: what does this pile of stones mean, what is its sense? Human traces, human products, point in a way to something that pure nature does not contain: sense.

We encounter other occasions in daily life where sense appears because of its absence: For instance, we read an email and we cannot understand what the sender is saying. Or: I fully understand the sense of an English text, but I have trouble to express it in German – even if the English text is my own: sense is present, but in a pre-language form, i.e. not (yet) put in words. Translating is interpretation, not exchanging words for other words. When, for example, Kikuyu expressions are literally translated into English, they sound strange and do not make sense. We also speak with gestures, accompanying our talking; in our common surroundings, this will be fully understood. But then we watch an Italian or an Arab and are puzzled by their gestures: what do they mean?

In our surrounding community as well as in our wider society we live in an interpreted world, in a world that contains innumerable forms of sense; and there, we are familiar with these forms of sense: from spoken and written language to codes of honour and ways of doing business, etc. We live within this sense-full world; through socialisation and education we grow into it; who belongs to this world represents it; interpretations happen on the foundation of *this* sense-full world. But there are many of these interpreted worlds, often quite alien to each other like the European and the African (sense-full) worlds. What does this mean for understanding, understanding the manifold forms of sense of the alien world?

On a few occasions, I have accompanied groups from Egypt to Germany. After arrival, most of them showed a behaviour one could describe as cultural shock. During the first days they would criticize everything they have experienced until they started to understand and to appreciate that things and behaviours in Germany were simply different. On the one hand, this can be explained as a way of self-preservation. On the other hand, the criticism was based on their *own* sense-full world from which they came. That German world did not fit for them; something was wrong. However, the same happens to European tourists, politicians, colonialists, aid workers and businessmen who travel to Africa. They see and interpret everything they encounter on their *own* background, on the foundation of their *own* sense-full world. With this closed attitude, understanding of the other side is impossible. First of all, it needs a readiness to acknowledge a *different* sense-full world; secondly, it needs an attempt to *understand*, to interpret the sense implications of the other world. A real hindrance to make an attempt to understand the counterpart is given by the fact that the other world may not appear to be sense-full in part or in total; it may seem to be '*sense-less'*, contradicting the sense of the own familiar world.

With this observation, we come across another important element *how understanding is happening:* We *always* understand based on our own familiar sense-full world. We cannot escape our background. From our standpoint, we perceive whatever we encounter. We understand with a pre-conceived idea of what we want to understand. We understand with a *prejudice.* (Gadamer 1975: 255–269) This is positive and negative at the same time. The usual meaning of a prejudice is negative because it hinders us to see the reality of what we encounter – we have our prejudices against persons from another country or tribe, against a certain car model, against the other gender. The *positive* meaning of a prejudice lies in the fact that we are depending on it when we understand. We read a book based on the knowledge we already have about the subject. A child is learning on the foundation of his/her previous experience. A businessman meets a business partner on the understanding of how business is done. In other words, we need our pre-experience, our pre-knowledge in order to understand a message, a new situation or text. This positive prejudice is part of the process of understanding. The question is: What has to happen so that the positive prejudice does not end up as a negative one?

Before we answer this question, we look at a third element of the process of understanding. For instance, when reading the autobiography of Njenga Karume (2009), a Kenyan businessman and politician, each of us may have different interests, different questions: What is the life story of this man? What does he tell us about his traditional origin? How did he experience the relationship between Africans and colonialists? Every question, every *focus* on the book, will provoke different answers. Another example: a tourist who travels to an African country will have a different focus on the country than a businessman. The tourist will look for landscapes, folkloric activities, wildlife or beaches, while the businessman will analyse the economic situation, political environment and business opportunities. And everyone looks at an African country under the almost exclusive perspective of development; an African country *is* supposed to be a developing country; an African society is no longer allowed to be a 'normal' society (Danner 2005). Each specific *focus* will guide the understanding in a certain way. We could also say that understanding happens under a certain *perspective*.

Understanding aims at grasping the *sense* – of a letter, a book, an email, of a joke, of a tool, of a rule. This 'grasping of the sense' depends on the existing pre-knowledge of the subject matter, on a *positive prejudice*. Understanding asks a certain question, is focussed, and happens under a specific perspective. Now we ask again: How does one ensure that the positive, necessary prejudice does not become a negative prejudice that already knows everything in advance and that terminates the process of understanding before it has started?

The positive prejudice is, of course, the expression of a will to understand. It is an essential element of the process of understanding. Looking carefully at this process, we can observe an interesting movement that characterises understanding: The person who intends to travel to an African country and seeks information about it – by reading, talking to other people, watching TV reports – does this with a certain pre-knowledge as we have said earlier. Somehow, the person has *to know in advance* what he/she is trying to understand; this knowledge may be vague and even wrong. But by reading, listening to other people, watching TV, the pre-knowledge will be *changed*; it will no longer be the same as before the reading, etc. This expanded and changed pre-knowledge will be the foundation for further efforts to understand. Everyone will have the experience that reading the same book or article for a second or even a third time is not the same as reading it the first time. The same applies to repeatedly watching a film; the understanding of the film is never the same. Travelling to the same country at repeated times will deepen the understanding.

The positive prejudice alters from one time to the other. However, the changed prejudice must not be mistaken as a quantitative addition of information, as an enlarged sum of facts. It is rather a widening of the personal and mental *horizon* that may result in a different attitude towards a country or towards any other subject matter. Contexts may be noticed, which may not have been apparent before.

In a way, the process of understanding where a movement happens from pre-knowledge to a text, a report, etc., and back to the (changed) pre-knowledge and from there again to the text, the report, etc., can be described as a *circle*. In a technical term, this is called the 'hermeneutic circle'. (Danner 1995: 235–237; Danner 2006: 60–67) It is important for our context to recognise that understanding happens in a circular way that it has to be distinguished from a quantitative adding up of data. In the process of understanding, a critical self-questioning will permanently be necessary: Do I understand the sense of what I am encountering, of *what* I intend to understand – or am I still caught up in my own original understanding of the subject matter? What does the author of a text mean? What does the social or the ethical behaviour of foreign people mean? Can I leave *my* understanding behind to give room to something different that emanates from the text or the foreign people?

The question that may arise here is: How do we know that we have *adequately* understood? Do we ever reach the 'truth' of the matter? The answer may be disappointing because we have no assurance that we will completely understand without any doubt and because there is no 'absolute truth', no formula, no final definition. This is the reason for a strong opposition against a theory of understanding. For, when we deal with data, facts and figures we get a doubtless result: 2 + 2 = 4, nothing else. However, if it is true that human beings have the 'irrational' attitude of giving their world in which they live sense and meaning and if sense and meaning are not quantifiable, then we have to live with the uncertainty that 'understanding' confronts us with. But we must not be lost in a chaos of relativity – everything goes, everything is true – because there is *'objectivity'* due to the 'resistance of the subject matter' (Bollnow 1966: 57–65). What we try to understand and to interpret does not allow us to judge arbitrarily on it. We have to give up our (negative) prejudice. In a figurative sense, we must allow the subject matter to 'speak'. And in a literal sense we have to *listen* to African partners if we intend to understand them.

'Understanding' in our context means a *process of cognition* which aims at grasping sense; it is, therefore, an intellectual effort. From this meaning, we have to distinguish an 'understanding' that means a good personal relationship, accompanied by positive feelings – 'we understand each other'. This can simply mean to tolerate another person's behaviour even without understanding it. From this, we also have to distinguish the *attitude* of understanding, the *readiness* to submit oneself to the strenuous intellectual process, which certainly is a prerequisite to understanding in the strict sense. It may be a very crucial, preliminary step in development cooperation: are we willing to understand the foreign other side?

Concerning 'understanding' as a process of cognition, we can discern three stages and forms: Unknowingly, we perform spontaneous acts of understanding in our daily life: we listen to somebody; we read an advertisement; we use a machine. Secondly, in this constant flow of acts of understanding, we may realise that we do *not* understand and that there is something missing. We have to ask the partner what he means; we have to read a newspaper article again; we may start to discuss it with another person. We *interpret* the sense of something. Thirdly, this situation of daily life may become the subject of theoretical reflection: We ask how understanding is happening, what we have to consider ensuring that we understand as adequately as possible. At this stage, we are in the middle of the question of systematic *interpretation* and of 'hermeneutics'.

7.2. Understanding the alien, a 'practical hermeneutics'

So far, we have put our emphasis on understanding as a process of cognition. In its centre we find 'sense' that we want to grasp. Although understanding usually happens unnoticed, in many cases the need of understanding becomes obvious. We understand from the point where we stand; i.e. we understand with a 'prejudice'. Here, 'prejudice' has a positive function contrary to the prejudice that hinders us to understand. There is a sort of circular movement going on between the (positive) prejudice and the subject matter that we want to understand, widening the (positive) prejudice and deepening the understanding of the subject matter. Understanding cannot achieve 'absolute truth', however 'objectivity' that is challenged by the 'resistance of the subject matter'.

In this theoretical context, I have mentioned for a few times the *attitude* that must motivate and guide understanding. We *want* to understand – or not; and we want to understand for a certain *purpose*. This practical approach has been elaborated by Theo Sundermeier (1996) in "Understanding the alien: A practical hermeneutics". For his approach, he also uses the expressions "intercultural hermeneutics" and "hermeneutics of the alien". The aim is the ability to *live* together in face of the very different, incompatible cultures that we find in the course of globalisation.

Sundermeier makes an important observation. So far, hermeneutics as a theory has concentrated on incidents of understanding and interpretation, where the interpreter, the understanding person, belongs to the *same* cultural background to the same mind-set, as the content that he tries to understand. Although there is always a 'hermeneutic difference' between understanding and the object of understanding – a text, a social rule, an educational aim – on the *common* cultural and mental background there is an (ideal) chance that the 'hermeneutic difference' will disappear. (Danner 2006: 63–64) Sundermeier calls this the understanding of the 'other' or the 'foreign' – e.g. when a European intends to interpret something that belongs to the European context. But the situation changes considerably where the understanding person and the content that is to be understood belong to different cultures and mind-sets. Then, we intend to understand something or someone *'alien'*. This is the case when, for example, a European wants to understand something that belongs to the genuine African context, or vice versa, an African is confronted with something typically European. The 'hermeneutic difference' remains an unbridgeable gap. The other side remains alien. A part of something that *cannot* be understood remains. How do we deal with it? How do we *live* with it?

The foreignness, the 'alienness', appears on two levels. I may meet people who are not from my own familiar world; at first, I will experience them through my senses: they look unfamiliar, they behave differently, they may even smell strangely. They may be exotic to me, repellent or attractive, frightening or inspiring. On another level, I may notice that they act within different patterns of life, that there is a foreign order that they follow. (140–144)[111] Thus, a subjective perception and an objective comprehension can be distinguished; both complement each other (76, 153). On either level, the differences between the cultures must be recognised and not be denied. This even strengthens the own identity. And this gives the strength to be open-minded towards the strange and the alien. (152)

For Sundermeier, the understanding approach towards the alien is not only an

111. Page numbers in this sub-chapter refer to Sundermeier (1996).

intellectual process. Acting, getting physically involved, living within the alien world, is necessary and complementary to understanding. Acting and understanding are related. "Who wants to understand has to accept the environment of the alien and has to live within it" (154).

Based on such insights, Sundermeier proposes four steps towards the understanding of the alien (153–173, 183–197):

1. On the level of the phenomena, i.e. how the alien appears and presents itself, the subjective attitude will be to abstain from opinions and judgements, from negative prejudices. The objective comprehension will provide a descriptive analysis. On the level of acting, one should attempt to perceive by keeping a distance. The foreignness of the alien must be preserved and must have its own validity.
2. On the level of signs, the subjective attitude will be sympathy. The objective comprehension happens as contextualisation. Participatory observation indicates the level of action.

   The signs (in this case of a culture) are addressing our senses – language, gestures and clothes. By perceiving them, we are tempted to label the other side. This must be avoided by learning how to read those signs. Sympathy is necessary to avoid (negative) prejudices, too quick comparisons or wrong conclusions. The readiness to learn goes together with sympathy. Signs have to be read within their own context. Participation, i.e. acting within the other culture, is a prerequisite for understanding. There is an important sequence: To participate comes first; second is to observe to achieve understanding. By that, one has to transcend the limits of one's own culture and community and to engage intensively in a foreign environment and foreign culture. (163) We Europeans are used to live within a culture that dominates others, and we are mentally trained by it. In order to understand, we have to become learners. We have to exercise listening and learning, patience and humility.
3. On the level of symbols, the subjective attitude is empathy. The objective comprehension will engage in comparative interpretation. The level of acting consists of partial identification.

   The veil of a Muslim woman may serve as an example for a symbol. It has to be interpreted within its cultural context. The veil may have a religious, social, cultural, emancipatory or communicative function. To recognise and acknowledge this, empathy is necessary. Empathy means to put oneself in the position of foreign world without being absorbed by it. The foreign has to be taken as the foreign. Also, this attitude has to be learned. Comparative interpretations support a step by step approach and have to weigh carefully the differences and the similarities. (170)

4. Respect characterises the subjective attitude on the level of relevance. The objective comprehension consists of translation and transfer towards our own world. 'Convivence' describes the level of action.112

This level is pure action. It has *relevance* with respect to our foreign and alien neighbours. "The aim of intercultural hermeneutics is to successfully live together where everyone can remain him/herself, nobody is suppressed and mutual exchange is still happening respecting and strengthening the dignity of the other person" (183). The life patterns and the order of his/her environment are recognised; our differences are respected. Respect means to balance distance and closeness, means to be patient and attentive, to observe and to participate (185). This respect has to be trained; it contains the return to one's own position. Understanding the alien can only be partial, never complete. 'Convivence', living together, is realised as a community of mutual help, as a community of learning and as a community of feasts. It is a shared life-world.[113]

Referring to the example of a European teacher, Kenyatta (1965: 124) reflects on the difficulty to understand an African:

> "The assumption of knowing the African's mind has been very often heard in the usual phraseology: 'I have lived for many years amongst the Africans and I know them very well.' Yet this is far from the actual fact, for there is a great difference between 'living' among a people and 'knowing' them. While a European can learn something of the externals of African life, its system of kinship and classification, its peculiar arts and picturesque ceremonial, he may still have not yet reached the heart of the problem [...] With his preconceived ideas, mingled with prejudices, he fails to achieve a more sympathetic and imaginative knowledge, a more human and inward appreciation of the living people, the pupils he teaches, the people he meets

112. The term 'convivence' simply means 'living together'; also the German 'Konvivenz' is unusual.

113. STEPS TOWARDS UNDERSTANDING THE ALIEN: Sundermeier (1996: 155).

Levels of Encountering the Alien	Subjective Attitude	Objective Comprehension	Level of Action
Phenomena	Abstaining	Descriptive analysis	Perception with distance
Signs	Sympathy	Contextualisation	Participatory observation
Symbols	Empathy	Comparative interpretation	Partial identification
Relevance	Respect	Translation/ Transfer towards ourselves	Convivence

> on the roads and watches in the gardens. In a word he fails to understand the African with his instinctive tendencies [...], but trained from his earliest days to habitual ideas, inhibitions and forms of self-expression which have been handed down from one generation to another and which are foreign, if not absurd, to the European in Africa."

Indirectly, Kenyatta demands what Sundermeier tries to develop in his "practical hermeneutics". At the same time, Kenyatta warns of misunderstanding 'living among a people' as 'knowing them'. There is no shortcut.[114]

7.3. 'Hermeneutics of development cooperation'[115]

Sundermeier's insights are summarised in this sentence: "Who wants to understand, has to accept the environment of the alien and has to stay within it" (154). What does this mean for a 'hermeneutics of development cooperation'? Does it have any meaning at all? Does development not mean to overcome backwardness? Why waste time on it? However, if it is true that the social and cultural context is determining how politics, economics and, last but not least, international relationships are perceived and functioning then there is no way to neglect the social and cultural context. We have to try to understand it to be able to talk about and work together towards 'development'; this applies to both sides of development cooperation.

---

114. See also: Wirz (1997) (Das Bild vom anderen. Möglichkeiten und Grenzen interkulturellen Verstehens). This chapter on 'understanding' and the whole essay on the relationship between Africa and the West refer to and are part of the more general discussion on *understanding other cultures*. During the more recent decades, scientists of various fields have begun to acknowledge that Eurocentrism hinders this understanding. The consequent discussion questions whether *'ethnocentrism'* is the proper alternative, whether 'universalism' has to be replaced by 'pluralism'. One core issue of this discussion is concerned with human rights. 'Intercultural hermeneutics' and *'intercultural philosophy'* try to overcome the one-sided approach of Eurocentrism. For example, see: Brocker/Nau (1997) (Ethnozentrismus. Möglichkeiten und Grenzen des interkulturellen Dialogs); Lütterfelds/Mohrs (1997) (Eine Welt – eine Moral?); publications of the Society for Intercultural Philosophy, Cologne. – *François Jullien* in an interview with Deutschlandradio on 23 August 2009: We cannot get to know the Chinese culture if we remain within the European categories [which certainly also applies to African cultures]. The term of the *'universal'* is the product of a singular history, i.e. of the European history. Also, the *human rights* are a product of the same singular history. Human rights have a positive side, i.e. the ideology of the Enlightenment (individuality, social contract, happiness as final goal, etc.) and a negative side, i.e. objection to suppression, the non-acceptable, revolt. The positive side of human rights (as European) is imposed on others while the negative side can be shared among cultures and history.

115. As far as I know, a 'hermeneutics of development' does not exist yet. Chabal (2009) presents an African political theory and is interested in *understanding* what happens on the ground, i.e. in the "interpretation of the meanings", because "all of us operate within our own context of meanings" (86). But Chabal is not concerned with hermeneutics in a strict sense (66). Chabal tries to leave Western theories aside, thinking outside academic analytical categories (128) and at the same time making use of interdisciplinary results (136). This descriptive and interpretative approach can be taken as a step towards a theory of development with a hermeneutic orientation.

Sundermeier's message is simple in its essence: Understanding the alien development partner can happen only gradually, takes time, needs patience and, above all, needs our willingness to learn – because we *do not know* the counterpart. In practical terms, this means that this learning process has to be recognised and incorporated in the development cooperation by carefully preparing its agents, that those who can only fly into a foreign country for a few days and who act only from a far distance should listen to those who have a chance to experience the alien side from within.

We have seen earlier that there are different schools and forms of hermeneutics: interpretation of the Bible, of laws, of classical texts; but there are also hermeneutic theories of education, of art, of music, and others. One distinguishing element of these 'theories of interpretation' is their *scope,* their focal point. The interpretation of legal texts happens with regard to justice and legality; the interpretation of literature in view of the message of the author; the interpretation in pedagogy with respect to education. Each hermeneutics is characterised by a specific scope.

In a different context, 'development' can be the *scope* and focal point, namely in a hermeneutics of development cooperation. Then, everything has to be understood and interpreted in view of 'development': Is the money involved serving the purpose of 'development'? Are the persons dealing with 'development' and 'aid' suitable for their task? Contrary to any document that is to be interpreted as something existing, 'development' represents an idea, an ideal, an aim to be reached, something that will be in the future – like the ideal aim of education and of an 'educated person'. However, a document and its sense stem from the past and it does not change. In the process of interpretation, one can go back to it.

Also, the idea of 'development' is something formulated and can be referred to. But it constantly changes. An economic crisis like in 2009 or the ecological necessities that have emerged exemplify how the idea of 'development' will have to *change* permanently. In addition, when we talk about development and development cooperation, it is not enough to understand the concept of *one* side and within this side. Understanding and interpretation have to reach out to the *other* side, too, and have to include its concept of development *as well as* the related factors of culture, mentality, etc. The foreign side represents a challenge in its own way. (Schmidt 2005: 9-11.) It shows that the encounter in development cooperation has to be a process of learning. Who is willing to accept this?

Without being able to present a definition of 'development' that would be generally valid and accepted, we can say that 'development' has acquired a very strong connotation to *under-development*, to developing countries. One hardly talks of 'development' with reference to America or Europe, although they are permanently changing economically, socially or politically. Then, 'development' means coming out from under-development and consequently the content and the aim of 'development' are defined by the status of the 'developed' West. Another consequence of this is that 'development' automatically includes 'aid' and, therefore, those who give and those who receive 'aid'. 'Development' is perceived in the context of 'development cooperation'. Is it because 'developing countries' are considered being unable to develop on their own? But do the 'developing' societies see the West as a model? Do they have a say in what *they* want as 'development'? Does the sum of the eight Millennium Development Goals[116] represent what 'development' is to be? Can 'development' be reduced to economic growth and related factors? These remarks and questions may give a hint to the problematic sense of 'development'.[117]

When 'development' represents the *scope* of interpretation, an important *limitation* of the hermeneutic approach has to be noticed: What should be understood as 'development' is not defined by interpretation as such. For, its content is determined by *pre-decisions* that become the subject of interpretation; it is the concept of 'development' the West may have and the concept Africans may have. Also, interpretations do not provide *decisions for actions* that result from them, although interpretations are a necessary basis for economic, social or political decisions, but decisions are a step beyond the process of interpretation and are something different. Therefore, we should make a distinction between: (a) concepts of 'development' which are pre-given to interpretation, (b) the interpretation of those concepts, and (c) decisions for actions that may follow the interpretation.

After this sketch of a 'hermeneutics of development cooperation' we can summarise a few aspects: Its specific scope is given by 'development'. This is a changing idea and ideal. Two sides – the 'developing' and the 'developed' countries – define what 'development' is to be. These definitions may differ considerably. Because of this and considering that 'development' has a wider sense than economic growth, the scope of a hermeneutics of development cooperation is not clearly defined; it is 'oscillating' and, therefore, represents a difficulty and an uncertainty for interpretation. Like any other form of hermeneutics, a hermeneutics of development cooperation depends on a pre-given content, and it has to be distinguished from subsequent decisions and actions. Concepts of 'development' are bound to surrounding social, economic and political *conditions* of the 'developing country', and those concepts of development are a result of these conditions. First and foremost, those conditions have to be understood. In many cases, they may be alien for either side of the development cooperation.

116. (1) Eradicate extreme poverty and hunger. (2) Achieve universal primary education. (3) Promote gender equality and empower women. (4) Reduce child mortality. (5) Improve maternal health. (6) Combat HIV/AIDS, malaria and other diseases. (7) Ensure environmental sustainability. (8) Create a global partnership for development with targets for aid, trade and debt relief.

117. See below 9.1.

Sundermeier's approach and specific practical steps of understanding provide guidelines for a hermeneutics of development cooperation.

Those conditions are the historic, mental, social, political, and economic underlying aspects of societies, the societies of the West and of Africa. In this essay, I am concentrating on the underlying *conditions* of development, not more. They are the core interest here; they have to be understood in order to give 'development' and the cooperation for 'development' a chance of success.

Based on the foregoing elaboration on understanding and interpretation, a few *rules of understanding* and interpreting issues of development may be formulated, with a strong emphasis on the readiness of understanding:

- Become *aware* of the alien, foreign, strange and unfamiliar and notice the occurrences of not-understanding and misunderstanding;
- Abstain from *judgements* based on your familiar background, experience and knowledge;
- Become conscious of your *own* background;
- Notice the *differences* to the foreign side; consider differences in thinking, language, gestures, social structures, values, ethics and beliefs;
- Be ready to grasp the *sense* of your own views and of what appears to be alien;
- Get more information about the *other side,* not only intellectually but also by encounter and experience;
- *Go 'back and forth'* between your view and the alien view;
- *Explain* your own perspective, understanding and view to your counterpart;
- Where it is possible, reflect on the differences together with the *counterpart*;
- Based on mutual respect, it is enough to *agree to disagree*; there is no need of and no benefit in assimilation.[118]

118. Geertz (2000: 13) "We are not [...] seeking either to become natives [...] or to mimic them."

Encounter and cooperation between Africa and the West will improve when both sides question their own attitudes towards the other, when they listen to each other, and when they talk freely about the undercurrent conditions of their relationship.

CHAPTER EIGHT

The encounter of two cultures

This and the following chapter on 'development' apply what has been theoretically elaborated in the last chapter on 'understanding and interpretation'. Here and in chapter 9, the issue is *understanding,* more precisely the understanding between Africans and Westerners. By focussing on understanding in a more concrete way, it gains social and political *actuality.* This becomes even clearer and more urgent by relating to development cooperation. For the guiding thesis is: development cooperation can become successful only when there exists mutual understanding or at least it has to be tried.

Our guiding questions thus far were: What constitutes the *undercurrent* African and the undercurrent Western *world view?* We talk of the 'undercurrent' or 'underlying' because there may either be hardly any visible difference on the surface – a European in a suit and a tie and an African in a European suit and a tie. Or the visible reality may be so different that we are lost – a village in

Germany in comparison to a *manyatta* of the Maasai;[119] the German is as lost in the Maasai settlement as the Maasai is lost in a German village, 'lost' in the sense of understanding and orientation. As we have seen earlier, the African in a European suit and a tie belongs to two worlds: to the 'City' and to the 'Village'.[120] The European encounters the African of the 'City', speaks in a European language to him, and assumes he is meeting him on an equal level of understanding and neither knows nor understands the reality of the 'Village'.

The more an African is acquainted with the 'City', the better he will understand the European because the 'City' has become the melting pot of African culture and European influence. In the 'City', the African encounters European ways of thinking and doing things through education, technology, work in foreign or westernised companies, through meeting foreigners or through travelling to Western countries. Presumably, a Westerner is more at a loss in understanding Africans than Africans in understanding Westerners.[121] For, the West has not encountered African ways of thinking and living in the same way as Africa has been confronted with Europe's ways of thinking and living. For many Westerners, encounter with African cultures did virtually not happen at all or very superficially; essentially, it is limited to those who work or live in Africa.

8.1. Differences

There are different underlying realities in the encounter of Africans and Westerners. Those realities represent different mind-sets – African and 'European'; they are neither tangible nor obvious nor are they quantifiable. They constitute what is *meaningful* for either side. I have highlighted the following aspects:

> The *human being* is defined and determined as 'brother' and 'sister', as a member of a community, in the African context – or as an entity on its own, as an individual in its uniqueness, in the European context. The African person is founded on his/her community. The European society is founded on individuals. African *ethics* and values are based on the relationship between persons, protecting and strengthening the concrete community, while European ethics is based on the individual, referring to mankind and, because of that, to abstract values and norms, claiming to be universal.
>
> Accordingly, an African person has *dignity* insofar he/she fosters the well-being of the community; the Westerner has dignity insofar he/she follows abstract norms. Dignity in the European context represents an 'internal value' (Kant), while dignity

119. A temporary settlement of a nomadic Kenyan tribe (Maasai), consisting of several huts made of branches, mud and cow dung, which form an oval or round court.

120. See above 3.3: 'Village' and 'City' – tradition and modernity.

121. Chimamanda Ngozi Adichie depicts in "The thing around your neck" (2009) how alien the life in America is for a Nigerian woman.

in the African context expresses an 'external value'. In other words, dignity in the European understanding rests in the individual, while dignity of the African person rests in his/her community.

In any case, the meaning of ethics is to regulate and harmonize the living together; the difference consists in the *foundation:* whether the community provides the foundation to the individual – as it is in Africa, or the individual provides the foundation to the community, which ideally is the whole mankind[122] – as it is in the West.'

Africa and the West also differ in their *spirituality.* Africans are counting on a ubiquitous supra-natural power; events are interpreted in the light of its presence; supra-natural powers are used and manipulated in manifold forms. "For Africans, the whole of existence is a religious phenomenon." (Mbiti 1999: 15) Westerners have organised and institutionalised their religious life, restricting it to one day of the week and to one place, or closing it into individual inwardness or excluding it from their life altogether.

African *history* is perceived differently by Africans and by Westerners. The period before the arrival of the Europeans is usually not appreciated as valuable by Westerners. The common history beginning in the 15th century, mainly during the time of transatlantic slavery, missionary, and colonisation, is experienced by Africans as *suppression,* while Westerners have perceived themselves as *superior masters* and partly still do today. By that, they are renouncing their moral ideals.

The consequential and contradicting attitudes are African distrust towards Westerners and Western arrogance towards Africans.[123]

122. In Schiller's 'Ode an die Freude' and then in Beethoven's 9th Symphony we read and hear: [...] alle Menschen werden Brüder [...] seid umschlungen Millionen [...] diesen Kuss der ganzen Welt"! - All humans become brothers. Millions, be embraced. This kiss to the whole world. This has nothing to do with a *concrete* community.

123. Etounga-Manguelle (2000: 68–75) presents a "typology" of African culture that has parallels to this summary and insofar confirms it:
African societies show *hierarchical distance.* There, "subordinates consider their superiors to be different – having a right to privilege", "strength prevails over laws".
Control over uncertainty "is exercised only through religion"; if Africans "immerse themselves in the present and demonstrate a lack of concern for tomorrow, it is [...] because of their submission to a ubiquitous and implacable divine will".
"Africans have always had their own *time*"; "nothing is done to prepare for the future."
Due to *indivisible power and authority* that is based on the force of religion, "the entire social body accepts, as a natural fact, the servitude imposed by the strong man of the moment".
The community dominates the individual. The subordination of the individual by the community characterizes the African culture. "The concept of individual responsibility does not exist in our hyper-centralised traditional structures."
"The African has an inexhaustible need for communication and prefers interpersonal warmth over content": *excessive conviviality and rejection of open conflict.*
The African is an *inefficient homo economicus.* Immediate consumption has priority over saving for the future and being forced to care of relatives hinders to accumulation of wealth.
Irrationalism has a high cost. "Witchcraft is both an instrument of social coercion [...] and a very convenient political instrument to eliminate any opposition". The "African is the intelligent being that uses his intelligence least".
African *totalitarianism* was not born with independence. Authoritarianism "is for us a way of life."
Despite of this widely negative picture of African cultures, Etounga-Manguelle argues to "preserve African culture, one of the most [...] humanistic cultures in existence."

Many additional cultural aspects and varieties play a role in shaping the African and the Western mind-sets. Also, geographical and intellectual differences must not be neglected. In addition, is it justified to see African and Western mind-sets as a dichotomy? More specific: In which way do African and Western rationality differ? Reality indeed is much more complex and allows and demands a variety of interpretations and contradicting perspectives.[124] However, the purpose has been to highlight aspects that need to be *understood*, i.e. aspects that cannot be grasped in a numerical, quantifiable way as those aspects constitute the mind-sets of both sides, the African and the Western mind-set. By that, I hope to have brought to light essential differences that demand understanding in the sense of *learning from each other*. If this has been achieved, the simplification may be forgiven.

Before I address the encounter of Africa with the Enlightenment, I should mention a few additional *observations* that have challenged my understanding as a foreigner in Africa. A well-known phenomenon is *'African time'*. You have an appointment in your office with a business partner; he appears half an hour late, two hours late or not at all. A seminar is supposed to start at 8:30 in the morning; that is the time when the first participants show up, the last one arrives at 12 o'clock. Gatherings at the village begin two, three hours after the agreed upon time. A car mechanic promises that the service will be finished on Wednesday morning, 'hundred percent!' you will be lucky to get your car in the evening. The stories are endless.

Mbiti (1999: 15–28) offers an explanation for what is 'going wrong' – according to the Western perception. The linear time of the West, i.e. the succession of past, present, and future is foreign to the traditional African thinking. Time is not something abstract; time is not in a vacuum, it is not measured by hours, minutes and seconds. On the contrary, *time is a composition of events,* i.e. time is concrete and it has to be experienced. Therefore, there is no future in an abstract sense because what has not yet happened cannot be experienced. *"Actual time* is therefore what is present and what is past. It moves 'backward' rather than 'forward'; and people set their minds not on future things, but chiefly on what has taken place." In the Western concept, time is utilised because it *exists* though in an abstract, non-tangible form. "In the traditional African life, time has to be created or produced. Man is not a slave of time; instead, he 'makes' as much time as he wants." We can say: It is not important *when* something happens but *that* it happens. The event is important, not something like 'time'. Of course, also ,Africans organize their life according to time; however, this is not bound to the clock, but to certain *events:* the sun rise, the necessity to rest, the milking of cows, etc. Being late may be explained by this kind of time concept (although very practical reasons may also be the cause like the lack of transport).

In the face of this interpretation of African time, Mbiti (1999: 18, 22–24) distinguishes two concepts of time. The one covers the 'now-period'; it is the *'micro-time'* and "has the sense of immediacy, nearness, and 'now-ness'; and it is the period of immediate concern for the people,

124. See Albert Wirz (1997: 165–166): The image of the other. Possibilities and limits of intercultural understanding (translated title).

since that is 'where' or 'when' they exist" (22). Mbiti calls this time 'Sasa', the other time concept the *'macro-time'* or 'Zamani'. 'Sasa' disappears into 'Zamani', i.e. the events disappear. "'Zamani' becomes the period beyond which nothing can go"; it "is the dimension in which everything finds its halting point". 'Zamani' is "the final storehouse for all phenomena and events"; the period of the myth. A consequence of this time concept may be that "African peoples have no 'belief in progress'; the idea that the development of human activities and achievements move from a low to a higher degree. The people neither plan for the distant future nor 'build castles in the air'" (23). Such a statement should be taken in consideration when we talk of 'development'. It is emphasised by Etounga-Manguelle (2000: 69): "In traditional African society, which exalts the glorious past of ancestors through tales and fables, nothing is done to prepare for the future."

I wonder whether Mbiti's and Etounga-Manguelle's interpretation of the African relationship to the future is still valid with respect to the young African generation and to the 'City'. The transition from 'tradition' to 'modernity' and from 'Village' to 'City' clearly is in the hands of the young generation. The demands of the North African and Arab revolutions of 2011 were uttered mostly by youths. Ayittey[125] distinguishes the 'Cheetahs' from the 'Hippos'. He describes the 'Cheetahs' as the progressive and future oriented young business people who are hindered by 'Hippos', the thick-headed political elites. I would like to maintain that the youth represent a new understanding of future.

At the same time, some Westerners' discomfort with their existence *in* the counted time, in the 'clock-time', should make us wonder; they notice that they are obsessed by time; and therefore, they plead for a deceleration of life.[126] This may be taken as a hint for the *relativity* of the Western mind-set and values. Mankell (2006: 228) expresses the difference in the Western and African concept of time in these words: In the eyes of the Blacks, hurry and impatience are a sign of lacking intelligence; the wisdom of the black man is based on long and thorough reflection.

I am often puzzled by the way Africans deal with *numbers*. They regularly combine numbers with 'about', 'almost', 'more than', etc.: The price of the car is *about* Kshs 2,543,995; there were *more than* 32 participants. Or: In Uganda I was told by a young man that the journey by car from Kampala to Mbale would take three hours; with a reasonable speed it took four and a half hours; the young man was part of the trip and for the return trip he again calculated three hours (notwithstanding that I had to catch my plane). Or: The date of a birthday traditionally is of no interest; the age of old people often is unknown, though one may be aware of the time and peer group of circumcision. For that reason, many people do not have an accurate birth date in their identification card.

As mentioned earlier (3.1), in the Kikuyu tradition counting persons or animals is a taboo because this would bring bad luck. Therefore, parents will not give an exact number of their children. And for the same reason, the sheep or herd of goats are not

125. http://www.ted.com/speakers/george_ayittey.html, July 2007

126. M. Gronemeyer (1996: 73–87); Sundermeier (1996: 166); Reheis (1996).

counted. However, the herd boy will notice when one or a few animals are missing, even if the herd amounts to a hundred sheep. The same would apply to a Maasai who guards a huge herd of cows. This is a most astonishing fact. How does he know? How can he have a quantitative insight without counting? Is it a *holistic* perception of his herd? Would it be too speculative to assume that traditional African recognition is rather holistic contrary to the quantitative perception and analytical recognition of Westerners? Do Africans prefer 'Gestalt' to 'numbers'? At least, it would be worth trying to better understand the African way of dealing with numbers. The West thinks in terms of numbers, today more than ever. If we had a look into Caesar's report on the Gallic War, which is two thousand years old, we would be astonished to notice the many figures that Caesar reports. Obviously, this does not match with African thinking.

I add a few more observations: It seems difficult for Africans to say *'no'* when they are not available or they do not know or they do not have what you ask for. Is it out of politeness, and they do not want to disappoint you – for the moment; the disappointment will come later?

A more serious question concerns the *value of human life*. Look at the Kenyan clashes of 2007/8; at the horrendous killings of millions in East Congo, of hundreds of thousands in South Sudan and Darfur; at the atrocities of Sierra Leone, and so on and so forth. The ritual sacrifices; the use of body parts of albinos and others for witchcraft. The stoning of women according to sharia law. The political murders, for instance, Ouko's death in Kenya in 1990, minister of foreign affairs, and the many who had to die after him.[127] Why? The readiness for lynching. What value does the human being have? Then there is the opposite: a *warmth* and hospitality that you can hardly experience in the West. There is also *forgiveness,* a strong African characteristic; one can apologise for a serious offence and one is forgiven; the 'truth and reconciliation' committees or courts in South Africa and in Rwanda exemplify its social value.

Such observations play a role in the encounter of Africa and the West; they cannot be ignored.

8.2. Enlightenment in Africa

Unfortunately, the picture of African characteristics is not as simple as it may appear according to what I have elaborated on so far. There is no longer a traditionally 'pure' African mind. The question arises, what influence does the West have on Africa's thinking and perception of the world; in other words: What does European Enlightenment mean for Africa?

The story of Kirimi Mbogo, a Kenyan lawyer, may illustrate the urgency of this question:[128] One of his clients claims that Mbogo owes him money. The client has

127. See *Daily Nation,* 30 March 2012, p. 9.

128. *Saturday Nation*, 4 December 2010.

approached a traditional court of elders ("Njuri Ncheke") to administer a curse against the lawyer. If guilty, the cursed person or a member of his family could die or face something terrible in his life. Mbogo has asked the (modern) High Court to stop the elders from administering the curse. He says he is not afraid of it, although it is satanic and a remnant of a traditional judicial system but the ceremony was unconstitutional; the traditional court had no mandate to resolve a lawyer-client dispute. So far the story! Its interesting part is that the *modern* court is to counter the *traditional* court and that Mbogo who is trained in modern law still *believes* in the traditional curse; otherwise he would not need to prevent it. Obviously, Africa's encounter with the Enlightenment creates confusion and conflict.

We remember how Enlightenment happened in Europe: Intellectuals discussed its principles and demanded their realisation; some rulers picked up the ideas and introduced reforms; revolutions enforced the rights of citizens; ordinary people were enlightened through education; scientific discoveries, improved technology, and economics changed the lives of the people; movements of emancipation fought for more rights of certain groups of the society. Enlightenment had its roots in earlier evolvements of the European mind. Therefore, this process took about 600 years.

The African history of mind with respect to Enlightenment is quite different to what has happened in Europe. In Africa, *elements* of European Enlightenment were imported *from outside*, mostly through missionaries and colonialism. There was no discussion and struggle on the basic ideas of Enlightenment, supported by African intellectuals and politicians. Its *results* were introduced in an indirect way. The missionaries introduced a form of Christian view of the human being and the world and told the Africans that their customs were devilish; the colonialists introduced administrative and political structures as well as technology that demanded foreign thinking and attitude – foreign in the African cultural context. Education was and still is the strongest agent to introduce enlightened thinking and ethics. In Africa, this process only started in the 18th and 19th century, which represents a very short period compared to the long process in the West.

In addition, originally this *second-hand* Enlightenment was an *enforced* process that reached only *a part* of the African population. The superiority complex of the West even *perverted the ideals of the Enlightenment.* There was no equality of the African individual, no respected dignity, no equal rights or better: no rights at all; Africans were treated as sub-humans, as slaves and after the abolition of slavery as servants, but never as 'citoyens', as 'citizens'. *Genuine* Enlightenment in the social and political sense that intended to liberate the ordinary people, to give them rights and to allow them the control over the rulers – did not happen.

After independence, the situation has changed with respect to the introduction of Enlightenment. There was a (virtual) chance for Africans to either reject Western thinking and ways of life or to adopt them deliberately and profoundly.

However, dependence on the West continued and with it the influence of *indirect* Enlightenment through economics, politics, military, education, and aid. African NGOs have learnt how to formulate a 'project proposal' and politicians know what the Western counterparts want to hear, which keywords have to be used; but this is a superficial adaptation. Above all, the African rulers followed in the footsteps of the colonialists and hardly cared for the ordinary people. Nyerere of Tanzania may be an exception in this respect, or Ian Khama, president of Botswana. But overall, the social and political ideals of the Enlightenment were not realised. The establishment of the master-servant society stayed on – until today.

Thus, outright rejection of Enlightenment never happened. Would it ever have been a realistic option? Let us speculate for a moment: What would it mean for Africa if the Portuguese did not arrive in the 15th century and there was no transatlantic slave trade? If later no 'discoverers' and no missionaries were interested in the continent? If the Europeans would not have colonised Africa? If Africa would have been left alone, an island within the rest of the world, just trading with the outside world, having partly been invaded by Islam? If, by that, European Enlightenment would never have influenced Africa or only very marginally – in its negative and positive consequences? Would Africa have developed or changed since the 15th century on her own or would she have remained the same? *In which form* would Africa have managed to cope with the rest of the world, mainly with the West, based on her own power and capabilities inherent to her traditions? For, globalisation is a movement essentially originated by the West; sooner or later, Africa would have been confronted by it.

History cannot be reversed. What has happened has happened whether it is good or bad and whether one likes it or not. Colonisation together with Enlightenment – though fragmented and distorted – have brought Africa closer to the development of the West and of the rest of the world – in terms of technology and economics, but hardly socially and politically. Africa cannot exist in isolation. Globalisation[129] demands to cope with it, exerting pressure on all countries, also on Africa. These are historic facts, again: whether you like them or not. The decisive and crucial matter is in which way *Africa* as a whole, African rulers and African ordinary people, will *deal* with this situation. Shall they put a (mental) fence around the continent and fight the West – as fundamentalist Islamist groups and states do, cynically using the technical achievements of the West that are a consequential product of Enlightenment – computers, cars, telephones, air planes, guns, bombs? Or shall Africans try to cope with the *ambivalence* of colonialism, Enlightenment, and globalisation and create out of it something constructive?

Africans generally convey the message that they are *eagerly catching up* with the technical, educational, economic, and even political status of the West, certainly also because the technical devices are attractive and practical. The mobile phone exemplifies

129. Here, 'globalisation' is used with an emphasis on its socio-cultural perspective, though its meaning is wider and it is perceived as positive as well as negative. In a cultural sense, globalisation is experienced as a threat and as 'cultural imperialism' (J. Müller 1999: 319–320). See 9.3.

the broad adaption of technology that includes all kinds of technical developments. Many Africans have understood the importance of education; those who can afford it will even study abroad; middle-class employees upgrade their qualifications beside their employment. Business does not know cultural barriers; everything goes that secures profits. African politicians face increased criticism from their citizens about their selfish, partly criminal and lawless dealings. Some have been hounded out of office because citizens appreciate freedom and justice not less than the people in the West. The events in Tunisia, Egypt, Yemen, and Libya have proven this.

African women have recognised the physical and emotional damage they suffer from female genital mutilation and fight against it – also on their own and without interference of foreign NGOs; in general, African women prove to be equal partners and citizens who actively contribute to their society.[130] All these are clear signs that Africans intend to be part of the global society. By that, they are willingly or unconsciously, though indirectly, adopting principles of Enlightenment.

Does this mean the sale of *African values?* Yes, if Africans allow themselves to be uprooted by the encounter with the Western ways of life. No, if they are aware of their own values and weigh their real value against what they gain or lose through the adaptation of enlightened values. This may indeed be confusing and conflicting as the example of the lawyer shows who wants a traditional curse to be stopped by a modern court. Not only from a European point of view, African society would gain in overcoming at least certain forms of witchcraft, like harming or killing of persons. African society would gain by empowering women by factually granting them equal rights. Africans as a whole would gain if the structure of the master-servant society could be abolished and the impunity of the so-called elites eliminated.

Thoughtful, responsible, active, and conscious adaptation of the Enlightenment and its values by Africans seems to be necessary in face of what has historically already happened and due to the need of further development on a global scale. That would have to be a gradual process; but it could be much faster than the development that took place in Europe from the period of the Renaissance to the Enlightenment. This adaptation does not necessarily mean a total abandonment of African values, though most certainly a *creative change.* 'African Renaissance', African traditional roots, the recollection of African values, should be the *counterpoint* of orientation for a responsible adaptation of Enlightenment. African values are based on the social structure where the community weighs more than the individual; where the other is a 'brother' and not an abstract entity among the 'millions'; where a personal relationship determines dignity of the person and moral behaviour; where spirituality, a certain concept of time and other particular traditions form the world view. These traditional values should be the counterpoint to an adaptation of Western values. The more consciously and thoughtfully

130. See for example: Susan Wakhungu-Githuku (ed.) (2010): Life Journeys. Seeking Destiny. Conversations with High Achieving Women in Kenya. Nairobi.

the encounter of African values and Western Enlightenment will happen, the more genuine and solid the outcome. The decisive matter will be what is more *meaningful* for Africans – their traditions or the Western set of ideas, norms and ideals. (Chabal 2009: 85–86). This will be *a decision of Africans themselves* and this defines African identity.

It appears indispensable that a *creative* African participation in science and technology demands an adaptation of the *principles* of the Enlightenment, not only its superficial results. For, it is one thing to *use* a machine and to be able to repair it; it is another thing to *understand* the physical laws that make the machine work; and it is still something else to *deal freely* with physical laws and even be able to discover new ones. Scientific discoveries and technical inventions need the *understanding* and the adoption of the principles of Enlightenment. This contains the application of independent, analytical, logical and mathematical thinking, i.e. accepting its foundation: reason and individuality. African scientists have proven that they are able to follow the 'rules of the game' of science. But exceptions are not enough.[131] Technology and science are mentioned here as an *example* for the dealing with Enlightenment and its principles. The same is valid for other areas; again as an example: democracy is only meaningful if its philosophical and ethical principles are accepted.

African conscious encounter with Western Enlightenment should be aware that intellectual understanding and accepting reason and individuality as foundations of Enlightenment are not the whole idea of Enlightenment. Enlightenment also means the *enforcement* of individual insights. In Europe and America, this resulted in revolutions and movements of emancipation. That is related to the fact that Enlightenment drives towards a change of *authorities.* In the West, this meant the loss of authority on the side of kings or the Church and the gain of authority on the side of citizens who had organised themselves in a new form of society that gave them individual rights and new laws. In Africa, individuals secretly rebel against elders for two reasons: first, they have better insights than them and second, they suffer from the injustice of the elders. But they keep quiet because they have to respect the elders' authority. Definitely, Enlightenment will create a conflict in this respect. But we have also seen that 'Village' and 'City' co-exist and that tradition and modernity are not necessarily a contradiction.

In their encounter with Africa, Westerners usually expect in a self-understood way that Africans have gone through the troublesome and partly bloody process of Enlightenment that has taken centuries in the West. Westerners forget that European Enlightenment can neither be ordered nor can it be implanted into a totally different, historically grown mind-set. The discourse between Africa and the West should happen on this level of a *different history of mind.* This discourse has and

131. The Nelson Mandela African Institute of Science and Technology that will be established in Arusha, Tanzania, and in other African countries takes care of the African will to cope with the West.

should have an open end; the result cannot be predetermined. Above all, European Enlightenment should not be glorified as the sole and best way of humanity. For, human catastrophes of the 19th and 20th century and global problems in the 21st century have their roots in Enlightenment, at least partly.

8.3. Perceptions

Africa's encounter with European Enlightenment happens as an undercurrent event. It does not show on the surface and is usually not reflected on; but it happens. For instance, it is present in the ways Westerners perceive Africans and how Africans perceive those foreigners. Perception contains more than what superficial facts show; perception is usually guided by one's standpoint; it also is *interpretation* that is guided by negative, i.e. obstructing prejudices. Africans perceive on the basis of their traditional background; Westerners look and interpret through 'enlightened spectacles'.

The West represents advanced science and technology while Africa represents underdevelopment in this respect. Westerners are blinded by their teaching and preaching – Africans say what those want to hear; the ones are imposing – the others blaming slavery, colonialism and aid; arrogance here – distrust there.

The African's image of the West and of Westerners has different faces. On the one hand, Africans *admire* the West and appreciate it as advanced, its standard of living and technology as desirable. In the eyes of Africans, a 'foreigner' must be rich in any case; prices miraculously double in front of him. On the other hand, those of the West *cannot be trusted,* they are dominating and bullying. Africans who reflect on the Westerners – like Shikwati and the contributors to his internet magazine "The African Executive" – suspect neo-colonialism, exploitation, neo-imperialism and conspiracy against Africa in *all* their doings. Politicians talk the language of the West – 'democracy', 'poverty eradication', 'human rights' and, by that, masterly fool their Western colleagues.

A *tourist* from the West enjoys the 'beauty of the landscapes', the traditional dances at the after-dinner programme of his hotel, and even his touristic visit to a slum. Everything is exotic for him. However, *Western media* transmit the 'real' picture of Africa: wars, landscapes in drought, dying old people and hungry children with bloated bellies. *Political scientists* count the 'failed states' of Africa and note that democracy does not work in Africa. *Business people* complain about the unreliability of Africans. Western *governments*, IMF and World Bank, and innumerous development organisations see the need of help and aid and complain that aid does not help. *Colonial descendants* quietly suffer because they have to live among these 'primitives'. The overall perception: Africa is backward, almost everything is going wrong.

By intention, I have depicted these mutual observations with some exaggeration. But they express something true concerning the ways of *perception*. Perhaps, it is rather on the side of the West to correct its picture of Africa. It would be helpful if the

West could adopt a neutral stance, stepping back from its own measures. For, "Africa works" though in a different way than the West expects.[132] The one-sided view on Africa that is in need of help distorts the reality. African countries should first of all be seen as 'normal' countries, not under the consistent perspective of 'development', i.e. overcoming under-development. This does not mean to deny the weak and ugly sides of Africa which is experienced and also reckoned by Africans themselves – poverty, the master-servant society, bloody and cruel conflicts. A blue-eyed view on Africa would not help either. But, the genocide in Rwanda *is* Africa and is *not* Africa in the same way as the cruelties of Srebrenica *are* Europe and they are *not* Europe.

Our mutual perceptions are guided by our information, expectations and prejudices. For this reason, our perceptions result in *different* images of a situation that should empirically be only *one*. A meeting, a development project, a business transaction or a diplomatic contact may be documented, let us say filmed and, therefore, should be accessible as 'totally objective' events; but they may have a different *meaning* for an African and for a Westerner. The one, 'filmed', situation becomes *two* situations, one for an African and one for a Westerner. Obviously, we have to be aware that one specific situation or event can be documented only superficially and its meaningfulness varies depending on the world view of who perceives it. There is hardly an identical situation for an African and for a Westerner. This is due to the African interpretation based on underlying aspects of the African world view and mind-set and due to the Western interpretation based on underlying aspects of the Western world view and mind-set.

8.4. Understanding and learning

Understanding and accepting are no pure intellectual acts; they also are *an attitude*. At least, I think I can deduce this insight from a personal experience: When I lived in Cairo, I used to visit any popular area, not only tourist sites. For instance, I walked through Boulaq Dakrour, a densely populated, crowded district of Cairo, not a slum, but quite simple. During the first few years of my stay, people would notice me there and greet me "hallo, mister", children would shout "how are you" or "money, money". After eight, nine years, walking in the same streets, nobody would care about me, not calling after me. I was just there, one of them. Certainly the people had not changed. *It must have been me,* the way I carried myself. The question is: What did I do to change? What happened to me?

Another similar, rather common observation: Germans – as an example – who have lived in Africa for many years develop perception problems with their home country. They do not fit anymore. They are found to be slow, too easy-going, and friendly. On the other hand, the 'African Germans' find their countrymen too hectic,

132. See Chabal/Daloz (1999); Danner (2000) and (2005).

over-punctual, perfectionist, too harsh, too un-cooperative, too humourless, too narrow-minded. Although an 'African German' will always remain a German, his attitudes have been influenced by an African environment. In a practical way, this demonstrates the *difference* in African and Western cultures and it reminds us that experience in a foreign world results in a partial alienation from one's own culture (Sundermeier 1996: 164). Another example: At the beginning, a white person may see African faces more like masks; he will not be able to notice differences and to recognise a certain African person, because 'they all look alike'. The same happens to Africans: 'these *wazungu* all look alike'. A Westerner may have finally 'arrived' in Africa when he can see a *'face'* in his African partner, a face that expresses and stands for a personality, when that face is no longer a black mask.

There is another type of foreigner: An expatriate may have lived and worked in Africa for years – but may not experience people and country in their originality. He spends his time among his foreign community, restricts his relationships to his foreign colleagues and to the group of people related to the children's foreign school, does his shopping in a high class supermarket close to where he lives, goes on safari with his own countrymen; the Africans whom he meets are more or less restricted to employees of his office and house. This is a form of refused encounter and learning.

Understanding has a lot to do with a willingness to *learn* about and to accept the foreign, sometimes alien side. Who lacks *willingness and acceptance* will live in a foreign country with a constant conflict and will not understand. On the one hand, understanding must not be mistaken by a Westerner to be or to become a 'professional friend of Africans' (Kenyatta) or by an African to blindly adopt what is European. But on the other hand, understanding opens up the possibility to *learn* and to *gain* from the other side.

All these 'wise' words are just good enough for a Sunday sermon as long as nobody sees the need to make a move away from *accustomed attitudes* – the Africans from blaming the West for their own misery, often indulging in an inferiority complex. Africans have to *respect themselves* before they can expect to be respected by others. Then, they can leave their negative historic experience behind them and overcome their distrust. Then, they will be able to *admit* their own failures and apologise for them; and this admittance will empower them to change.

Also, the Westerners would have to move away from accustomed attitudes. If they could forget their imagined superiority they would notice that Africans, given the same chances, are not less capable, intelligent and successful than themselves. The African brain drain to the West demonstrates the high qualifications Africans have; otherwise they would not get a job in the West. Over the last two hundred years, Africans have indirectly learnt the results of the Enlightenment, originally alien to them. Did the Westerners have to learn something similarly alien and so much at the same time? Any Kenyan with school education can speak three languages – which Westerner is able to do that? Some of the colonial descendants are hardly able to speak more than their inherited dialect.

Encounter and cooperation between Africa and the West will be improved when both sides start to question their own attitudes towards the other, when they are able to admit to their own failures, when they are willing to learn from each other, and finally, when they would be able to talk freely to each other about these undercurrent conditions of their relationship. The West should understand and accept that the *real damage* it has inflicted on Africa is a *mental* one, namely to *deny Africans dignity*. This damage is great compared to the material and physical losses. The Western alleged superiority has justified the transatlantic slave trade, mission, and colonisation. It still justifies the patronising attitude of development agencies and Western governments towards Africans; some foreign ambassadors excel in it. As a start, the West should have the decency to acknowledge the harm that it has done to Africa. For example, the British would have to *admit* the atrocities committed during "Britain's Gulag".

The learning process, the transfer of knowledge, has been in one direction over the last centuries; it happened from the West to Africa. "But what shall we get from Africa?" a Westerner may critically ask. Certainly, Africa offers business opportunities, but has not much to offer with respect to scientific and technological progress, though Africans are involved in research, too. However, a serious encounter with African traditions and ways of life may encourage one to pause and *to contemplate* the Western routines. For, doubts in and strong criticisms of the Western way of life are manifold; the most actual questions arise with respect to the ecological damage we are confronted with.[133] Is Africa an alternative then? Certainly not in the sense of simply copying her traditions. But there is no denying the fact that Africans have different, more personal dealings with each other including an ethics with personal orientation; traditionally and originally, there is respect for nature due to a spiritual relationship to it; the understanding of time – as founded on real events – is totally different to the Western time concept. What could all this mean for the West? This is not about copying Africa, but simply, to respect Africans and their traditions and to notice that the Western world view and life-style are not unique and not necessarily the most human ones.

To be willing *to learn* and to abandon teaching and preaching to others may not be easy, for it needs some training to become a *listening* and *learning* person (Sundermeier 1996: 165). The global society largely depends on developing 'learning communities' amongst the cultures; by that, innovative potentials can be enhanced. The industrial societies of the West that have traditionally conceived themselves as 'teaching and preaching societies' have to become learning societies. (W. Lepenies 1995: J. Müller 1999) Learning means understanding. Genuine

133. See below 9.3.

understanding will end the Western arrogance and African distrust.

This has to be seen as an important first step which has to be followed by decisions on norms and values and on what can be accepted and what has to be rejected.

'Development' must lose the connotation of under-development in comparison to the West. Rather, African societies must improve, change, and reform – according to intrinsic laws, rules, and necessities of society, economy, politics and education.

CHAPTER NINE

'Development'

The relationship between Africa and the West strongly focuses on 'development'. One talks of 'development' and has Africa in mind. 'Aid does not work' means: there is no success in Africa. As the African-Western relationship is at the centre of our reflections, we should now ask what 'development' means for this relationship and how 'development' should be understood from the point of view of Africa. We have to question the Western standard of civilisation and whether it can be a model for Africa, although, at the same time, Africa's 'development' has to be seen within the global context. Finally, we have to look at the political side of 'development', at democracy as a political system and at the political players, whom I will call 'pseudo-elders'.

9.1. What is development for Africa?

At first, I will confront two African exemplary events with the Western approach to development cooperation. The one is an ordinary event, a funeral in an African village; the other one refers to the terrible clashes in Kenya in 2007/8.

An old lady has died. She has lived up-country somewhere west of Nairobi in Kikuyu land. It is very hilly there as small rivers cut deep valleys into the red soil. A Christian funeral mass takes place on a steep slope within the village. There, on an almost plain area, close family members and some honourable persons of the village are seated under a shade that is constructed from thin raw wooden posts supporting used plastic sheets with imprints on them. The lovingly decorated coffin is placed in front of the shade. A large framed picture of the deceased stands on it. A big crowd of villagers is seated in groups on the grassy slope, men with men, women with women, several are standing. Some young mothers have come with their babies whom they breast-feed when they start to whine. One group of men has taken up space in a cattle dip. A cow stands in an open shed on one side of the plot. There is the master of ceremonies who guides the event with the help of crackling loud speakers: prayers, songs, eulogy, reading from the Bible, sermon, prayers, speeches, songs ... After this mass, men carry the coffin to a prepared grave at the family's plot into which it is lowered accompanied by more prayers and songs.

What is wrong here? Nothing! Relatives, friends, and neighbours accompany one of their own to rest, paying her their last respects and keeping her as their ancestor close to them. Nothing is wrong with respect to the *meaning* of the event.

However, an 'enlightened' Westerner may find the whole situation 'primitive' and 'backward'. He might think that the villagers should erect a suitable community hall for such occasions, avoid an unhygienic environment; the people should be seated in proper chairs; the loud speakers should function better; maybe, the priest needed a more thorough training for his task; above all, burying people in a private ground is wrong and, therefore, the village should provide a communal cemetery. These people are in need of 'development!'

We can imagine dozens of other everyday situations in African life like this one. They might provoke a similar reaction from Westerners. Once the idea of 'development' has taken charge, a *pattern of development ideology* readily supports the good will to 'civilise those Africans': In this context, 'development' means to fight *under*-development; obviously, Africans need us Westerners; we can tell them what development is and what they have to do; and we know what *we* have to do; we give them advice and money; we arrange projects; the projects are structured according to goals and means, time and finance plans; we formulate action plans and teach Africans to do the same; we teach them how to write project proposals; there, key ideas of 'development' that are in fashion have to be mentioned, for instance, poverty eradication, informal sector promotion, structural adjustment, help for self-help, civil society, Millennium Development Goals, ecology; projects have to be controlled and evaluated; therefore, we have to formulate logical frameworks with indicators and sources of verification; the best instruments have to be discussed, micro-finance or budget aid, government or private sector; we talk of partnership on an 'equal level'; as we do not notice any success, we now tell Africans that they have to develop themselves; Africans come and say: 'I have an idea, now I need a donor!'; critics demand 'no aid' and 'more aid' and attack 'dead aid'; a development industry of hundreds of thousands of people are involved in bustling activities, government institutions, ministries, NGOs, churches ...

A funeral in a village may not necessarily provoke a 'development project' by a foreign organisation. However, it poses a principle question: Shall foreign-driven 'development' change or even eradicate African *tradition* and customary ways of life? In the case of the funeral, an important aspect of tradition is included: burial 'at home' to keep up the relationship with the ancestors. 'Enlightened' foreigners will not see and understand the importance of this aspect and will impose something contradicting the position of the 'Village'.

The bloody clashes in Kenya at the beginning of 2008 present another and quite different example to demonstrate a contradiction between Kenyan/African reality and Western 'development'. The presidential election at the end of 2007 was the superficial cause for the clashes. The election result was tight (and rigged) in a way that both main competitors claimed victory – Kibaki with the core tribe of the Kikuyu and Odinga with the core tribes of the Luo and Kalenjin. The Odinga side called for 'mass demonstrations'. However, there seems to be indications that displacement of Kikuyu from the Rift Valley had been planned and organised long beforehand. After having been attacked, the Kikuyu fought back; police played another apparently destructive role. All this resulted in the destruction of shops, residential houses, roads, and railway tracks, in looting and arson, in killing and raping, in displacing about 650,000 people and killing 1,133 and injuring many more. Obviously, this was a tribal war and a fight for land that lasted for two months.[134]

In the eye of a foreigner, many 'development' efforts had been undertaken in advance that should have prepared the Kenyan people to avoid such a horrendous conflict. Dozens of foreign and local organisations had been involved in civic, political and voters' education for at least two decades. 'Leaders' and ordinary people should have been enlightened about good citizenship and conflict resolution, democracy and good governance, multiparty system and party structures, the

134. This is the overall picture that innumerous newspaper reports, the Kriegler Report (see 4.4) and accusations of the ICC suggest.

electoral system and voting, human rights and rule of law, patriotism and tribalism and land reform. There were workshops for media people, for youth, women, entrepreneurs and farmers, discussions on development, paralegal training, and excursions abroad for 'leaders'. And so on. The foreigners together with their African colleagues did a professional job, were didactically and educationally well prepared, used brochures, manuals, pictures, graphics, cartoons, statistics, tables, schemes, figures and different colours, overhead projectors, films and Power Point Presentations. They applied participant-centred methodology and group sessions, paid for transport, food, and accommodation. The seminars were documented, evaluated and improved. And so on.

But still, the ideological pattern of development as well as the content and methodology of political and civic education – applied by development agencies – could not prevent the Kenyan clashes though they may have reduced their intensity. Although a clear output cannot be expected from a certain input, facing the contradiction between Western development efforts and the reality of the Kenyan clashes, the Western approach towards the contemporary African world view has to be questioned. This world view is defined by a pseudo-elder system, tribal identity, disrespect of the ordinary people, by an appreciation of land that goes beyond its material value, but certainly also by greed for power and wealth. Did the foreign educational development efforts touch those cultural aspects? Did they take them into consideration at all? Were they *able* to do this?

What we are discussing here is the essential question: What is development?[135] What is development for Africa? *Why* is Africa today what and where it is? This question cannot be answered in a straight forward way. As we have talked extensively about the *traditional* set-up of African societies, one may conclude that the indigenous, cultural mind-set provides the explanation. I can see it only as *one* factor, though a valid one. *Colonialism* definitely also has a share in Africa's current situation because of the humiliation it brought about, the exploitation of manpower and resources, the reduction of the population in certain countries through the transatlantic slave trade. "Things fell apart" because of missionaries and the influence of Enlightenment, i.e. Africans became alienated from their cultural origins. But as Etounga-Manguelle (2000: 66) says: "[...] we can no longer reasonably blame the colonial powers for our condition [...] The need to question our culture, the African culture, is evident."

---

135. Concerning *'development'*, we have to distinguish between (a) development *aid*, (b) development *cooperation* and (c) development *politics*. The latter means the political decisions and programmes through which industrialised countries intend to support developing countries, e.g. which countries shall be supported, through governments or through NGOs, how much money shall be spent, etc. 'Development co-operation' includes the concrete actions in developing countries -- projects, infra-structural support, activities of NGOs and government organisations, advice to governments, etc. 'Development aid' shall be limited to immediate help in cases of natural disasters or other emergencies such as starvation or sicknesses, having relief in mind and no sustainable development.

Also, the *internal* relationships have hindered and still hinder growth – the conflicts between countries, tribalism within countries and last but not least the suppressive and uncaring relationship of elites towards ordinary people. Neither African traditions nor foreign influence alone can explain where Africa stands today. Mainly her *leaders* have to take considerable blame – since independence up to date.[136] Certainly, *poverty* has to be seen as one of the dominant characteristics of Africa, and poverty bears the same features all over the world, independently of cultural traditions. Poverty has two faces: It is the *result* of political and social conditions; and at the same time it is part of their *causes*.

Independently of all attempts to understand and to explain, the West has to learn and to accept that Africa is not just 'backward' – it is *different*, different to the West and to Asia. The West has to make some effort to *understand* the difference. Because of the fundamental mental difference, it is wrong and too superficial to maintain that Africa is fifty, hundred or three hundred years behind Europe. One hundred years ago, for example, Europe was totally different to Africa today because Africa's traditions are not comparable to and not compatible with the European mind-set at that time. When we take the Western contemporary standard of science, technology, social, economic and political structures as the *only* measure – then, of course, Africa is under-developed and 'behind'. However, African traditional life and world view are simply a *different* way to live. But as globalisation pressurizes Africa and as Africans themselves *want* to cope with the West, there is a need to close the scientific, technological, social, economic and political gap. This can be done by Africans and in cooperation with the West in a dignified and effective way if both, Africans and Westerners, make an effort to *understand* the other side and even their own, including the 'undercurrent'.[137]

We can assume that Africans themselves are interested in improvements and reforms; partly, they have adopted Western thinking and life-style of their own choice. By that, they define 'development' in the sense of the 'City'. We can notice

---

136. Etounga-Manguelle (2000: 75): "Was African totalitarianism born with independence? Of course not! It was already there, inscribed in the foundations of our tribal cultures. Authoritarianism permeates our families, our villages, our schools, our churches. It is for us a way of life."

137. This, of course, is a challenge to African philosophers and to intercultural philosophy, namely to reflect on the relationship between African traditions and Enlightenment, on their compatibility or incompatibility. Which tradition can be preserved in the process of adopting Enlightenment and vice versa; which aspects of Enlightenment have to be rejected in order to preserve tradition? How does this go together with the process of globalisation and economic, social and political development? What has already happened in this respect considering 'City' and 'Village'? E.g., see Kimmerle (1997: 103–104), and publications of the Society for Intercultural Philosophy, Cologne. In this context, see Chabal (2009: 71–76, 130), who states that rationality and spirituality go together in modern Africa, the same as formal and informal politics: "[...] informalisation here is not synonymous with 'traditional' [...] Just as the dichotomy between 'modern' and 'traditional' does not make much sense in the context of post-colonial Africa, that between formal and informal is equally uninformative, when not downright misleading [...] What is required is the ability to explain how a hybrid life that encompasses all these normative categories makes sense to people who are striving to survive in difficult circumstances."

a dialectical process and understand the position of the 'Village' as the 'thesis' and the position of the 'enlightened' foreigner as the 'anti-thesis'; then, the 'City' will have to create a position that forms a 'synthesis' – preserving tradition in a changed environment, which is 'development' driven by Africans. However, should the aim consist in *preserving* tradition, preserving it by the letter? Or does the encounter with a different culture mean to *respond* to that culture under the perspective of the own tradition? In the process of this response, tradition will be modified, 'modernised'. Is this not what is anyway happening in the 'City'?

What is development?[138] A thorough discussion of this term – in the West as in the South – is a basic condition to find common ways to overcome poverty, as Jürgen Haushalter argues[139]. Any development of a society is based on indigenous and historically grown models, not on external and foreign models of society. For quite some time, the West has been aware that the industrial model not only faces clear limits but also threatens foundations of life. Haushalter asks whether a technologically-oriented society would accept that the African life-philosophy 'Ubuntu' should be imposed on it. This philosophy appears to be exotic for the West; it is based on tribalism, spirituality, subsistence economy, solidarity and humanity and on the conviction that the human being becomes a fellow-being only through a human being. Its foundation and quality of life does not depend on self-realisation, individualism, growth and profiteering. Africans intuitively reject this kind of ideas. According to Haushalter, this rejection by Africans implies a wise, far-sighted care for life. They feel that the industrial model is alien to them and not compatible with the archaic elements of their own philosophy of life.

In other words, Haushalter is pleading for a development in an *African* way. How should this look like? Insisting on archaic traditions, perpetuating the 'Village', as Haushalter seems to suggest? This would no longer be possible because too much has already happened since the encounter with the West. Colonialism and globalisation have contributed a considerable part towards development in the sense of the Western model. But then, Africans' genuine will to adapt to Western technology and ways of life as well as their insight that certain traditions are harmful to them – e.g. female circumcision or witchcraft – have brought them closer to the West. We can conclude that Africa's future rather lies in the 'City' than in the 'Village'. Is there a place for 'Africaness', for 'négritude'? What role can tradition play in a development steered by Africans? To which extent can tradition survive and positively contribute to a genuine African development? For instance, there are new ways for initiation of girls into adulthood instead of circumcision; in Ghana, the people and the king of the Ashanti try to combine old forms of tribal rule with democracy.

138. See also above 9.1.

139. www.bonner-aufruf.eu <Accessed 4 June 2010>

9.2. The West as the model?

We are referred back to the question: What is development? This can easily be answered if 'development' means: become like the industrialised countries, follow their political, economic, social, technological pattern! Then the goals of development are defined and pre-given. But as soon as a country and the whole of Africa are taken seriously as responsible for their fate, the answer must come from *there* and not from the West; responsibility is given back to them, and development is no longer defined, but a task to be mutually worked on.

If it is correct that an empirically explicit situation can be perceived in different ways according to the standpoint, then this also applies to the above mentioned example of political and civic education that was inspired by the West. This education did not take into consideration the situation as it existed for the Kenyans; they obviously had not shared the developmental perspective of the West. This begs the question: What do cultural underlying aspects mean for development and development cooperation? How do they affect it? The African social structure with hierarchy and peer groups, elders and master-servant relationship, with orientation towards clan and tribe, may – in the eyes of Westerners – result in *informal* decisions, nepotism in business and politics, autocratic management, and neglect of ordinary people. Ethics with a priority on personal relationships may have an effect on the disregard of the 'objective' law and on impunity, on different decisions depending on whether they relate to something within or beyond a certain community. Spirituality based on the belief in supra-natural powers and in witchcraft may result in 'irrational' decisions and appear as a hindrance to development.

On the other hand, cooperation with societies that are guided by Enlightenment may demand action based on 'reason', i.e. to think in terms of cause and effect; to act based on individuality and equality, e.g. to cooperate in team work; science and technology will require the application of these enlightened aspects, i.e. reason and individuality as well as accuracy; 'African time' will have to adapt to reliability and planning for the future; African 'soft' relationship to numbers will have to adopt to 'hard' facts, data and accurate figures.

This brief and rough sketch does not claim to be complete. But what should be demonstrated is the influence of a world view on development-related behaviours and actions. However, a critical look at this sketch will reveal that it is also one-sided: *African* actions are evaluated according to Western measures and *not vice versa.* We do not ask what the African world view could mean for the *West,* what it would mean for the West to adapt to African cultural measures. Does this tell us that *'development'* is a *Western* concept, a Western ideology? That 'to develop' means to become Western – the West as the aim and model of development? Ulrich Menzel (1993: 5) asks whether development has to be considered as a world-historical, one-dimensional process which affects all societies and ends up with similar results, though at different times. Or, are different types of social development possible due to national, cultural, and social particularities?

The West cannot and should not be a model to be copied for Africa's development for three major reasons: African and Western mind-sets and world views are *not directly compatible;* the evolution of the 'City' shows that compromises and changes here and there are required. Secondly, African cultures have their *own strengths* based on which they may find their genuine ways to a standard that will allow them global communication and competitiveness.

Finally, Western societies *question themselves,* their life-style and its consequences. As an example, I refer to Fritz Reheis (1996) who notices alarming signs: on the individual level, one can observe an increase in diseases such as cancer, asthma and allergies, heart and circulation problems, and depression. People flee from everyday life, resulting in a boom of tourism. Also, drug and consumption dependency, social recklessness, egocentrism, and divorces increase. On the society level, rich and poor drift apart more and more; crimes become more; birth rates and consequently populations decrease; an over-aged society creates problems for pension schemes; ethical ideals of the Enlightenment, e.g. the categorical imperative, seem to be forgotten in daily life. Information and stimulations exceed the human capacity for absorption. Communication means threaten privacy. The production of consumer goods exceeds the actual need: "Many people buy things they do not need with money they do not have in order to impress people whom they do not like." (Reheis 1996: 96)

On the level of nature, species of animals and plants disappear, water, fossil fuels and other resources become scarce, and emission of carbon dioxide destroys the atmosphere and changes the global climate, resulting in natural catastrophes. Because of the exploitation of natural resources, nature is no longer able to regenerate water, air, forests or soil.

It seems to be obvious that such symptoms of the industrialised societies do not inspire striving towards their *life style* and to set it as a development goal. The Western mistakes should not be repeated by others. In addition, it shows that the Western life-style cannot be copied due to the *scarcity* of natural resources and due to the *destruction* of nature caused by the West. The Earth can simply not meet the demands of an exploding and 'developing' global population. In face of these facts, a fight for natural resources may happen, resulting in the 'survival of the fittest'. And there is the other possibility – and I think, the human necessity – that the industrialised nations will *reduce* their consumption according to the availability of resources; by that, they would give less developed societies a chance to develop their economy and technology.

A *revision* of *global* development goals is necessary, inclusive of *all* global regions and everywhere in the same way. This revision should be guided by a *revised orientation of values and norms*. Specifically, the industrialised societies have to reconsider their values and norms. For instance, what value has consumption for the sake of consumption? Which value does over-perfection have? The mentioned negative effects of industrialised countries on nature and on society should give African countries a hint that they should free themselves from a development goal that blindly mimics the West. Their reform should be guided by their genuine values and norms. But in any case, a global compromise concerning the consumption of natural resources seems to be essential if humanity and the globe are to survive.

If the West can no longer be the model for African development, then the *comparison* with the West can be abandoned. Then, 'development' loses the connotation of *under*-development, a 'development' that aims to catch up with the West. Instead of setting the goals of a society exclusively outside of itself, the goals can now evolve from inside. Instead of overcoming 'under-development', one can think in terms of *reforms* on all levels: reform of economy, politics, education, society, etc. This is what happens in Western societies and as they are perceived; nobody talks of 'development' of Sweden or America or Germany in the same way as one talks of 'development' in Africa or South America. Western states improve, change, and reform their systems. The German state of Bavaria was an agricultural society after the Second World War; today it is a high-tech economy; but nobody considers this to be 'development'. In other words, African societies should be given the chance to improve, to change and to reform – according to *intrinsic* laws, rules, and necessities of economy, politics, education and society.

If African countries are not defined in comparison to the West and, therefore, are seen to be improving and reforming as any other state or organisation in the world, then they can be perceived as *normal.* 'Normality' means, firstly, that African life of individuals and of the society happens without being under the verdict of being 'under-developed'. For, "understanding a people's culture exposes their normalness without reducing their particularity" (Geertz 2000: 14). Secondly, everywhere it is also normal that individuals, organisations and state administration try to improve and to modernise. Thirdly, if Westerners were able to perceive Africans as normal people – and not as 'under-developed' ones – then also their relationship could relax and become natural; 'normality' would mean that they are not meeting as 'donors' and 'receivers'. Maybe, the Chinese are just treating Africans as normal: doing business with a strong selfish bias.

Africa shall be given back and shall seize her normality and, by that, her dignity. This must not deny the extreme problems Africa is facing – wars, despots, poverty... But being perceived as under-developed and existing as beggars is choking the whole continent and distorting its intrinsic forces for reform. "Africa works" (Chabal/Daloz 1999), though more 'informally' than the West expects.

Rejecting the West as the goal for Africa's future, pleading for intrinsic reforms instead of overcoming under-development, Africans may agree with this kind of approach. But Westerners may consider it as romantic and idealistic. The core concern I try to bring forward is that Westerners have to step down from their self-made pedestal. The first step has to be an attempt to *understand* African world view and mind-set.[140] Africans should attempt to understand Western world view and mind-set. Understanding the other side will *change the parameters* and benchmarks of the mutual perception and dealings.

Having said this, I do not blindly argue supporting issues that fully contradict Western conviction. Accordingly, there will hardly be any essential progress in African societies:

If *witchcraft* continues as an expression of envy and utter irrationality, people are accused to be witches and killed and, therefore, prosperity is hindered;

If *elites* continue to suppress ordinary citizens in a master-servant society and politics is considered a source of income, politicians enrich themselves by stealing from state coffers and enjoy impunity by help of an inefficient judiciary;

If *ordinary people* have no say and are bulldozed and misused by despots;

If *suffering* of the ordinary citizens is not addressed as the main concern of the state that is more than 'poverty eradication';

If *traditions* are not questioned when they are a source of suffering and a hindrance to open up the society towards the future.

Although this may look like a typical intervention by a Westerner who prescribes what Africans have to do, ordinary African citizens want nothing else; a quick look into newspapers will confirm that.[141] Such remarks should also be an opportunity for sober *discourse*.

9.3. Global contexts

Africa is part of the global world, which can be felt today more than ever before. Cocoa, tea and coffee are shipped abroad from several countries; flowers and vegetables are flown to Europe; young city people dress not differently to their

140. Dietschy (2011) emphasises that development cooperation without regard to religion has to fail. This considers only *one* aspect; it is the *whole* cultural dimension that has to be regarded. But Dietschy also demands: "The players in development from the West have to change their thinking. Also in the area of world views and interpretations of the world, they have to gain professionalism. How can development cooperation be successful if the conditions for communication with the religiously and culturally 'other' are missing?"

141. For example, Peter Mwaura (*Saturday Nation*, 14 May 2011) argues that the Kenyan development plan "Vision 2030" "needs to confront the ghosts of our witchcraft culture, as no modern society can be built on sorcery or the use of supernatural and magical powers [...] Vision 2030 is anchored on a science culture. It proposes to apply science to raise productivity and efficiency. Yet, that cannot be done unless we free people from belief in witchcraft and popularise science."

Western peers; cars are imported from Japan, Korea or Europe; Chinese and others are interested in Africa's oil and more natural resources; Egyptians are partner in the Kenyan-Ugandan railway; French run a Kenyan telephone company, Arabs another one; you listen to a music CD via a music system from Japan and speakers from America, the CD has been produced in Holland, the composer had been born in Germany and lived and worked in Austria, the performing musicians are French, the titles of the music are in Italian, and the recording is licensed by an American company. This is *globalisation.* If we would know the background and origins of all the things surrounding us, we could discover more and more international connections. Globalisation is a fact and it is nothing new. Economic and cultural exchanges among continents date back five thousand years. But periods of globalisation faded away and ended (Borchardt 2004).

Today, we experience an acceleration of globalisation that has hitherto been unknown. As individuals, we are usually not the actors of globalisation but its passive observers, its 'victims'. This combined with the foreign influence that comes with globalisation creates fears in many people; they are afraid of 'westernisation' and alienation, of losing economic, political and social control and, above all, losing their traditions. Balser and Bauchmüller (2003: 230) try to show that those *fears are not justified* and that the reaction of counter-globalisation often has to be judged as ideological. They argue: International trade provides more wealth and freedom for many people; new technologies can spread faster; worldwide competition limits the power of enterprises and forces them to solicit customers; countries can specialise on their strengths and buy missing commodities in other countries for less money; and globalisation enriches our lives, mixes cultures, ideologies and fashions. We are not at globalisation's mercy: As individuals, we can often decide what we consume and which values we intend to realise; governments can open or close their markets; but it needs well-functioning institutions to balance the effects of globalisation such as the World Bank, International Monetary Fund and World Trade Organisation (Balser and Bauchmüller 2003: 41–68).

Senghaas (2002: 7) does not share this optimistic outlook on globalisation. He sees a clear difference between the 'OECD world'[142] and developing countries. There is an asymmetric competition, supplanting developing countries. They experience the foreign influence of the 'OECD world' as superior in economy, technology and media efficiency. This is understood as a *direct attack* on their own identity, which often may have become unsteady. Three ways of reaction can happen: regression due to overcharge; rebellious resistance as expression of defence; or occasional innovative reaction, i.e. creating something new as a result of a challenge that was originally felt as overpowering.

142. "Organisation for Economic Cooperation and Development", founded 1948, roughly containing Europe, USA, Canada, Australia, Japan, Mexico.

According to Senghaas, the 'OECD world' is in the driving seat of globalisation. 'Developing countries' are in the position rather to *react* to it than to act creatively. Obviously, globalisation is the modern challenge for the relationship between Africa and the West. Jimnah Mbaru (2003: 58–65), former chairman of the Nairobi Stock Exchange for ten years, takes globalisation head on. "Globalisation of economics is a sound development", he says as an African. "Indeed, globalisation is hailed for the new opportunities it brings, such as access to markets and technology transfer, which hold out the promise of increased productivity and higher standards of living." But Mbaru knows that African governments and institutions have to give *strategic responses* to the challenges inherent in globalisation. The most important challenges "are severe competition and the danger of financial crisis due to volatility of capital flows". Mbaru's advice – mostly for the financial sector – is more than just a reaction: strategic mergers and partnerships; investment in ITT; development of skilled manpower; regionalisation of stock exchanges; reforming the banking sector and especially improving the regulatory framework; admit foreign banks and increase the level of foreign investor participation; finally, "African countries will need to devise an orderly sequencing of capital account liberalisation".

Without having to go into more technical details, we can take Mbaru's position as an example of how an African banker is able to creatively face the challenge of globalisation. But Mbaru would not be an African if he were not also concerned about the *social and cultural side* of globalisation.[143] Mbaru (2003: 66–68) is also aware of dangers that may come with it. One is the rising level of *social inequalities*, another the threat of *cultural shock:*

> "The cultural values and morals of the developing world will be greatly eroded and even lost as people imbibe Western, and particularly American, mannerisms and behaviour. The transmission of cultural values is taking place on a massive scale through today's information technology. This cultural change could be disastrous as it could undermine the family and encourage promiscuity."

Here, Mbaru expresses a certain fear of globalisation: it might *destroy African culture*. An alternative to 'westernisation' would be the isolation from foreign influences. However, Breidenbach and Zukrigl (2002: 24) emphasise that culture is not something static; it changes in the encounter with different cultures. Therefore, "culture is not something that one can lose or win, but rather a process by which people give meaning to the world in which they live". 'Giving meaning' refers to the values that determine a society. The fear which Mbaru

143. In general, globalisation is seen as an *economic* process and 'cultural globalisation' as a result of it. See, for instance, Kappel (2004): "Winners and losers of globalisation"; Meier-Walser/Stein (2004) as a systematic inventory of this discussion. More recently, also, *ecological* aspects play an increasing role in the discussion about globalisation.

expresses can diminish if the values of his society are strong and genuine. For instance, in America or in Europe there are many groups of immigrants who preserve their indigenous cultures, sometimes to an extent that they are in conflict with the culture of their new home. An example is the Turkish people in Germany who are Moslems and who, for instance, in certain cases commit 'honour killing'. This is a clear contradiction to European values. In other words, immigrant groups demonstrate that the encounter of different cultures does not necessarily extinguish one of them because the immigrants choose and decide to *uphold their values* and culture. This should also be true for African societies.

Peter Burke (2002: 26) draws the attention to the fact that as individuals we represent *several collective identities*. We have a gender identity, a religious, a professional identity, also identities that are regional or geographical. In the African context, these collective identities may be even more distinct than in a Western context. One belongs to an extended family, to a clan, a village, a tribe, a nation, and finally to Africa. The question arises, which identity or identities are affected by the encounter with Western values and cultures. In my opinion, what I have described as the 'City' is a proof of a *creative integration* of African and Western culture. Modernity and tradition co-exist there.

Burke (2002: 30) gives an example that is worth mentioning: The *Japanese* have a long tradition of learning from other cultures, above all from China and the West, also of *transforming* what they have learnt to something very own. Since the middle of the 19th century, a tradition exists that is called 'double life' – traditional and Western at the same time. Today, many Japanese eat two kinds of food, wear two kinds of clothes (a Western suit in the office and a kimono at home) and live in two kinds of homes (in a Japanese furnished apartment with a Western room or in a Western furnished apartment with a Japanese room). This example shows that it is possible to live within different cultures or to shift from one to the other. Is this not the way many Africans are living today, at least in the city? Is Jimnah Mbaru's fear justified?

Today, more than ever, globalisation provides the general *framework* for Africa's development in an international context. Africa's development can no longer be imagined without the global context – with or without 'aid'. Development cooperation is one aspect of it. For, development agencies – big ones and small ones – confront Africans with Western ideas and concepts and expect Africans to realise them. Under another aspect, international trade introduces technology to Africa in overwhelming varieties, kinds and quantities: cars, television, mobile phones ... All those devices are welcomed as their use is helpful and fascinating. There is no serious objection and no consideration whether their use is harmful for the society and for traditions. But technology and its use exert changes to everyday life. They demand skills for operating them, knowledge, consequently education, finally science; *they change the way of thinking.*

If trade and technology boost change, the question arises: What has to be considered as the *driving power* of development in Africa? Should we not expect *politics* to set the direction and the speed? Is economy not depending on regulations and laws, support and infrastructure which politics has to provide in order to allow business to flourish? This is true in theory and in a political environment where all arms of the government function to do exactly that. But where politics is abused for the benefit of a few players and because of this has other priorities, economy has to function according to its *intrinsic* rules and laws; Mbaru's above mentioned guidelines for the financial market are an example for this. Under the circumstances of an unfavourable political environment, it is *business* that has to drive development. An anecdote may illustrate this: At the time, when email was new, a businessman in Cairo showed me on his computer how it worked. He also opened his address book. There, I noticed something which had not much to do with email, but with business relations: half of the addresses were in Israel. Considering that the Egyptian government for political reasons did not want their citizens to have any contact with Israelis, this cursory observation taught me: business has to go its own way to be successful, with or without political support.

Ecology has become one of the most important aspects of global development. Already in 1979, Hans Jonas warned the world society that it has to adopt the 'imperative of responsibility', a new kind of responsibility. This has to be directed towards nature and humanity and their relationship. For, the way humans are exploiting and destroying nature steers towards a global catastrophe. Jonas (1979: 8) says, we have to know *that* something is at stake in order to know *what* it is. Not only the fate of humanity is in danger, but also the *image* of the humans, not only their physical survival, but also the intactness of *human essence*. We need an ethics that preserves both, an ethics that includes prudence as well as reverence. Destruction of rain forests, extinction of species of plants and animals, and global warming, are clear signs of what Jonas has been talking about.

Discussing African development and globalisation, it becomes obvious that the issue of *protection of environment* cannot be left out. This constitutes another dubious 'gift' of the West to Africa. Although Africa also contributes to the destruction of nature through deforestation, CO_2 emission or water pollution, the blame goes mostly to the West with respect to the past and the present. However, globalisation imposes the need to solve the ecological problems *together*. Africa has to join what has been named *'sustainable development'*, not in order to do a 'favour' to the West, but to survive, too. According to UNESCO,[144] *'development'* has two meanings in this context: firstly, as catching up with technological, social, political and economic development, and secondly, as social and political promotion of scientific and technological progress to protect and restore nature.

144. UNESCO and Sustainable Development 2005:
http://unesdoc.unesco.org/images/0013/001393/139369e.pdf.

Two quite different terms of 'development' are combined here. This contributes to a vagueness of the term 'development'. In addition, alone the meaning of 'development' as overcoming under-development is very wide and blurred as it depends on regional situations and ideological positions.

Unfortunately, the term *'sustainability'* is not really helpful either. In the context of 'sustainable development', it is loaded with the meaning of 'durability', with future effects, being agreeable with nature and, in addition, with justice in a global sense and among generations, with human rights and dignified human life, etc. Thus, 'sustainable development' has in mind a wholesome, ideal world where humans and nature live together in perfect harmony. It is not astonishing that an East African committee has packed all possible problems under the headline of 'sustainable development';[145] the specific orientation in 'sustainable development' is lost. The reason for this may be that the concept of the UNESCO-Programme is Eurocentric and designed top-down. The East Africans could no longer follow what the headquarters of UNESCO had in mind. In other words: The problems of a certain region are not necessarily similar to those of the world organisation. If UNESCO and the West in general want African governments to join 'sustainable development', they have to include Africans on the design table. (Danner 2011b)

9.4. Democracy and 'pseudo-elders'

Globalisation in general and development cooperation in particular are challenging Africa's *political systems*. The West expects an adoption of *'democracy'* with all its features: political parties, constitution, division of power between legislature, judiciary and executive, regular elections, etc. To a certain extent, African countries have introduced all that. But do they have 'democracy'? The Ghanaian George Ayittey (2008) is a fierce critic of African leaders and governments: "Only 16 out of the 54 African countries are democratic and fewer than 8 African countries are 'economic success stories'. Intellectual freedom remains in the Stalinist era: only 8 African countries have a free and independent media." "[...] there are bright spots in Africa where countries are well governed: Benin, Botswana, Ghana, Malawi, Mali, Mauritius, and South Africa, among others. But they are pitifully few."[146]

Although some African states do not even have those superficial elements of democracy, one can generalise and maintain: Democracy often serves as a *facade*

145. "Salient issues to be covered under the three pillars of ESD are: Society - human rights, gender equity, peace and human security, health, HIV/AIDS, governance, cultural diversity and inter-cultural understanding; Economy – poverty reduction, corporate responsibility, market economy; Environment – natural resources, climate change, rural development, sustainable urbanisation, disaster prevention and mitigation." (The UN-Decade of Education for Sustainable Development: 2005–2014, pp. 21–22, S. 21f.)

146. See also Kabou (1991), Ayittey (1993, 1999, 2006).

for politics in Africa, last but not least in order to satisfy donors. Behind the democratic facade, things are done the African way. If Western democracy is taken as the formal way of politics, then African politics is functioning *'informally'*; it is "the politics that [lies] outside the workings of the country's constitutional arrangements". But 'informalisation' should not "be taken as an indication of what is not working in Africa but rather as the conceptualisation of that which is effectively taking place – the norm rather than the exception". Also, 'informal' does not mean to be 'traditional'. It refers to "the process whereby the 'modern' and 'traditional' interact in a dynamic of agency that seeks to overcome existing constraints to living a 'decent' life." (Chabal 2009: 129–130) In "Africa Works", Chabal and Daloz describe *'disorder'* as the political instrument in Africa. 'Informalisation' as well as 'disorder' has to be understood as a Western perspective. 'Disorder' "is in fact a different 'order', the outcome of different rationalities and causalities" (Chabal and Daloz 1999: 155).

What does the 'informal' way mean – 'how things are done in Africa'? An example of the social sphere may demonstrate this: A golf club close to Nairobi has elected a young businessman as their golf captain. As the majority of the members are Kikuyu, it is mandatory that a leading position is occupied only by an elder. Before his election, the new captain had to go through certain procedures and ceremonies to establish him as an elder of his *home* village, not of the town of the golf club and not of Nairobi where he works. This example is elucidating in so far as a golf club represents an institution that has been introduced by the British colonialists; it is something 'modern' and alien to African tradition. Club regulations demand a captain, for instance, an organising *function*. That is the Western perspective. The African perspective, however, perceives more than this function and relates it to a communal context. The captain must be an acknowledged and respected person of *his community*. Only then can he be accepted to take over a leadership mantle. In the Western understanding, both have nothing to do with each other; it is enough to be a respectable member of the club to qualify for a captaincy.

In a similar way, state and state functions are not separated from the society, i.e. from the community to which a politician belongs to. A councillor, a member of parliament, a minister, and even the president, first and foremost belong to their community and to their tribe. As within their communities, the relationships between politician and his clientele are personalised and hierarchical, although they are dealing with each other in modern 'democratic' institutions on the county or the national level. What counts are personal, tribal and peer connections but not political functions and tasks of the politician. That is why a tribe protests when one of their politicians is suspected to be involved in a crime, for instance, in corruption or a drug deal. Not the crime *per se* is of concern to the community, but that *'one of us* has been attacked'. This also explains why communities have proposed to pay for the legal fees of the six Kenyans who have been named by the International Criminal Court as the major suspects of the 2008 clashes. (But they are not concerned of the victims).

Politicians on all levels are considered to be 'leaders' with the connotation to be 'elders'. Their constituents look up to them as such and expect all manners of help and favours – from school fees to a job for a daughter. A member of parliament is to repair roads and establish schools and hospitals at his or her constituency. What the members of the community do not see is that the politician has to – or should – fulfil functions and tasks that are not directly related to their locality. On the other hand, the politician expects his constituents to support him when it comes to elections. Politician and constituents behave *as if* they were related within a traditional community. But this is no longer the case and it does not work. The politician does not and cannot deliver what his clientele expects; and he has to bribe them to get their votes as they do not vote for him based on genuine loyalty.

What has existed and still exists on the community level has no real equivalent on the level of state administration, particularly on the national level. A traditional elder has his place within a community where everyone knows the other members and where an elder has responsibilities and can be controlled. An elder will not be elected in a democratic process, but he will be chosen on merit and other criteria. The situation of a politician is quite different. Usually, he decides on his own to go into politics because he sees a chance to enrich himself. With some exceptions, politicians are not motivated to *serve* the society; they want 'to *eat*'. If a community decides to send someone into politics then it is for similar reasons, i.e. to gain an advantage in the tribal power game. Further, the abstract and functional level of government administration, specifically on the national level, cannot be compared to the concreteness of a community – of a clan, a village, a sub-tribe. In the modern context, the politician does not know the citizens for whom he is supposed to work; they are anonymous to him as he is abstract to them. There is no traditional control over the leader. But still, the politician pretends to be an elder and behaves accordingly, and the citizens perceive him as such. He no longer is an elder; he is a *pseudo-elder.*[147] The traditional meaning and importance of elders have been lost, i.e. the respect to elders that represented a value because of the leadership, the wisdom, and the guidance that a concrete community could expect from them.

Democracy and pseudo-elders contradict each other. A pseudo-elder cannot act democratically; and democracy cannot host pseudo-elders. This is so, strictly speaking. However, pseudo-elders are very skilful in playing with democratic elements. Each element serves their purposes: elections, parliament, constitution, judiciary... The game consists in arranging elections, bribing members of parliament, changing constitution in time, nominate 'suitable' judges.

The North African revolutions in Tunisia, Egypt and Libya (and in the Middle East) at the beginning of 2011 show: Whether *democracy* is a suitable political

147. See above 3.4.

system for non-Western countries cannot be judged from the view of rulers, i.e. pseudo-elders, alone. Obviously, the *people* demand democracy, chasing dictators out of office and claiming justice, equality, freedom of expression and participation, which are features of Enlightenment. The time has to show whether those states will represent democracies in the Western understanding.

When the motivation to join politics consists either in the individual interest to 'eat' or in the tribal interest to be in power – which is interdependent – then a *political party* has to fulfil a certain function, namely to secure power. This may be true for any political party all over the world. However, in the Western context, a party usually represents an ideology, values, convictions and, based on them, a programme how a country should be managed. This seems to be totally missing in the African context. Here, parties are expected to bring a tribe and individuals to power, not more. Therefore, at times of elections, political parties are used like *matatus* (minibuses); if the one does not bring the candidate to the desired destination, he jumps on to another one. For a party member of the West, this would not be an option.

Usually, an African party does not represent a programme; it 'belongs' to a tribal leader. Party and the man at the top are almost identical. It is a *personal and tribal* power instrument. Therefore, mainly at times of elections, followers of parties may be instigated by their 'leaders' to physically fight it out with their opponents. This includes killing, destruction and displacement. Kenya has been affected by this kind of 'politics' for the last twenty years, the most terrible event was the election at the end of 2007 with the subsequent tribal clashes. *Violence* is part of politics (Mehler 2003). Kenya is not alone on the African continent in this respect. When elections and the related battles are over, politicians across the political parties behave like a peer group. They form a human species of their own, a political caste. For instance, when it comes to prosecution because of fraud or corruption or other crimes, they protect each other; impunity thrives.[148]

Why do African politicians behave like this? Because they are pseudo-elders and, therefore, have lost their responsibility and the contact to reality and fellow-citizens? Because the colonial period broke the "link between power and obligation by forcing chiefs to work for, and to account to, the imperial authorities", contrary to the past when "chiefs were expected to redistribute their wealth for economic, political or symbolic reasons" (Chabal 2009: 123)? Because they are simply 'human' in the sense that they follow their greed and hunger for power? Probably, the reason is a mixture of all of this. (Mair and Mehler 1999) In any case, African politicians quite often give the impression that they are *not caring* for the ordinary people. It is rather the foreign donors who want to help the poor, but donor funds will be embezzled by African politicians.

---

148. Also witchcraft plays a role in politics as we have seen above, 5.3. See also: Kempkey (2010).

"'Government' doesn't care about the people, let alone provide them with basic social services (clean water, electricity or health). In fact, the role of government is not to serve but to fleece the people. It has been hijacked by a cabal of gangsters, who use the state machinery to enrich themselves, their cronies and tribesmen. The richest in Africa are heads of state and ministers." (Ayittey 2008)

A traditional elder is chosen, not elected, and he will not step down, he will die as an elder. Also pseudo-elders do not really believe in proper democratic elections. Therefore, they manipulate elections – a 'democratic' feature – at any stage: sue a counter-candidate under false pretence, hinder an opposition party to get access to media or forbid it altogether, set up a 'suitable' electoral commission, stuff the ballot boxes with 'correct' votes, change the results after counting, etc. If all this does not work, they do not accept the result. And if they manage to get in power, they are unable to step down, in spite of the constitution – or according to the constitution (!) after they have had it changed through the 'parliament'. Mugabe, Museveni, Mubarak, Ben Ali, Gbagbo ...[149]

Introducing some elements and features of democracy does not guarantee democracy. By and large, democracy in Africa can be judged as a facade behind which things are done 'the African way'. The dealing with democracy

"has not resulted in a form of liberalisation favourable to the advent of Western-style liberal democracy. Instead, it is the Western democratic blueprint that has been adapted to African 'traditions', creating in the process a *hybrid* political dispensation that is essentially informal, and that strengthens further the centrality of *networking.*" (Chabal 2009: 143–144)

The essential question is: Does this kind of politics support an improvement and reform of the existing society and economy in Africa? The Kenyan Jaindi Kisero is sceptical: "The political class is the biblical millstone hanging on the neck of the ordinary man in this country. This economy is at the tipping point for robust growth, but the problem is the distortion at the top."[150] If this is so, how can the 'millstone' be removed or transformed to become supportive instead of drowning "the ordinary man"? Ayittey (2008) sees the solution in institution building: an independent central bank; independent judiciary; free and independent media; independent electoral commission; efficient and professional civil service; and a neutral and professional army and security forces. This sounds quite convincing – *but* the establishment of all these institutions and the guarantee of their independence need

149. See the "African Presidents Index: The good, the bad and the ugly", in *The East African*, 27 December 2010 – 2 January 2011. The seven highest rated are in this order: Ramgoolam (Mauritius), Pires (Cape Verde), Khama (Botswana), Mills (Ghana), Pohamba (Namibia), Zuma (South Arica), Michel (Seychelles); the seven lowest rated: Afwerki (Eritrea), Al-Bashir (Sudan), Mbasogo (Equatorial Guinea), Itno (Chad), Ahmed (Somalia), Mugabe (Zimbabwe), Yangouvonda (Central African Republic).

150. *Daily Nation*, 29 December 2010.

a willing and able *government,* a political good-will. According to the metaphor of Ayittey, the governments consist of "Hippos", of "nasty, ornery and unrepentant hard-knocks. Wedded to seats of power, not even bulldozers can dislodge them." Therefore, they will not build independent institutions. The proposed institution building sounds convincing from a Western point of view – without taking the 'Hippos' into account.

According to this point of view, the ball of 'development' remains in the court of ordinary Africans: farmers, women, business people, the informal sector, intellectuals, employees, artists... They have to be the motor of reforms and improvements, with or without government support. They are the ones who have to push for democratic reforms – see Tunisia and Egypt at the beginning of 2011. At the same time, it would be wrong to maintain that governments do nothing at all. It depends on which one we have in mind and at which time. Ghana does definitely better than Chad, and the first Kibaki government in Kenya made a big difference to the previous Moi regime.

Critics of aid like Moyo (2009) blame *external* causes for Africa's unfavourable economic and political performance – slavery and colonialism as historic burden, apartheid, bad trade conditions and aid as such. The Senegalese Dembélé (2010: 158–172) is a convinced 'externalist'. He admits that African politicians have a considerable responsibility for the existing situation, but he refuses to put the main responsibility for the African crisis on them. "Who does this, insults the intelligence of Africans." In Dembélé's view, colonialism was an efficient enterprise of destruction. It drained Africa and suppressed the natural growth of flourishing societies. In many respects, African societies were more developed than the European. "Kingdoms like Ghana or Mali were guiding not only in the area of economy, but also in science, technology and culture. A city like Timbuktu in Mali was an internationally recognised place of exchange for economy and intellectual life." Colonialism destroyed all this; therefore, the colonial heritage remains one of the main causes of the African crisis.

According to Dembélé (2010: 159–165), the post-colonial era has created an unfavourable economic environment for Africa, for instance through price fluctuations of basic commodities, through subsidies for cotton and other agricultural goods, through negative trade conditions, through indebtedness caused by structural adjustments and the financial policy of the World Bank and IMF.

> "The liberalisation of trade and investments, privatisation of state companies and public services as well as the austerity policy imposed on African governments resulted in the collapse of several business branches, in the weakening of the state, growing injustice and the increase of poverty to an unimaginable extent." (Dembélé 2010: 165)

We do not have to decide the debate between 'internalists' and 'externalists', namely whether Africa suffers from self-made or imposed causes. Certainly, both sides have valid arguments. In our context, where we are pleading for mutual understanding and, on the side of the West, for an end of arrogance, 'externalists' can demand with good reasons that understanding and the end of arrogance must have *consequences*. A change of attitudes must result in a change of economic politics; respect for Africans must materialise in fair economic conditions. Concerning the European development politics Vaatz (2010: 205) remarks that the local people are mentally not taken in consideration and they are not included in the decisions on the use of development funds.

> "This is today's postcolonial arrogance. The most embarrassing of it is that it is not noticed and permanently repeated. [...] To really understand what is going on in the target countries one has to set aside own practices and orders as well as value systems. Europeans are still teaching and preaching too much although colonialism is overcome. Only the people themselves can change their situation."

As there are considerable *internal* causes, too (Ayittey 2006), it cannot be denied that a big hindrance to progress consists of the unwillingness of African politicians to *serve* their nations and to leave personal and tribal interests behind them. Exceptional politicians exist, unfortunately they are not sufficient; it needs a 'critical mass' of serious servants of the people. African critics of 'development cooperation' should have their failing leaders in mind; it is one-sided to blame Western 'neo-colonialism' for the present status of Africa. Also, it is up to African politicians to stand up against Western economic and ideological interests and not to play profitable games with Western aid. At the same time, we have to consider that the attitudes of politicians is an expression of the *whole* society. In other words: to what extent are the *citizens* of an African country ready to *serve* their society and their state?

On the other hand, if the West has a serious interest in the 'development' of Africa, then Africans can be reminded of their own proposal for 'a new partnership': NEPAD. There, the basics for African-driven reforms are clearly formulated.[151] The West does not have to dictate what Africans have to do.

Further, *real partnerships* between state and state – which is different to donor and receiver – do not have to build on 'aid'; money is not the primary issue:

> "The African people and governments have to free their thinking and to de-colonise mentally, in order to rediscover their dignity and pride and to take decisively care of their fate. The Africans have to dominate the debate on the development of their continent and must not allow that others talk in their name or dictate what Africa has to do. It is time to get rid of structures inherited from colonisation and to end the interference of the international financial institutions. It is necessary to overcome the mentality which is shaped by foreign dependence. And it is necessary to discredit the idea

151. See specifically No. 49 of the NEPAD Framework.

> according to which Africa's development depends on 'aid' from abroad." (Dembélé 2010: 183)

If indeed mutual understanding and respect between Africa and the West is to be achieved, emphasis should be laid on Africa-driven *reforms and design.* Then, the *roles* and the *concept* of cooperation in this process have to be defined anew.

It is crucial that Africa takes responsibility for her own progress and that the West accepts that it is an *integral part* of this 'development', not just through 'helping', rather through adjusting their life-style to the capacity of the globe and to the needs of others.

Instead of teaching and preaching, Westerners ought to get into the habit of modesty. For their own progress, Africans should overcome their distrust towards the West. Arrogance and distrust keep captive.

CHAPTER TEN

End of arrogance

The criticism of development cooperation between Africa and the West gave a hint that its failure might be caused, at least partially, by a *mutual non-understanding* of the partners. Westerners may not be aware of the rich and lively African history of the pre-colonial time, of the harm that slave trade, mission and colonialism have done to Africans and the distrust towards the West it has implanted in them. Or Westerners may be well aware but cannot admit it out of pride and arrogance. They also may permanently misunderstand Africans because of ignorance of the African social structure, which is based on the extended family, clan and tribe, on the strict respect for age and elders, on the close relationship of peer groups. From there, the ethical orientation follows; it emphasises personal relationships within the tribal community against abstract ethical rules and laws; also this may create misunderstandings. Finally, African spirituality may often be alien to Westerners, including its tendency to witchcraft, the constant presence of a supra-natural power and the contact to ancestors. If the relationship between Africa and the West shall improve, then the Westerners have to make an effort to *understand* their African counterparts and, above all, they have to overcome their superiority complex towards Africans that they often harbour. Instead of teaching and preaching, they ought to get into the habit of *learning*.

On the other hand, Africans also have to come to terms with their history. They have good reason to be proud of their past. And they have all reasons to despise the Western despicable treatment of their ancestors and of themselves up to date. Their distrust towards the Westerners because of this experience is understandable. However, for their own progress, they should find a way out of this position because it keeps them captive – not just based on one-sided forgiveness, rather based on self-respect. At the same time, Africans should make an effort to understand from where the Westerners come, i.e. their mind-set, which is based on individuality, on reason and rationality. Individual reason explains the Western progress in science and technology, their social and government structures, and, last but not least, the Western relationship to religion. Also, it is important to perceive Enlightenment as an idea and an *ideal* that is permanently *betrayed* in practice, mainly when it comes to ethics. The Western double standards may have an explanation in this. To understand is not the same as to excuse.

The end of the Western arrogance and of the African distrust and inferiority complex should be the base of mutual trust and of normalising the relationship. 'Normal' would mean, among others, normality with respect to 'development', i.e. an improvement and reform of society, economy and state as it happens also in the West, without focussing on 'under-development'. It is also normal that each side pursues selfish interests. However, mutual respect and understanding should help to balance the claim of interests, giving the counterpart a chance, too.

Considering Western and African partners in business and governments, the ordinary people may be ignored. Due to the way African politicians in cooperation with business are focussed on their personal interests, it has to be feared that ordinary Africans will continue to suffer. Obvious forms of suffering are hunger, sickness, poverty and suppression, discrimination by and subjection to politics. (Müller and Wallacher 2004: 340) If a clear orientation for development cooperation exists, then it is the endeavour *to overcome suffering* which is even more essential than 'poverty eradication'.

I am of the strong conviction that *education* is the foundation of all kinds of reform, including the struggle against suffering: education designed by Africans, and education for all which at least covers primary education. In addition, it urgently needs *vocational training*. For, at the moment there is the problem of jobless academicians on the one hand and unqualified workers on the other hand. Vocational training would be suitable in bridging this negative alternative. But quantitative coverage is also not good enough; it has to be *qualitative* education. For me, this is teaching and *learning by understanding;*[152] children and youths have to be taught to think and, by that, to become independent and creative. A consequence of this necessity is teacher training. High school and university education should be seen under the quality perspective, too. Graduates should be educated in a comprehensive way, being more than specialised narrow-minded experts.

Also, the Western educational systems have to take the challenge of quality and have to provide comprehensive education ("Bildung") and not only specializing training. It is time that a theory of comprehensive education includes the ability and willingness for *intercultural dialogue*. This is not meant in the sense of responsibility that the West takes responsibility for other people. No, Westerners have to learn to take a step back, *learn* about other cultures, *know* them, *listen* to what they have to offer, try to *understand* them and to accept their alienness, and seek *dialogue* with them whenever and wherever it is possible. This educated open-mindedness for other cultures has to be more than touristic curiosity and superficiality. Mainly Westerners – and not only anthropologists – should liberate themselves from a narrow-minded Eurocentrism and take the chance of an "enlargement of the universe of human discourse" (Geertz 2000: 14).

Comprehensive education is not a question of an educational system only, but a matter of personal engagement and of life-long learning. Therefore, intercultural dialogue is part of adult responsibility. This dialogue must be based on the (exemplary) knowledge of a foreign culture, in our context: of African culture; dialogue means to strive to understand and respect it. It needs statesmen as well as intellectuals[153] and ordinary citizens on both sides who are ready for an *informed and open-minded dialogue*. The former president of Germany, Horst Köhler (2010), set an example by offering dialogue with African leaders. Kofi Annan as the Secretary General of the United Nations initiated a "Dialogue among Civilisations" (Aboulmagd 2001).

Talking about understanding the counterpart, about Westerners overcoming their arrogance towards Africans and about Africans overcoming their distrust towards Westerners, cannot be more than an *appeal*. But it needs a *change of attitudes* in order to come out of the shadow of arrogance and distrust. Both hinder to see the facts and to judge in a sober way. The appeal for it sounds idealistic, and there is no 'programme' to make it work. As there are Africans, Europeans and Americans who have taken the decisive steps long ago, such an appeal must not be in vain.

---

152. See Danner, Helmut: Educational Foundations for Curriculum Development. Learning by Understanding. Amman 2007, www.helmut-danner.info.

153. Küng (1998); Lütterfelds/Mohrs (1997); Brocker/Nau (1997); Society for Intercultural Philosophy, Cologne; Fornet-Betancourt 2000.

However, we must not close our eyes to existing Western conceit towards other societies and cultures. For example, William Pfaff (2010) elaborates on how America's foreign policy is guided by a *Manifest Destiny,* by a consciousness of a mission to create a better world. The former Secretary of State, Condoleezza Rice, allegedly has said that it is America's job to change the world and this should happen according to America's image. This brings the sense of mission of a dominating Western nation to the point: It has good intentions, decides what is good for the rest of the world, and imposes what the rest of the world not necessarily wants and actually often rejects. In that lies a certain tragedy. America's sense of mission is nurtured by a secular utopian ideology; the aim ought to be a universal democracy – whether it is compatible with a society and its culture or not. The 'manifest destiny' is also inspired by religious beliefs. President Woodrow Wilson was convinced that America had to fulfil a divine commission to reform civilisation and to bring to the globe the benevolent principles of American democracy and religion. In more recent times, President George W. Bush recognised his government's responsibility in ridding the world of evil. These kinds of convictions justify the use of power and force; this explains why America entertains more than a thousand military bases all over the world. Pfaff (2010: 130) concludes that America's Manifest Destiny is "the hubris of an attempt to deliver a form of Western values at gunpoint".

Another example of a condescending attitude is Nicolas Sarkozy, president of France, here especially towards Africa. He gave a speech at the Cheikh Anta Diop University of Dakar, Senegal, on 26 July 2007, addressing Africa's youth: "I have come to speak to you in the frank and honest way how you speak to friends whom you love and respect. I love Africa; I respect and love the Africans." However, African intellectuals received this speech as hardly veiled insults and accusations. Achille Mbembe, Cameroon, can find invitations for exchange and dialogue in this speech only in the form of pure rhetoric. "What is expressed between the lines, are demands, orders, appeals for order (among them appeals of censorship), cheap provocations, insults packed in hollow flattering – in addition to an unbearable high-handedness." Mwatha Ngalasso reports: "The speech was ranked as arrogant, paternalistic, and neo-colonialist, as blurred, old-fashioned, and out-dated, as demagogic, loaded with historic errors and incomprehensible memory lapses, culpable omissions and false judgements on black people and their relationship to the actual world of today" (Cichon 2010: 37, 61, 102). These quotes shall be sufficient to represent a whole book of angry responses of educated Africans to a leading Westerner.

Obviously, it is time for an end of arrogance and for genuine dialogue.

Bibliography

Hist. Wb. Philos: Historisches Wörterbuch der Philosophie. Vol. 1–12. Basel, Darmstadt, 1971–2004.

Aboulmagd, A. Kamal et. al. (2001): Crossing the Divide – Dialogue among Civilisations. South Orange, N.J.

Achebe, Chinua (1994): Things Fall Apart. 1st ed. 1959. New York.

Anderson, David (2005): Histories of the Hanged. Britain's Dirty war in Kenya and the End of the Empire. London.

Ansprenger, Franz (2002): Geschichte Afrikas. München.

Assmann, Jan (1995): Ma'at. Gerechtigkeit und Unsterblichkeit im Alten Ägypten. 2nd ed. München.

Ayittey, George (1993): *Africa Betrayed.* New York.

Ayittey, George (1999): *Africa in Chaos*. New York.

Ayittey, George (2006): *Africa Unchained.* New York.

Ayittey, George (2008): Obama's Victory Shames Africa. In: *The Huttington Post.*

Balser, Markus/Bauchmüller, Michael (2003): Die 10 Irrtümer der Globalisierungsgegner – wie man Ideologie mit Fakten widerlegt. Frankfurt am Main.

Barth, Boris et. al. (2007): Das Zeitalter des Kolonialismus. Darmstadt.

Behrens, Gerd (1999): Ein Segen namens Melanin. In: Süddeutsche Zeitung. 20 October 1999.

Berg-Schlosser, Dirk (1997): Menschenrechte und Demokratie – universelle Kategorien oder eurozentrische Betrachtungsweise? In: Brocker, Manfred/Nau, Heino H. (eds.): Ethnozentrismus. Darmstadt, 289–306.

Bidima, Jean-Godefroy (1995): La philosophie négro-africaine. Paris.

Bielefeldt, Heiner (1997): Menschenrechte – universaler Normkonsens oder eurozentrischer Kulturimperialismus? In: Brocker, Manfred/Nau, Heino H. (eds.): Ethnozentrismus. Darmstadt, 256–268.

Bierschenk, Thomas (2005): Die Lehren von Coulibaly. Ein Schweizer Castaneda in Westafrika. In: Tsantsa, November 2005.

Binswanger, Ludwig (1962): Grundformen und Erkenntnis menschlichen Daseins. München, Basel.

Birus, Hendrik (ed.) (1982): Hermeneutische Positionen. Schleiermacher, Dilthey, Heidegger, Gadamer. Göttingen.

Bitala, Michael (2002): Die Macht der Vampire. In: Süddeutsche Zeitung, 17. Juli 2002.

Blom, Philipp (2010): A Wicked Company. The Forgotten Radicalism of the European Enlightenment. New York.

Bollnow, Otto-F. (1966): Zur Frage der Objektivität in den Geisteswissenschaften. In: Oppolzer, Siegfried (ed.): Denkformen und Forschungsmethoden in der Erziehungswissenschaft. Vol. 1. München, 53–79.

Borchardt, Knut (2004): Globalisierung in historischer Perspektive. In: Meier-Walser, Reinhard C./Stein, Peter (eds.): Globalisierung und Perspektiven internationaler Verantwortung. München. 21–49.

Borgstedt, Angela (2004): Das Zeitalter der Aufklärung. Darmstadt.

Bouchentouf-Siagh, Zohra (2010): Doppelbödigkeit und Geschichtsschacher. In: Cichon et. al. (eds.): Der undankbare Kontinent? Afrikanische Antworten auf europäische Bevormundung. Hamburg. 73–100.

Breidenbach, Joana/Zukrigl, Ina (2002): Widersprüche der kulturellen Globalisierung: Strategien und Praktiken. In: Aus Politik und Zeitgeschichte B 12/2002. 19-25.

Brocker, Manfred/Nau, Heino H. (eds.) (1997): Ethnozentrismus. Möglichkeiten und Grenzen des interkulturellen Dialogs. Darmstadt.

Buber, Martin (1962): Das dialogische Prinzip. Heidelberg.

Burke, Peter (2002): Globale Identitäten aus der Sicht eines Historikers. In: Aus Politik und Zeitgeschichte B 12/2002. 26–30.

Césaire, Aimé (1968): Über den Kolonialismus. Berlin.

Chabal, Patrick (2009): Africa. The Politics of Suffering and Smiling. London.

Chabal, Patrick/Daloz, Jean-Pascal (1999): Africa works. Disorder as political instrument. Oxford.

Chabal, Patrick/Daloz, Jean-Pascal (2006): Culture Troubles: Politics and the Interpretation of Meaning. London.

Cichon, Peter et. al (eds.) (2010): Der undankbare Kontinent? Afrikanische Antworten auf europäische Bevormundung. Hamburg.

Connah, Graham (2006): Unbekanntes Afrika. Archäologische Entdeckungen auf dem Schwarzen Kontinent. Darmstadt.

Courtenay, Bryce (2005): White Thorn. A Novel of Africa. Camberwell/Australia.

Danner, Helmut (1995): Hermeneutics in educational discourse: Foundations. In: Higgs, Philips (ed.): Metatheories in philosophy of education, vol. I: Introduction. Johannesburg.

Danner, Hemut (2000): Afrika funktioniert, aber anders. In: epd Entwicklungspolitik 23/24; complete text in: www.helmut-danner.info.

Danner, Helmut (2005): Kenia ist kein Entwicklungsland. In: www.helmut-danner.info.

Danner, Helmut (2006): Methoden geisteswissenschaftlicher Pädagogik. Einführung in Hermeneutik, Phänomenologie und Dialektik. 5th ed. München.

Danner, Helmut (2010): Verantwortung in Ethik und Pädagogik. Oberhausen.

Danner, Helmut (2011a): Dambisa Moyo's ‚Dead Aid' – Ein Kommentar und die afrikanische Reaktion. In: Nebe, Johannes M. (ed.): Herausforderung Afrika – Gesellschaft und Raum im Wandel. Baden-Baden. 393–410.

Danner, Helmut (2011b): Verantwortung und Bildung für eine 'nachhaltige Entwicklung'. In: www.helmut-danner.info (Bildung).

Dembélé, Demba Moussa (2010): Unkenntnis, Unverständnis oder bewusste Provokation? In: Cichon, Peter et al. (eds.): Der undankbare Kontinent? Afrikanische Antworten auf europäische Bevormundung. Hamburg.

Dietschy, Beat (2011): Abschied vom säkularen Heilsversprechen. In: Welt-Sichten 2/2011.

Diop, Cheikh Anta (1974): The African Origin of Civilisation. Chicago.

Dittmer, Jörg: (1999): Jaspers' "Achsenzeit" und das interkulturelle Gespräch – Überlegungen zur Relevanz eines revidierten Theorems. In: Becker, Dieter (Hg.): Globaler Kampf der Kulturen? Analysen und Orientierungen. Stuttgart, 191–214.

Eckermann, Johann P. (1994): Gespräche mit Goethe in den letzten Jahren seines Lebens. Edited by Otto Schönberger. Stuttgart.

Eckert, Andreas (2007): "Bin ich nicht ein Mensch und ein Bruder?" Die Abschaffung der Sklaverei im 19. und 20. Jahrhundert. In: Barth, Boris et. al.: Das Zeitalter des Kolonialismus. Darmstadt. 61–68.

Eisenhofer, Stefan et al. (eds.) (2000): Mein Afrika. Die Sammlung Fritz Koenig. München et al.

Elkins, Caroline (2005): Britain's Gulag: The Brutal End of Empire in Kenya. London.

Erdmann, Gero/Engel, Ulf (2006): Neopatrimonialism Revisited – Beyond a Catch-All Concept. Working paper no. 16 of the German Institute of Global and Area Studies, February 2006. Published as: Neopatrimonialism reconsidered – Critical review and elaboration of an elusive concept. In: Journal of Commonwealth and Comparative Studies, Vol. 45, No. 1, 2007

Etounga-Manguelle, Daniel (2000): Does Africa need a cultural adjustment program? In: Harrison, Lawrence E./Huntington, Samuel P. (eds.): Culture matters. How values shape human progress. 65–77.

Flaig, Egon (1995): Sklaverei. In: Hist. Wb. Philos. vol. 9. Basel. 976 – 985.

Flaig, Egon (2009): Weltgeschichte der Sklaverei. München.

Fornet-Betancourt, Raul (2000): Philosophical Presuppositions of Intercultural Dialogue. In: polylog: Forum for Intercultural Philosophy 1.

Gadamer, Hans-Georg (1975): Wahrheit und Methode. Tübingen.

Gebrewold-Tochalo, Belachew (2003): Indigenous culture and development. The case of the Kambata/Ethiopia. In: Imunde, Lawford (ed.): Kein Leben ohne Wurzeln. No Life without Roots. Loccum. 97–126.

Geertz, Clifford (2000): Thick Description: Toward an Interpretative Theory of Culture. In: Geertz, Clifford: The Interpretation of Cultures. 1st ed. 1973. New York. 3–30.

Gerhardt, Kurt (1988): Bildung statt Bulldozer. Konsequenzen aus dem Scheitern der öffentlichen Entwicklungshilfe in Afrika. In: Entwicklung und Zusammenarbeit, H. 11, p. 8–11.

Gichure, Christine W. (1997): Basic Concepts in Ethics. Nairobi.
Gichure, Christine W. (2000): Fraud and the African Renaissance. In: Business Ethics 9 (4): 236–247.
Gronemeyer, Marianne (1996): Das Leben als letzte Gelegenheit. 2nd ed. Darmstadt.
Hancock, Graham (1992): Lords of Poverty. The Power, Prestige, and Corruption of the international Aid Business. New York.
Harden, Blaine (1993): Africa. Dispatches from a Fragile Continent. 1st ed 1990. London.
Hergé (1931): Les aventures de Tintin, reporter du Petit Vingtième, au Congo. Bookform by Les Éditions du Petit Vingtième. Brussels.
Hinske, Norbert (1980): Kant als Herausforderung an die Gegenwart. Freiburg, München.
Hinske, Norbert (1981): Was ist Aufklärung? Beiträge aus der Berlinischen Monatsschrift. 3rd ed. Darmstadt.
Huntington, Samuel P. (1997): Der Kampf der Kulturen. The Clash of Civilisations. Die Neugestaltung der Weltpolitik im 21. Jahrhundert. 6th ed. München, Wien.
Hunwick, John (2006): West Africa, Islam, and the Arab World. Princeton.
Jaspers, Karl (1949): Vom Ursprung und Ziel der Geschichte. München.
Jonas, Hans (1979): Das Prinzip Verantwortung. Frankfurt am Main.
Kabou, Axelle (1991): Et si l'Afrique refusait le développement? Paris.
Kant, Immanuel (1966a): Beantwortung der Frage: Was ist Aufklärung?. 1st ed. 1783. In: Kant, Immanuel: Werke in sechs Bänden, edited by Wilhelm Weischedel. Vol. VI. Darmstadt. 53–61.
Kant, Immanuel (1966b): Grundlegung zur Metaphysik der Sitten. First ed. 1785. In: Kant, Immanuel: Werke in sechs Bänden, edited by Wilhelm Weischedel. Vol. IV. Darmstadt.
Kant, Immanuel (2008): Groundwork for the Metaphysics of Morals. Translated, edited and commented by Jonathan Bennett. Last amendment: September 2008. In: www.earlymoderntexts.com/pdf/kantgw.pdf.
Kappel, Robert (2004): Gewinner und Verlierer der Globalisierung. In: Meier-Walser, Reinhard C./Stein, Peter (eds.): Globalisierung und Perspektiven internationaler Verantwortung. München. 266–303.
Karume, Njenga with Mutu wa Gethoi (2009): Beyond Expectations. From Charcoal to Gold. Nairobi.
Kempkey, Kristina (2010): The Political Relevance of Religion in Africa: Case studies of Nigeria and Rwanda. In: Bologna Centre Journal of International Affairs.
Kenyatta, Jomo (1965): Facing Mount Kenya. New York.
Kesselring, Thomas (2003): Ethik der Entwicklungspolitik. Gerechtigkeit im Zeitalter der Globalisierung. München.

Kimmerle, Heinz (1997): Die interkulturelle Dimension im Dialog zwischen afrikanischen und westlichen Philosophien. In: Brocker, Manfred/Nau, Heino H. (eds.): Ethnozentrismus. Darmstadt, 90–112.

Kimmerle, Heinz (2002): Interkulturelle Philosophie zur Einführung. Hamburg.

Köhler, Horst (2004): Why should others concern us? Fourth Global Ethic Lecture, 1 December 2004.

Köhler, Horst (2005): "Wir brauchen Afrika" ("We need Africa"). Interview with Die Zeit, 13 Oct. 2005.

Köhler, Horst (ed.) (2010): Schicksal Afrika. Reinbek.

Koller, Christian (2007): Der Wettlauf um Afrika. Wirtschaftliche und politische Motive bei der Aufteilung des Kontinents. In: Barth, Boris et al. (eds.): Das Zeitalter des Kolonialismus. Darmstadt. 69–76.

Kourouma, Ahmadou (1999): En attendant le vote des bêtes sauvages. Paris.

Küng, Hans (1998): Weltethos für Weltpolitik und Weltwirtschaft. 3rd ed. Darmstadt.

Lepenies, Wolf (1995): Das Ende der Überheblichkeit. In: Die ZEIT, 48/1995.

Lévinas, Emmanuel (1983): Die Spur des Anderen. Freiburg, München.

Livingstone, David (1857): Missionary Travels and Researches in South Africa. London.

Lütterfelds, Wilhelm/Mohrs, Thomas (eds.) (1997): Eine Welt – eine Moral? Eine kontroverse Debatte. Darmstadt.

Machamer, Peter (2009): "Galileo Galilei". The Stanford Encyclopedia of Philosophy (Spring 2010 Ed.), Edward N. Zalta (ed.).

Mair, Stefan/Mehler, Andreas (1999): Zehn Jahre Demokratisierung in Afrika – außer Spesen nichts gewesen? In: SWP aktuell. 1-8.

Makumba, Maurice M. (2007): Introduction to African Philosophy. Nairobi.

Mana, Kä (2005): Wiederaufbau Afrikas und Christentum. Afrikanische Theologie für eine Zeit der Krise. Luzern.

Mankell, Henning (2006): Das Auge des Leoparden. 3rd ed. München.

Marks, Robert B. (2006): Die Ursprünge der modernen Welt. Eine globale Weltgeschichte. Darmstadt.

Masoga, Mogomme A. (2003): Contesting Space and Time: The West and Africa in conversation. In: Imunde, Lawford (ed.): Kein Leben ohne Wurzeln. No Life without Roots. Loccum. 267–280.

Mazrui, Ali A. (1969): European Exploration and Africa's Self-Discovery. In. The Journal of Modern African Studies, 7, 4. 661–676.

Mazrui, Ali A. (1990). Cultural Forces in World Politics. London et al.

Mbaru, Jimnah (2003): Transforming Africa. New Pathways to Development. Nairobi.

Mbeki, Moeletsi (2009): The Architects of Poverty: Why Africa's Capitalism needs Changing. Johannesburg.

Mbiti, John S. (1999): African religions and philosophy. 1st ed. 1969. Nairobi.
Mbugua, Njeri (2005): Joki. Enumclaw.
Mehler, Andreas (2003): Politische Parteien und Gewalt in Afrika. Systematische Überlegungen vor empirischem Hintergrund. In: University of Leipzig Papers on Africa. Politics and Economics. No. 64.
Meier-Oeser, Stephan (2004): Wissenschaft. In: Hist. Wb. Philos., vol. 12. Basel/ Darmstadt 902–915.
Meier-Walser, Reinhard C./Stein, Peter (eds.) (2004): Globalisierung und Perspektiven internationaler Verantwortung. München.
Menzel, Ulrich (1993): Geschichte der Entwicklungstheorie. 2nd ed. Hamburg.
Meredith, Martin (2006): The State of Africa. A History of Fifty Years of Independence. London et al.
Moyo, Dambisa (2009): Dead Aid. Why aid is not working and how there is another way for Africa. London.
Müller, Johannes (1999). Weltkirche als Lerngemeinschaft – Modell einer menschengerechten Globalisierung? In: Stimmen der Zeit 217. 317–328.
Müller, Johannes/Wallacher, Johannes (2001): Entwicklungszusammenarbeit im Zeitalter der Globalisierung. In: Entwicklungspolitik 7/2001, 21–25.
Müller, Johannes/Wallacher, Johannes (2004): Entwicklungszusammenarbeit im Spannungsfeld von Eigeninteresse und Solidarität. In: Meier-Walser, Reinhard C./Stein, Peter (eds.): Globalisierung und Perspektiven internationaler Verantwortung. München. 339–350.
Müller, Klaus E. (1971): Animismus. In: Hist. Wb. Philos., vol. 1. Basel, Darmstadt. 315–319.
Naipaul, Vidiadhar S. (2010): The Masque of Africa. Glimpses of African Belief. New York, Toronto.
Nebe, Johannes M. (ed.) (2011): Herausforderung Afrika. Gesellschaft und Raum im Wandel. Baden-Baden.
Nietzsche, Friedrich (1966): Die fröhliche Wissenschaft. In: Nietzsche, Friedrich: Werke in drei Bänden. 2nd vol., edited by Karl Schlechta. 1st ed. 1882. Darmstadt.
Oelmüller, Willi (1980): Versuch einer Orientierungshilfe für sittliche Lebensformen. In: Oelmüller, Willi et al. (eds.): Philosophische Arbeitsbücher 2. Diskurs: Sittliche Lebensformen. Paderborn. 9–86.
Oliver, Roland (1992): The African Experience. Major Themes in African History from Earliest Times to the Present. New York.
Osterhammel, Jürgen (2007): Vom Umgang mit dem 'Anderen'. Zivilisierungsmissionen – in Europa und darüber hinaus. In: Barth, Boris (ed.): Das Zeitalter des Kolonialismus. Darmstadt. 45–54.
Oxford Advanced Learner's Dictionary. 7th ed. (2006). Oxford.
Pakenham, Thomas (2003): The Scramble for Africa. White Man's Conquest of

the Dark Continent From 1876 to 1912. 1st ed. 1991. New York et al.
Palmer, Karin (2010): Spellbound. Inside West Africa's Witch Camps. New York et al.
Palmer, Richard E. (1969): Hermeneutics. Interpretation Theory in Schleiermacher, Dilthey, Heidegger, and Gadamer. Evanston.
Pfaff, William (2010): The Irony of Manifest Destiny. The Tragedy of America's Foreign Policy. New York.
Reheis, Fritz (1996): Die Kreativität der Langsamkeit. Neuer Wohlstand durch Entschleunigung. Darmstadt.
Rodney Sand, Walter (2001): How Europe Underdeveloped Africa. Nairobi et al.
Schalk, Fritz (1971): Aufklärung. In: Hist. Wb. Philos. Vol. I. Basel. 620–633.
Scharf, Matthew (2008): The Enlightenment and Economic Development: The Roots of Growth in Europe and its Prospects in Africa. In: The Bologna Centre Journal of International Affairs, online.
Schmidt, Stephan (2005): Die Herausforderung des Fremden. Interkulturelle Hermeneutik und konfuzianisches Denken. Darmstadt.
Seitz, Volker (2009): Afrika wird armregiert oder Wie man Afrika wirklich helfen kann. München.
Senghaas, Dieter (2002): Kulturelle Globalisierung – ihre Kontexte, ihre Varianten. In: Aus Politik und Zeitgeschichte B 12/2002, 6–9.
Shakespeare, William (without year): The complete works of William Shakespeare. London (Odhams Press).
Shikwati, James (2006): Fehlentwicklungshilfe. In: Internationale Politik. April 2006, 6–15.
Shleifer (2009), A.: Peter Bauer and the Failure of Foreign Aid. In: www.economics.harvard.edu/faculty/shleifer/files/bauer.
Signer, David (2002): Ökonomie der Hexerei. In: Weltwoche 24/2002.
Signer, David (2004): Die Ökonomie der Hexerei, oder Warum es in Afrika keine Wolkenkratzer gibt. Wuppertal.
Sobel, Dava (2000): Galileo's Daughter. London.
Sundermeier, Theo (1996): Den Fremden verstehen. Eine praktische Hermeneutik. Göttingen.
Thiong'o, Ngũgĩ wa (1975): The River Between. 1st ed. 1965. Nairobi et al.
Thiong'o, Ngũgĩ wa (2007): Wizard of the Crow, 5th ed., London.
Thiong'o, Ngũgĩ wa (2009): Re-membering Africa. Nairobi.
Thiong'o, Ngũgĩ wa (2010): Dreams in a time of war. Nairobi.
Thwaites, Daniel (1936): The Seething African Pot. A Study of Black Nationalism. London. http://plato.stanford.edu/archives/spr2010/entries/galileo/.
Uzgalis, William (2007): John Locke. In: Zalta, Edward N. (ed.): The Stanford Encyclopedia of Philosophy.
Vaatz, Arnold (2010): Postkoloniale Überheblichkeit. In: Development and

Cooperation. 204–205.
Walker, Robin (2006): When we Ruled. The Ancient and Mediaeval History of Black Civilisation. London.
Warah, Rasna (2011): Red Soil and Roasted Maize. Selected Essays and Articles on contemporary Kenya. Bloomington.
Weiß, Ulrich (1997): Menschenwürde/Menschenrechte: Normative Grundorientierung für eine globale Politik? In: Lütterfelds, Wilhelm/Mohrs, Thomas (eds.): Eine Welt – eine Moral? Darmstadt, 217–243.
Wirz, Albert (1997): Das Bild vom anderen. Möglichkeiten und Grenzen interkulturellen Verstehens. In: Brocker, Manfred/Nau, Heino H. (eds.): Ethnozentrismus. Darmstadt, 153–169.

Index

A
Abu Ubaid Al-Bakri 14
Achebe, Chinua 23
African Renaissance 65, 67-69, 125
African Union 61
Aid 1-4, 6-7, 18, 21, 24, 28, 65, 103, 113-114, 126-127, 131, 133, 143, 150-151
Aksum 16
Al Bashir, Omar 61,149
Alien 23, 26, 29, 31, 40, 47, 68, 72, 83, 85, 105, 108, 115-117, 128-129, 134, 136, 141, 146, 153-154
Altamira 13
America 3, 8, 10-11, 18, 20, 22, 24-25, 30, 48, 61-63, 81-82, 94-95, 97-100, 113, 117, 125, 139-142, 154-155
Ancient Ghana 13-14, 16
Animism 79
Ansprenger, Franz 12, 17, 26
Anti-Enlightenment 99
Apartheid 2, 24, 27, 29, 31, 53-54, 83, 150
Arab 19, 21-22, 105, 120
Aristotle 20, 87, 91
Arrogance 7, 18, 28, 52, 65, 118, 126, 130, 150, 152-155
Asian 55, 62-63
Assmann, Jan 90
Attitude 3, 6-8, 10, 21, 31-32, 49-52, 65-66, 102, 105, 107-111, 116, 118, 122, 128-129, 150-151, 154-155
Augustine of Hippo 80
Authority 28, 35, 37-38, 50, 57, 88-91, 94-95, 98-99, 118, 125-126
Axial period 89-90
Ayittey, George 2, 120, 145, 149

B
Balser, Markus 141
Bauchmüller, Michael 141
Behaviour 6, 34-36, 39, 41, 44, 52, 56-59, 61, 66-67, 81, 105, 107, 125, 137, 142
Belgium 7, 24
Belief 6-8, 23, 25, 37-39, 45, 57, 62-64, 72, 74, 77-86, 89, 92
Belonging-to 38
Benin City, Kingdom of 14, 16
Berlin Conference 20, 24, 29
Bible 23, 26, 81, 83, 87, 94, 104, 113, 132
Bielefeldt, Heiner 93
Bierschenk, Thomas 73
Bitala, Michael 71, 73
Botswana 13, 67, 123, 145, 149
Brahe, Tycho 87, 89
Brandt Commission 6
Breidenbach, Joana 142
Bribe 50, 66-67, 147
Brother 12, 40, 46, 57-58, 62, 79, 117-118, 125
Burial 16, 37, 39-40, 43-45, 66, 133
Burke, Edmund 25
Burke, Peter 143
Bush, George W. 155
Business 2, 7, 9, 28, 46, 48, 58, 60-61, 66-68, 73, 85, 105-106, 120, 124, 127, 129, 137, 139, 143-144, 150, 153
Buxton, Thomas 25

C
Calvin, John 95
Césaire, Aimé 29
Chabal, Patrick 31, 33, 37-40, 46, 49, 57-58, 66-67, 81-82, 84, 99, 104, 112, 135, 146
Change 2-4, 7, 21-22, 25, 31-32, 46, 48, 50, 52, 63, 66, 68, 74, 80-81, 89-91, 94-95, 98, 102, 107, 109, 113, 122-123, 125, 128-129, 131, 133, 138-140, 142-143, 150-151, 154-155
Charity 59, 65, 83-85
China, Chinese 14, 16, 30, 62-63, 89-90, 112, 139-140, 143
Christian/ity 17, 22, 25, 28, 38, 43-44, 59, 63, 70, 73, 78, 80-85, 88-89, 94, 96, 122, 132
Church 18, 59, 75-76, 81-84, 87-91, 94-95, 99, 125, 131, 135
Circle, hermeneutic 107
Circumcision 35, 46-47, 60, 121, 136
City 33, 40, 45-47, 60, 66, 68, 72, 78, 117, 120, 126, 135-136, 138, 143
Civilisation 13, 16-17, 22, 25-26, 30, 45, 62, 91, 131, 154-155

Civilising mission 25-28, 30
Cognition 103, 108
Cold War 28
Colonial/ism 2, 8, 11, 13, 17, 20, 22, 24-31, 38, 51-55, 58, 65, 82, 99, 105-106, 122-124, 126, 127, 129, 134-136, 146, 148, 150-152, 155
Colonies 20, 23-24, 26, 28, 97
Columbus, Christopher 89
Commerce 16, 22, 25-26
Community 6, 34-35, 38-46, 52, 57-63, 66-67, 74, 78-79, 81, 83-84, 86, 88, 90, 93, 105, 110-111, 117-118, 125, 128, 132, 137, 146-147- 152
Compassion 65
Conditions 2-3, 6, 15, 19, 23, 89, 98, 103, 114-116, 129, 134-136, 140, 150
Congo 7, 11, 17, 19, 24, 28, 81, 121
Connah, Graham 15, 17
Constitution 51, 61, 63, 94, 97, 122, 145, 147, 149
Consumption 119, 138-139
Context 2, 4-6, 11, 16, 21, 31, 37-39, 46-48, 56, 59-61, 79-73, 80, 89, 92, 94, 98, 103, 105, 107, 109-114, 117-118, 122, 131, 135, 143-144, 146-48
Convivence 111
Copernicus, Nicolaus 87-89
Corruption 2-3, 50, 58, 66-67, 146, 148
Cradle of mankind 12
Criticism 1-2, 6, 35, 49, 91, 92, 95-96, 103, 105, 124, 129, 152
Culture 3, 6-8, 14, 16, 22-23, 25, 27, 29, 31, 43, 46-47, 62-65, 67-68, 75, 83, 93, 99, 101, 103-104, 109-110, 112, 113, 116-119, 128, 130, 134, 136, 138-143, 150, 154-155
Curse 35, 40, 71-72, 75, 78, 88, 122, 124

D

d'Alembert, Jean-B. 96
Daloz, Jean-P. 104, 146
Decision 29, 61, 92, 100, 114, 125, 134, 137
Deism 95
Dembélé, Demba M. 2, 5, 150
Democracy 29, 67, 94, 103, 125, 127, 131, 133, 136, 145, 147, 149, 155
Dernburg, Bernhard 26
Descartes, René 99
Development 1-4, 6-9, 12, 14-15, 18, 21-23, 25, 28, 30, 32, 38, 46, 48, 60-61, 63-64, 72, 88-90, 93-94, 97, 99, 102-103, 105, 107, 111-115, 119, 122-123, 125-126, 128, 130-134, 149-153
Devil worship 69, 75,
Dialogue 6, 63, 87, 154-155
Diderot, Denis 20, 95
Difference 6, 8-9, 37, 49, 60, 63, 70-72, 82, 87, 89, 108-110, 114-119, 127, 134, 140
Difference, hermeneutic 108
Dignity 21, 47, 49, 58, 62, 92-94, 97, 100, 110, 116-117, 121, 123, 128, 138, 150
Diop, Cheikh A. 16
Discovery 17, 31
Distrust 130
Donor 1, 29, 49, 102, 132, 138, 144, 147, 150
du Preez, Max 53
Dutch 17, 19-20, 24

E

East Africa 16-17, 20, 22, 24, 29, 70, 141
Ecology 132, 143
Economy 25-26, 50, 53, 62, 66, 72, 130, 135, 137-138, 140, 143-144, 148-149, 153
Education 6, 22-23, 25-26, 28, 30-35, 38, 40-41, 44, 48, 56, 71-72. 82, 90, 96-97, 99, 104, 108, 112-113, 116, 121-123, 128, 130, 131-133, 136, 138, 142, 144, 150, 153-154
Egypt 16, 19, 70, 80, 104, 123, 140, 143, 146, 149
Elders 15, 33, 41-44, 50-51, 56, 89, 120-121, 124, 130, 136, 144-148, 152
Election 49, 57, 65, 132, 144-148
Elites 2, 19, 21-22, 46, 119, 123, 134, 139
Elkins, Caroline 27
Emancipation 45, 47, 96-97, 99, 121, 124
Empathy 109-110
Encounter 5-7, 9, 16, 31, 45, 53, 55, 60-61, 63, 66, 83, 92, 100, 102, 104-106, 110, 112, 114-116, 118, 120-121, 123-125, 127-128, 135, 141-142
England 24-25, 90, 93-94
Enlightenment 8, 21, 47, 49, 51, 58, 62, 89-100, 111, 118, 120-125, 127, 133-134, 136-137,147, 153
Equality 21, 46, 48, 50-51, 58, 83, 92, 94-95, 97, 100, 113, 131, 136, 147

Ethics 21, 25, 27, 31, 55-65, 68, 81-82, 85, 92, 99, 101, 114, 116-117, 121, 128, 136, 143, 153
Ethiopia 12, 15, 26, 35, 80, 82
Etounga-Manguelle, Daniel 8, 79, 117, 119, 133-134
Eurocentrism 18, 31, 59, 111, 144, 154
Europe/an 3, 8-13, 16-31, 33-35, 47, 51, 53, 56-62, 70-71, 77, 80-83, 85-100, 104, 108-112, 115-117, 120-127, 134, 139-140, 142, 149-150, 154
Externalist 149

F
Flaig, Egon 18-19
Focus 105
Forgiveness 74, 120, 153
France 13, 19, 24-26, 43, 90, 95-96, 140, 155
Frederick the Great 95-96, 98
Freedom 39, 89-91, 94-95, 123, 140, 144, 147
French Revolution 51, 90, 93, 96

G
Galilei, Galileo 86-90, 94
Gebrewold-Tochalo 35-36
Gede 16
German/y 7, 17, 24-26, 54, 60-61, 63-64, 90, 95-96, 98-99, 104, 116, 126-127, 138, 142, 154
Gichure, Christine 59, 66-68
Goethe, Johann W. v. 24, 99
Golden Rule 56, 61, 63, 92, 100
Great Zimbabwe 15-16
Greece, Greek 18, 77, 81, 88-89, 99

H
Hadar 12
Haiti 20
Haushalter, Jürgen 135
Hegel, Friedrich W. 95
Herbalist 74-75
Hergé 11
Hermeneutics 101-103, 106-108, 110-113
Hierarchy 37, 40, 87, 136
History 7-33, 36-37, 40, 51, 54, 58, 83, 85-86, 88-90, 92, 97, 101, 103, 111, 117, 121-122, 124, 152-153
Hobbes, Thomas 93-94
Holocaust 62
Homo sapiens 12
Horace 89
Horizon, mental 44, 67, 106
Hospitality 61, 120
Houphouët-Boigny, Félix 79
Human rights 18, 21, 45, 58, 60-63, 92, 111, 125, 133, 144
Humanity 26, 28, 38, 59, 92, 96, 125, 135, 138, 143

I
Ibn Khaldun 13-14
International Criminal Court 60, 132, 145
Identity 22, 30, 36-38, 46, 54, 64, 80-81, 108, 124, 133, 140, 142
Immaturity 91, 100
Impunity 49, 51, 66, 123, 136, 139, 147
Independence 24, 28, 31, 37, 50, 94, 96, 117, 121, 134, 148
India/n 17, 19, 24, 30, 52-54, 88-89
Individual/ism 5-6, 18, 21, 32-33, 35-43, 47, 55-56, 58-59, 62, 72, 81, 85-96, 99-101, 111, 116-117, 121, 123-124, 135-138, 140, 142, 147, 153
Industrial revolution 25, 94, 97
Informal 48, 132, 134, 136, 138, 145, 148-149
Inquisition 86-88
Intercultural Philosophy 111, 134, 154
Internalists 149
International Monetary Fund 3, 102, 125, 140, 149
Interpretation 42, 45, 62, 79-81, 88-89, 91, 101, 103-104, 107-115, 118-119, 125-126, 139
Islam 16, 19-21, 25, 37, 45, 61, 69, 72, 77, 79-81, 83-84, 122
Ivory Coast 37, 79

J
Japan 140, 142
Jaspers, Karl 88-89
Jinn 75-76, 83
Jonas, Hans 62, 143

K
Kabou, Axelle 2
Kalenjin 22, 37, 132
Kamba 27, 34, 70, 74
Kant, Immanuel 91-92, 95-96, 100, 116
Karume, Njenga 27, 30, 44, 50, 72, 105
Kenya 7, 9, 12, 16, 22, 24-32, 35, 37, 40, 42-44, 51-54, 60, 62, 65-66, 70, 73-78, 80, 105, 116, 120, 123, 128, 131-133, 136, 139-140, 145, 147-149
Kenyan clashes 29, 37, 52, 65, 70, 120, 131-133, 135
Kenyatta 9, 22-23, 26, 33-39, 56, 110-111, 127
Kepler, Johannes 86, 88
Kibaki, Mwai 32, 149
Kikuyu 9, 24, 26, 28-30, 32-38, 40-42, 56, 70, 73, 104, 119, 131-132, 135
Kimmerle, Heinz 78
Kisero, Jaindi 148
Kithitu 74
Koenig, Fritz 16
Köhler, Horst 63-64, 154
Koobi Fora 12
Koran 83
Krapf, Ludwig 22
Kriegler Report 65, 132
Küng, Hans 61

L
Land 7, 24-30, 33, 36-38, 52-53, 57, 74, 132-133
Lascaux 13
Leader 2-3, 43, 50, 53, 56, 66-67, 76-77, 82, 132, 134, 144-147, 150, 154
Learning 1, 9, 33-35, 96, 105, 109-110, 112, 118, 126-128, 134, 142, 153-54
Leibniz, Gottfried W. 94
Lincoln, Abraham 20, 93
Livingstone, David 17, 22, 25
Locality 36-37, 146
Locke, John 93-96
Logics 28, 48
Logos 88-89
Lord's Resistance Army 5
Luhya 42-43, 56
Luo 29, 37, 42-43, 73, 132
Luther, Martin 88, 93

M
Maasai 29, 73, 116, 120
Macharia, Keguro 66
Makumba, Maurice M. 56
Malawi 80, 144
Mali 13-14, 16, 144, 149
Mana, Kä 83-84
Mankell, Henning 119
Mapungubwe 15
Marriage 34-35, 40-41, 43, 46, 59, 74
Masters 21, 47-51, 117
Master-servant 7, 46, 48-51, 122-123, 126, 139
Mau Mau 27-28, 53, 73
Mauritania 13, 20
Mazrui, Ali 17
Mbaru, Jimnah 141-143
Mbembe, Achille 155
Mbiti, John 38-39, 70, 72, 78, 81-82, 84, 118-119
Mbugua, Njeri 48-49
Meaning 4, 8-9, 13, 16-17, 26, 32, 34, 37-38, 44-45, 56, 58, 77, 81-83, 90, 93, 103-105, 107, 111, 116-117, 122, 124, 126, 131, 141, 143-144, 146
Measure 56, 62-63, 125, 134, 136
Measuring 6, 51, 101-103, 118
Medicine man 71, 74
Mendelsohn, Moses 97
Mental 5, 7, 29-30, 97, 102, 106, 108-109, 113, 122, 128, 134, 150
Mentality 51, 102, 112, 150
Menze, Ulrich 136
Metaphysical 77, 103
Mijikenda 70, 78
Mind-set 2, 4-6, 9, 86, 108, 116, 118-119, 124, 126, 133-134, 137, 139, 153
Missionary 7, 17, 21-31, 42, 80-84, 98, 117, 121-122, 128, 133, 152, 155
Modernity 32, 39, 44-45, 66, 119, 124, 142
Moral 6, 18, 21, 25, 28, 33, 35, 55-61, 63-68, 85, 92, 95, 111, 117, 123, 141
Morality 27, 36, 38, 58, 60, 63, 66-67, 82, 88, 92
Moyo, Dambisa 2, 102, 149
Mozambique 23
Mshindi, Tom 65
Mugabe, Robert 52, 57, 148
Mythos 88-89

N
Namibia 13, 24, 48
Natural law 58, 62, 77, 89, 92, 94
Nature 58-59, 77-79, 90, 94, 100, 104, 128, 137-138, 143-144
Négritude 64, 135
Neopatrimonialism 50
NEPAD 64, 150
Ngalasso, Mwatha 155
NGO 3, 122-123, 132-133
Nietzsche, Friedrich 94
Niger 13-14, 16-17, 20
Njuri Ncheke 120
Norm 6-7, 35, 47, 55-65, 68, 85, 102, 116, 124, 129, 130, 138
Norm orientation 55, 57-59, 63
Normality 138, 153

O
Obama, Barack 10-11
Objectivity 107-108
Odinga, Raila 42, 44, 132
OECD 140-141
Oelmüller, Willi 57
Old Djenné 13
Olduvai 12
Oliver, Roland 13
Olorgesailie 12

P
Palestine 88-89
Park, Mungo 17
Participation 31, 49, 124, 141, 147
Partnership 45, 55, 59, 67, 113, 132, 141, 150
Party, political 132, 147-148
Peer group/age-group 34-35, 37, 40-41, 43, 119, 136, 140, 145, 147, 152
Perception 3, 7, 18, 22, 48, 77, 80, 89, 108, 110, 118, 120, 125-126, 139
Personal relationship 31, 59, 85, 101, 123, 136, 152
Perspective 2-3, 17, 18, 29-30, 46, 83, 99, 103, 105, 114, 118, 122, 126, 135-136, 145-154
Pestalozzi, Heinrich 96, 99
Petraitis, Richard 76
Pfaff, William 155
Plato 59, 77
Politics, politician, 1, 29, 36, 49-51, 55-57, 62, 65-67, 74, 77, 90, 93, 95, 99-100, 102, 104-105, 111, 121-123, 125, 130, 133-134, 136, 138-139, 143-150, 153
Polygamy 46, 59
Popper, Karl 88
Portuguese 12, 17, 19, 22-24, 29, 80, 122
Poverty 1, 42, 48-49, 66, 113, 125-126, 132, 134-135, 138-139, 144, 149, 153
Prejudice 30, 63, 91, 95, 98, 105-110, 125-126
Ptolemaeus 86

Q
Quakers 20

R
Racism 12, 26-28, 31, 52, 82, 95
Rationality 36, 88, 95, 98-100, 118, 134, 139, 153
Reality 7, 36-37, 58-59, 61, 63, 65, 69-71, 76-79, 83, 88-90, 99, 101-103, 105, 115-116, 118, 126, 132-133, 147
Reason/ing 23, 64, 85, 95, 98-99, 101, 124, 136, 153
Rebmann, Johann 17, 22
Reciprocity 36-38, 40, 57, 65, 67
Reform 7, 67, 88, 96, 98, 121, 130, 133-134, 138-139, 141, 148-150, 153, 155
Relationship 3, 5-11, 13, 17-18, 21, 23, 26, 30-32, 37-39, 41, 46, 48-51, 53-55, 57, 60, 63, 77, 79, 85, 98, 101-102, 105, 111, 115-116, 119, 127-128, 130, 132, 134, 136, 138, 141, 143, 145, 152-153, 155
Religion 23, 29, 36-37, 56, 59, 61, 74, 78, 80-81, 83, 90, 94-95, 98-99, 117, 139, 153, 155
Respect for 3, 5, 7, 9, 13, 23, 27, 31, 34-35, 39, 42-43, 49-51, 53, 56-58, 61-62, 65, 78, 96, 110, 114, 121, 124, 127-128, 131, 133, 145, 149-150, 152-155
Responsibility 2-3, 21, 33, 35, 58, 62-64, 79, 91, 117, 136, 143-144, 147, 149, 154-155
Rousseau, Jean-J. 20, 24, 93, 95-96
Rule of law 93, 133
Rules of Understanding 114
Rwanda 24, 120, 126

S
Sacred trees 73, 78
Sarkozy, Nicolas 155
Sarrazin, Thilo 60
Science 18, 71, 77, 86-87, 89-90, 94, 98-100, 124-125, 134, 136, 139, 142, 149, 153
Scope 3, 112-113
Senghaas, Dieter 140-141
Sense 64, 71, 101-107, 112-114, 118
Senses 59, 87-89, 94, 103-109
Servants 11, 21, 30, 47-51, 53, 95-96, 121, 150
Settlers 24, 26, 50-53
Shikwati, James 125
Signer, David 70, 72-73
Slave/Slavery 5, 13, 15-16, 18-22, 24-25, 31, 49-57, 62, 97, 117-118, 121-122, 125, 128, 133, 149, 152
Smith, Adam 49
Social contract 93, 95, 111
Social structure 7, 22, 32-33, 36, 47, 49-51, 78, 83, 94, 101-103, 114, 123, 136, 152
Socrates 89
Sokoto 20
Somalia 61, 148
Songhai 14
Sorcery 69-72, 83, 139
South Africa 7, 12-13, 15, 24, 26-27, 46, 79, 82, 120, 144
Speke, John 17
Spinoza, Baruch 98-99
Spirit 26, 30, 56, 70-71, 73-75, 77-79, 82-84, 102
Spiritual 26-27, 30, 56, 69-73, 77-79, 83-84, 128
Spirituality 46, 69-70, 72, 77, 80, 82-84, 97, 99, 101, 117, 123, 134-136, 152
Stanley, Henry 17
Sudan 20, 26, 60, 80, 120, 148
Sundermeier, Theo 39, 108-113
Superiority 18, 26, 30-31, 54, 98, 121, 127-128, 153
Superstition 70-71, 84, 95
Suppression 7, 27, 49, 97-98, 100, 111, 117, 153
Sustainability 113, 144
Swahili 22, 70
Swartkrans 12

T
Technology 25, 30, 44-45, 62, 90, 94, 99-100, 116, 121-122, 124-125, 134-137, 140-143, 149, 153
Thinking 6-7, 9, 62, 78, 85-91, 94-95, 99, 111, 114, 116, 118, 120-121, 124, 134, 139, 142, 150
Thiong'o, Ngũgĩ wa 23-25, 34
Timbuktu 16, 149
Time, concept of 5, 117-119, 123, 128, 136
Tradition 1, 5, 7, 13-14, 18, 22-23, 27, 30, 32-34, 36, 38-39, 41-46, 48, 51, 56, 58-59, 62, 64-67, 71, 74, 80-83, 87, 89-90, 92, 102, 105, 116-125, 128, 132-135, 139-140, 142, 145-146, 148
Tribal 23, 33, 37, 42-44, 52, 56, 65, 71, 132-135, 147, 150, 152
Tribe 9, 22-23, 26-27, 34-35, 37, 40, 42-43, 50-52, 56-57, 65, 67, 70, 105, 116, 132, 136, 142, 145-148, 152
Tylor, E.B. 78

U
Uganda 5, 77, 80, 119, 140
Under-development 112, 126, 130-131, 138-139, 144, 153
Understanding 3-4, 6, 8-9, 11, 25, 39, 46-47, 51, 54, 57, 59-60, 62-64, 69-71, 77, 81, 88, 92, 94, 101-119, 124, 126-129, 138-139, 144-145, 147, 149-150, 152-154
UNESCO 78, 143-144
Universal 21, 25, 56, 58-63, 92, 111, 113, 116, 155
Uprisings 27, 53

V
Vaatz, Arnold 150
Value 6-8, 35, 37, 45, 48, 51, 55-62, 64, 66-68, 82, 92, 102, 114, 116-117, 119-120, 123, 129, 133, 138, 140-142, 146-147, 150, 155
Village' 32, 39, 44-46, 59, 67, 71, 116, 119, 124, 132, 134-135
Voltaire 93, 95

W
Wamalwa, Michael 43-44
Wedding 40-41, 44, 65

West Africa 13, 18-20, 24, 26, 70, 72-73, 77, 117
Western societies 47, 137-138
Wilson, Woodrow 155
Witch 70, 72, 75-76, 79, 82
Witchcraft 36, 39, 46, 69-79, 83-84, 117, 120, 123, 135-136, 139, 147, 153
Witchdoctor 70, 72, 74-75, 79
Women 18-19, 28, 35-37, 40-43, 45-46, 76, 97, 99-100, 113, 120, 123, 131, 133, 149
World Bank 3, 65, 102, 125, 140, 149
World view 4, 6, 9, 77, 79, 83, 85-87, 89, 98, 102, 115, 123, 126, 128, 133-134, 136-137, 139

Z
Zanzibar 20, 24
Zimbabwe 15, 26, 52, 148